SHIFTING TOWARD
UNORTHODOXY

SHIFTING TOWARD UNORTHODOXY

Ten Unconventional Mindsets That Help Healthcare Leaders Succeed in a Complex World

MICHAEL S. HEIN, MD, MHCM, ACC

MEDI Leadership Senior Vice President and Executive Coach

Shifting Toward Unorthodoxy
Ten Unconventional Mindsets that Help Healthcare Leaders Succeed
in a Complex World

Michael Hein

For information about this title, to obtain permissions, or to order other books and/or electronic media, contact the publisher:

MEDI Publishing
https://medileadership.org/unorthodoxy/
MEDIpublishing@medileadership.org

Disclaimer: The situations and individuals described in this book are inspired by real-world experiences. However, names, details, and circumstances have been altered to protect confidentiality. Any resemblance to actual individuals or events is purely coincidental unless explicitly stated otherwise.

ISBNs:
979-8-9922803-0-2 (hardcover)
979-8-9922803-2-6 (softcover)
979-8-9922803-1-9 (eBook)

Printed in the United States of America

Cover and interior design: 1106 Design
Illustrations by Virpi Oinonen (Businessillustrator.com)

DEDICATION

I dedicate this book to four fierce women
who've taught me the most about life:

Julie, Connie, Alissa, and Caitlin

TABLE OF CONTENTS

PREFACE

The healthcare industry in the United States is traversing unprecedented and unfamiliar territory as it journeys into the second quarter of the 21st century. The financial and clinical service challenges are well-known and widely experienced. Working in and leading healthcare organizations is never easy, often quite difficult, and sometimes traumatic.

As an executive leadership coach, I've had the privilege of working with hundreds of healthcare leaders in profoundly personal and professionally transformational ways. Their developmental journeys gift me deep insights into their lives, leadership, and institutions; something I'm immeasurably grateful for and continually humbled by. They have taught me more about leadership than all my degrees, courses, training, and experiences combined. As a result, I have grown along with them, which is the most remarkable of gifts.

Human suffering in healthcare leadership is real. Leaders share with me how difficult their professional lives have been and continue to be. In pursuit of recovery, restoration, or an attempt to find something less traumatizing, many leaders move on to other roles, retire, or remove themselves from the industry. Sometimes leaders remain in their positions and do enough to get by, checked out—yet still working. Their suffering touches me deeply, stirring profound empathy, just as the suffering of my patients moved me when I practiced medicine. It also raises alarm and sometimes my ire. Our healthcare organizations need excellent leaders; the industry is losing and sometimes abusing them. My highest hope for this book is that leaders like those described above find hope and help between its covers.

Not every leader is suffering or merely surviving. Some are thriving. The contrast between those who are thriving and those who aren't is striking and fascinating. It isn't a new fascination for me. For decades I've been inquisitive about healthcare leadership and what makes it work well; drawing me deep into the science behind human and leadership development and behaviors, organizational design, and management theory. Through formal and informal education, I have read, studied, and compiled shelves full of books and folders stuffed with journal articles. I've asked other leaders and coaches questions about their and others' leadership in healthcare organizations, compiling their insights and perspectives. Over decades of focused inquiry and experience, some explanations emerged for the striking disparity between struggling leaders and their more content counterparts. More recently, I began to share those explanations with other coaches, client organizations, and leaders. Many have found them valuable.

This book introduces you to those explanations and insights, with the hope that they will be helpful for you too.

This is a book about excellent results. I imagine that you care about those. Nearly every healthcare leader does. It is also a book about how leaders go about achieving those results. But it isn't a how-to-do-it book. It's a how-to-think-it book. The explanation for how leaders who thrive in healthcare "do it" is that they "think it" differently. To paraphrase Ralph D. Stacey, a thought leader in organizational theory and management, *coaching is exploring how coach and client are thinking together about how they are thinking about leadership.* That, in a nutshell, describes this book and my intentions. So, as you are reading, we will be thinking together about how we are thinking about leadership.

To be accurate, it isn't just how they think that separates the leaders who do better. It's what lies underneath the way they think. Thinking flows from mindsets, and certain mindsets divide the suffering leaders from the thriving ones. Mindsets are our brain's way of quickly making sense of the world, including leadership and healthcare organizations. They are the fountainhead of the thriving leader's success and at the root of what trips up the one who is suffering. From mindsets flow thinking, thinking leads to doing, and doing leads to results. The book is, indeed, about results; but it is really about mindsets, because mindsets are the beginning place of results for everyone.

The book begins with an introduction to three critical topics foundational for the mindsets that follow. These brief chapters will help you understand mindsets, get us on the same page about systems, and describe what I mean by *shift* and its importance for healthcare leaders.

After that, I introduce, describe, and compare ten mindsets, chapter by chapter. They are each presented in a coupled way: an "orthodox mindset" and an "unorthodox mindset" about the same topic. I use *orthodox* to mean the conventional, prevailing, most common mindsets of leaders in today's U.S. healthcare industry. *Unorthodox* mindsets offer a new and unconventional approach to leadership and healthcare organizations, better aligned with the complex world that healthcare leaders face today.

Mindsets One through Six are related to systems. They build on each other, beginning with a mindset about complexity. Mindsets Seven through Ten are specific to leading and thriving in complex systems. The last chapter envisions all the mindsets together, offering forward-looking learning and development guidance.

A couple of overarching themes tie all the mindsets together. First is *complexity* as a field of science that informs healthcare leaders how to make better sense of and lead today's healthcare organizations. Complexity is a unifying arc, differentiating what is orthodox from the unorthodox. Unorthodox mindsets fit with complexity, while orthodox mindsets do not. Secondly, *shifting*, as discussed in each chapter, refers to growing and developing as leaders, drawing upon late-20th and early-21st century theories of adult development and leadership. Shifting moves us from the familiar to the unfamiliar, toward complexity, and into the next developmental stages.

Developmental science shows that we can grow toward complexity-fit mindsets. The gap between where most of us are and where many of us could be is more than a theoretical one. I experience that gap daily with my clients as I partner with them in their growth, and I grow along with them. My experience aligns with the literature and provides a significant measure of my motivation for writing this book.

From the beginning, I want to be careful and straightforward with you about shifting. I am not suggesting that there's something wrong or right, good or bad, about orthodox mindsets. I am, however, suggesting that the unorthodox ones are more useful in your daily world. While I invite you to shift toward the unorthodox, that is not an invitation to throw away or leave the orthodox entirely behind. I'm asking you to *add* the unorthodox mindsets, widening your options to help you make better sense of the world around you. It is a crucial point, this being additive and not subtractive. I will make it more than once. The redundancy is not because I think you'll forget or don't get it. I'm intentionally addressing our brain biology, which is inclined to either/or thinking, not both/and thinking. Without intention, given our brain's predilections, we will both slip into thinking about swapping unorthodox mindsets for orthodox ones. That won't do, so let's not.

The chapters flow from one to the other, carrying the concepts forward and building on the precedent ones. But the reader may be more interested in one mindset than another, and each chapter can stand alone. So feel free to read them in whichever order interests you.

No matter your journey through the book, each chapter invites you to make a shift at the end. I've intentionally written that section to be more like a nudge than a road map. It's almost like I provide you with a small bag of food, enough for the first day of a long journey, and a compass, but no map or directions other than telling you to head northish and to get on with it. I know that will leave many wanting, and that is my hope.

It's good to be hungry for a journey into the unknown. It keeps us curious. It helps us ask for more help or more learning. I want to introduce you to this leadership journey, the trip of a lifetime, and guide your early steps. The rest of the "map" is yours to create as you live it out. If I told you what to do or how to do it, I would do you a great disservice. I'm confident in your intelligence and resourcefulness, so you do not need my advice. Your path on this journey is one paved by self-awareness and curiosity. The curves and valleys are yours to explore and learn from. I am convinced that staying with orthodoxy will not serve you well, and that gives me confidence that this is the best journey for a healthcare leader to begin. So let's get on with it, then.

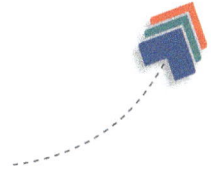

ACKNOWLEDGMENTS

Leadership is a lifetime of learning, and I have a lifetime of people who taught, mentored, and shaped me. I could not mention them all, and I will undoubtedly overlook many. Through four advanced degrees from three universities and multiple professional certificates, all my mentors, attendings, colleagues, professors, students, residents, and friends shaped my understanding of leadership. A few stand out and deserve mention: Mr. Mark Johnson, Dr. Jack Williams, Dr. Michael McVay, Dr. Max Farver, Dr. Laurel Preheim, Mr. Al Washko, Dr. Randy Petzel, Ms. Janet Murphy, Dr. Gordon Schectman, Dr. Richard Stark, Mr. Dan McElligott, Ms. Beth Bartlett, and Mr. John Fraser.

Those individuals shaped my development as a leader, but my friends, colleagues, and clients from MEDI Leadership have taught me and inspired me the most. They have challenged and encouraged my thinking, making me a better human, coach, and author. Much of the book reflects the accumulated work of MEDI Leadership coaches and the many learnings from working with thousands of U.S. healthcare care leaders for decades. MEDI Leadership's experience of and knowledge about leadership and healthcare is unparalleled, and this book benefits from that rich and remarkable heritage. Several people from

MEDI Leadership have helped and encouraged me to write this book, including Mr. Eric Norwood, Ms. Chery Foss, and Mr. Robert Porter. Other colleagues have contributed, including Dr. Michael Skoch, Dr. Frank Rosinia, Dr. Kathleen Amyot, Ms. Katie Peters, and Dr. Ronald Robinson.

The book would never have come to fruition if it weren't for Mr. Lee Angus and my colleagues at Navvis Healthcare, the parent company of MEDI Leadership. For their support and encouragement, I'm deeply grateful.

As a coach, I value coaching. Tracy Hume served as my book coach throughout the writing process. What is found in these pages would have been impossible without her.

For those I did not mention but deserved mentioning, I beg your pardon and acknowledge your double gift of forgiveness and contribution.

Lastly, I want to express my deepest gratitude to my wife of 40 years and my grown daughters, who patiently read and commented on many drafts of the same chapter every time. They are the ones who lived my leadership journey with me, sometimes suffering the most as I stumbled and bumbled along, learning about leadership. They have provided endless encouragement, precious insights, and unwavering support for this book and me.

PART ONE

INTRODUCTION

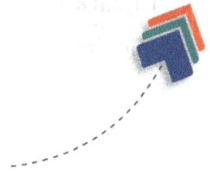

INTRODUCTION

Healthcare leaders face unprecedented challenges today. They must maintain the financial stability of their organizations in a tumultuous post-pandemic era. They must continuously adapt to rapidly changing technological advancements. Patient safety, experience, and access and quality of care demand constant attention. Workforce demographics, preferences, and expectations challenge leaders. The pressure to perform is unyielding.

The issues are so pressing and the expectations so high that it is difficult for leaders to find harmony between their professional and personal lives. Leading healthcare is a wearying daily battle in pursuit of the common good.

There's a reason for this: the fast-paced, dynamic demands result from complexity.

INTRODUCING COMPLEXITY

Complexity arises when numerous interconnected elements within an organization interact unpredictably. When complexity is present, it creates both a challenge and an opportunity, compelling leaders and their organizations to innovate and adapt. Understanding and navigating complexity is critical to effective leadership. Below are four key ways to understand and identify complexity.

Complexity Has Many Interacting Parts

Something is complex if it has many interconnected parts that interact in ways that are not fully knowable. That makes it difficult to predict the result of all those interactions. In short, if something is complex, it is hard to figure out how it works.

Suppose leaders had difficulty fully understanding and predicting the clinical performance of their multihospital organization. There were so many interconnected elements that it was hard for them to know what contributed to the outcomes they were puzzled about. This situation suggests complexity.

You Can't Reduce Complexity

Imagine those leaders looking to individual hospitals to figure out what was happening with those patients. With so many patient interactions, it would be hard to understand what each hospital, clinic, or provider contributed to the overall patient outcomes. This illustrates a key characteristic of complexity: when something is complex, a leader's understanding is not improved by breaking the whole into its parts.

This contradicts what science and philosophy have taught us for centuries—that examining and learning about the parts is the best path to understanding the whole. In other words, the whole is the sum of the parts. Reducing the whole into its parts is called "reduction." Believing reduction is the path to understanding is "reductionism." Reductionism has been, and is, a powerfully valuable tool in many scientific and philosophical contexts.

However, reductionism doesn't help us understand complex things. As a result, our tried-and-true approaches to understanding, managing, and leading complex healthcare organizations are less helpful than they once were. When leaders try to understand their complex organizations by reduction, they increase their *misunderstanding*.

Complexity Is Nonlinear

Underlying reductionism is the belief that when we do *A*, *B* always follows. This kind of direct, cause-and-effect interaction between various parts is called *linearity*. Certainty about linearity gives us confidence in predicting or expecting what happens next. For example, believing in linearity helps us build plans for the future that we have confidence in.

However, complex systems don't work that way. Instead, the interactions among the parts are nonlinear. *A* may lead to *C* instead of *B*. Or maybe *A* leads to *B* this time, but next time it leads to *D*. When things are complex, we can't extrapolate cause-and-effect relationships into the future, because they are nonlinear. This means we can't anticipate what will happen when things are complex, and we can't fully attribute results and outcomes to the efforts we deployed to achieve them. In other words, complexity is characterized by a high degree of ambiguity and uncertainty.

For example, the leaders above cannot attribute patient outcomes or experiences to a single provider, nursing unit, department, or hospital. The nonlinearity of relationships in complex environments makes it exceedingly difficult, if not impossible, to attribute results or outcomes to any particular cause.

It doesn't take much to realize how disruptive the notion of nonlinearity is to conventional beliefs about leadership and organizational performance. How do you hold people or organizations accountable for results and outcomes if you can't fully attribute outcomes to any particular cause? As we can see, nonlinearity is another reason leading complex healthcare organizations is so difficult.

Our Brains Struggle with Complexity

Complexity generates a tsunami of information, a byproduct of all the interactions. Our brains, struggling to take it all in, create cognitive shortcuts, simplifying what we're experiencing. That allows us to make swift, efficient judgments and decisions. In addition to our brains' propensity to simplify is a preference for noticing what we expect. That leads us to only notice the information that affirms our beliefs. Simply put, we only see what we believe.

The result is an oversimplification of complex situations coupled with a blindness to the unexpected. Consequently, our understanding of what is happening around us is always imperfect. That means a healthcare leader's knowledge of the organization they lead is overly simplified and always incomplete, which makes leading difficult.

The interaction of multiple elements, reducibility and linearity, and the quirks of human cognition are important concepts throughout this book. I refer to them often, as they are definitive qualities of complexity, and they help differentiate various kinds of systems.

INTRODUCING UNORTHODOXY AND MINDSETS

Introducing Orthodox and Unorthodox Thinking

The examples above are a few of the many reasons why complexity requires different thinking. To be well suited for complexity, leaders must shift from conventional, linear thinking to more adaptive, holistic, and agile thinking. Conventional thinking and its approaches can diminish a leader's effectiveness in complex organizations. Therefore, shifting toward unconventional thinking, aligned with complexity, is vital.

Conventional thinking includes beliefs and opinions that adhere to traditional, established, or generally accepted rules, principles, or practices; in a word, thinking that is *orthodox*. Ways of thinking that aren't orthodox are, by definition, unorthodox. The focus of this book is to help healthcare leaders move away from conventional thinking and toward unorthodox ways of thinking, which helps leaders succeed in a complex world.

The Connection Between Thinking and Mindsets

Shifting to unorthodox thinking only happens if we shift toward unorthodox mindsets first. That's because mindsets underpin our thinking. Therefore, to shift toward unorthodox ways of thinking about healthcare leadership requires identifying and carefully considering different mindsets and their merits.

Leaders may be more interested in better results and outcomes than unorthodox mindsets. But let's examine that a bit more closely. Most people agree that results and outcomes are linked to a leader's approaches, actions, and behaviors—what leaders do. It is important to understand that what leaders decide to do is based on how they think. If different results or outcomes are needed, different thinking must come first. Since thinking flows from mindsets, to think differently mindsets must change. Therefore, reaching different or better results and outcomes depends on changed mindsets. Leaders must shift toward unorthodox mindsets if they want to do better with complexity.

Leadership behaviors matter, but mindsets matter more. That makes leadership mindsets the epicenter of transformation and why this book is about ten unconventional *mindsets* rather than ten unconventional *behaviors*.

LAYING THE FOUNDATION FOR MINDSETS, SYSTEMS, AND SHIFTING

Before delving into the ten mindsets, three important topics need further exploration: first, a deeper dive into what mindsets are; second, a clear understanding of systems—including systems thinking and the concept of "systemness"; and third, an explanation of "shifting" and why it's important. These topics form the foundation for the rest of the book.

MINDSETS AND WHY
THEY MATTER

Mindsets Shape Actions, Which Shape Results

WHAT MINDSETS ARE

Mindsets are a set of combined beliefs, paradigms, and mental models informed by our emotional intelligence. They exist in our minds and affect our thinking, ultimately influencing our approaches, actions, and behaviors. Like a computer's operating system, mindsets work quietly in the background, often beyond our conscious awareness.

Mindsets are interconnected, interdependent, and mutually reinforcing. They are deeply ingrained and difficult to identify. Additionally, as we interact with our surroundings, our experiences shape our mindsets. Mindsets also determine how we make sense of those experiences. It's essential to see the self-reinforcing loop this creates. Mindsets determine what we notice, and what we notice shapes our mindsets. The cyclical nature of mindsets can trap us in a loop. When that happens, it hinders our growth and adaptability.

Because mindsets shape our sense of reality, they also shape a leader's approaches, actions, and behaviors. By *approaches*, I am referring to structural, programmatic tools and techniques such as Lean management techniques and other established industry management norms. By *actions*, I am referring to specific actions, such as making the decision to fire someone, or sending out blanket email directives. By *behaviors*, I am referring to the emotional content and attitude of a leader's behaviors; for example, a leader's tendency to make decisions quickly and assertively.

A leader's approaches, actions, and behaviors influence the results and outcomes they and their organization achieve. In other words, mindsets shape how we show up, and how we show up impacts the organization. If we want to change results and outcomes, we must change how we show up. If we want to change how we show up, we must first shift our mindsets. Without a mindset shift, change is unlikely.

WHERE MINDSETS COME FROM

Mindsets Come from Personal Experiences

Our mindsets and the ways we think develop from our personal experiences. From childhood onward, we strive to understand the events occurring around us. Over time, our understanding shapes our thoughts about how the world functions. Those beliefs eventually become ingrained in our subconscious, informing our mindsets. Once entrenched there, it takes intentional effort to bring those mindsets back to the surface for reconsideration.

For example, Jonathan grew up in an autocratic, paternalistic household. In high school, he became a mechanic and started racing cars. His boss successfully ran the mechanic shop and race team in a command-and-control fashion. Twenty years later, Jonathan became a nurse and, in short order, a nurse manager. A few years after that, he noticed his career trajectory plateauing but wasn't sure why. Jonathan participated in an executive leadership coaching program, where 360-degree style feedback confirmed his challenges: people were tired of his direct, commanding demeanor.

Jonathan found this feedback hard to digest. His life experiences had taught him that others expect good leaders to be direct and commanding. He had internalized this assumption and never thought to question it.

Another example is Amanda. Amanda grew up in a single-parent home. She idolized her mother, who was smart and resourceful. The ideas she internalized about leadership came from her experiences with her mother: no matter what questions Amanda had as she was growing up, her mother always seemed to have the right answer. Her mother advised her on everything from how to fill out college scholarship essays to how to handle household maintenance when she bought her first home.

From these experiences, Amanda internalized her belief that good leaders usually know the best course of action. When she became a leader in her healthcare organization, she adopted this approach without thinking about it. Whenever someone faced a problem, she provided them with a solution. She was skilled at this, being both intelligent and approachable. People admired her and considered her an exceptional leader, resulting in a promotion. But as her responsibilities expanded, so did the number of issues people brought to her for resolution. The pressure to solve all those problems became overwhelming, yet Amanda never questioned her basic belief about leadership: good leaders know all the answers.

Like Jonathan and Amanda, our mindsets come from our experiences. However, it is important to note it's not the experiences themselves that shape our mindsets. It's how we *make sense of* those experiences. Jonathan made sense of his experiences with his father and shop boss by believing good leaders give orders. Amanda made sense of her experiences with her mother by believing good leaders have the right answers. How they both made sense of their experiences solidified their beliefs, and they incorporated those beliefs into their leadership mindset.

To be clear, what Jonathan and Amanda thought about leadership was not their mindset. Mindsets determine how we think, which determines what we do. What they thought *came from* and reinforced their mindset. The mindset they both held is called a "heroic leadership" mindset by many. A heroic leadership mindset supports the belief that good leaders are direct and commanding and know or can find the right answers.

Like Jonathan and Amanda, how we make sense of our experiences depends on our mindset, and our mindset depends on our experiences— a self-reinforcing loop. That's one reason why it is difficult to change.

Mindsets Come from Insights

It can be difficult to escape the self-reinforcing loop of mindsets. But insights are potent disruptors. They can instantly alter our mindsets. Sometimes an experience we have births a new realization about ourselves or others or how the world operates. These insights represent "Aha!" moments. Insights can serve as profound learning instances that quickly reshape mindsets.

For Jonathan, insight into his leadership style came in the context of a leadership coaching program. With his coach's help, Jonathan began to see how his life journey had shaped his mindset about leadership. One insight was that he led similarly to how his father raised him and how his boss led the mechanic shop.

Jonathan's insight helped him notice his thinking. Once he became aware of his thinking, Jonathan noticed his mindset and summarized it as, "Good leaders get things done by telling people what to do and how to do it well." So that's what he had always done (nicely, he would add).

Because the approaches tied to his mindset no longer worked well for him, Jonathan tried to shift his mindset toward something more useful. Along with the shift in mindset, he had to learn new ways of thinking about leadership. And Jonathan needed to practice behaviors that fit his new thinking and mindset.

Amanda gained insight in a less formal way. One day, she confided in Beth, her supervisor, expressing doubts about her leadership abilities. Amanda was considering resigning due to the immense pressure of always needing to have all the right answers. Beth suggested, "A great leader doesn't always know what to do. They help others know what to do."

Amanda instantly grasped how her mindset about leadership—that good leaders have the right answers—had been holding her back. With this newfound insight, her mindset quickly shifted, and her thinking and behaviors followed suit. Amanda's story underscores how insights can be potent catalysts for permanently reshaping mindsets.

HOW TO "SEE" MINDSETS

Just like Jonathan and Amanda, leaders can only shift their mindsets if they know what they are or "see" them. But seeing them is not always easy, because mindsets are often deeply entrenched in our subconscious. Below are four ways leaders can see their mindsets.

Notice How You Show Up

A leader can see their mindsets by observing their approaches, actions, and behaviors—how they show up. How a leader shows up depends on how they think, and how they think is knowable with inquiry and curiosity.

For example, Michael shouted at his boss, angry about a request to reduce his department's labor expenses by 15 percent. After an apology, Michael reflected on his strong negative emotional response. Practicing self-inquiry, he asked himself, "Isn't that interesting how you showed up? What was that about for you?" Michael noticed his behavior and was curious about it rather than judgmental.

Explore Your Thinking

After some reflection, Michael noted the patterned thinking about executive leaders that had precipitated his behavioral response. He believed executive leaders never have the organizational awareness they should. When Michael was told to reduce his expenses, he thought the request was ridiculous and unfair—they had no idea what they were asking—which resulted in his emotional response.

But thinking is not the same as mindsets; mindsets determine thinking. So Michael needed to do more to understand the mindset influencing his thinking.

Discover Your Mindset

To see his mindset, Michael had to stay curious about why he thought about executive leaders the way he did. Only then did he discover the mindset underlying his thinking. After considerable reflection, with help from his coach, Michael realized he held a heroic leadership mindset. That mindset informed him that executive leaders should know everything about the organizations they lead—being all-knowing is a "heroic" notion. In Michael's mind, leadership should have known that their request imperiled his ability to achieve the performance targets for which he was accountable. The perceived threat to his competency as a leader stirred Michael's emotions and drove his behavior. We can see how Michael's pursuit to understand his mindset unfolded in Figure 1.

| Mindsets | → | Thinking | → | Approaches, Actions, Behaviors |

FIGURE 1. *Seeing Mindsets*. By analyzing observable approaches, actions, and behaviors, we can infer the underlying ways of thinking that shape them, ultimately revealing a mindset. This illustration does not depict feedback loops, where actions, in turn, can influence our thinking or mindsets. (Source: Michael Hein, 2025.)

Michael's mindset determined his thinking. His thinking determined his approaches, actions, and behaviors. To see his mindset, Michael began by observing how he showed up. That led him to notice his thinking. And with deeper inquiry, he understood his underlying leadership mindset.

See Mindsets Through Expressions

Like Michael, we all display our mindsets through how we show up. Commonly called "leadership style," the way leaders show up is a window into their mindsets.

Imagine two leaders who are both CEOs. Denzel thinks most people are not inclined to work—a few are, and they've worked for the positions and higher ranks they have. For Denzel, an important part of leadership is finding those people who have the innate desire to work. Denzel has a fixed mindset about human motivation. For him, most people lack internal motivation, and that is something that can't be changed. Denzel thinks most people are innately lazy.[1]

Imani, another CEO, believes that while a few may be disinclined to work, most people can learn to work hard and try their best. When their best fails them, something has gotten in their way. For Imani, an important part of leadership is inspiring and motivating others to work hard and to remove the barriers getting in their way. Imani has a growth mindset about human motivation. For her, most people have and can develop internal motivation. Imani thinks most people are innately industrious.[2]

Now imagine the company is in severe financial difficulty. Company data showed low workforce productivity compared to industry benchmarks. Both leaders interpreted the information through their mindsets. Denzel thought that the workforce wasn't working hard—people are lazy. To eliminate the "dead weight," he responded with a workforce reduction. Imani thought differently about the same data. She thought outdated technologies and facilities hindered productivity—people want to be industrious. In response, Imani updated critical infrastructure rather than reducing the workforce.

Both leaders "expressed" their mindsets by how they showed up, (i.e., through their approaches, actions, and behaviors.) Denzel showed up in ways that led to a workforce reduction. Imani showed up in ways that led to more capital investment. The same situation with different mindsets led to different thinking. Different thinking led to different expressions. And different expressions led to different outcomes. We can see Denzel's and Imani's mindsets through those expressions.

In the following chapters, I use this ability to see mindsets, listing three orthodox and unorthodox expressions for each mindset. My intent is to help you notice the mindsets you and others hold. In the last chapter, I bring all the expressions together to portray both an orthodox leader and an unorthodox leader.

Expressions are important. They provide a starting point for self-reflection. Your journey toward unorthodoxy begins by noticing your expressions. Then, you can be curious about your underlying thinking and where that comes from. You can't make a shift if you don't see the mindset you have. You can't see the mindset you have unless you notice your thinking. And you can't notice your thinking unless you notice your expressions first.

A FEW CAVEATS ABOUT MINDSETS

Mindsets Are Complex

A clear and direct cause-and-effect relationship between experiences, insights, mindsets, thinking, expressions, and results doesn't exist. The connections between them are complex. Therefore, while it's doable, it isn't easy to derive mindsets from thinking and behaviors.

Moreover, we sometimes behave in inexplicable ways. Some of those puzzling behaviors stem from mindsets that clash. Consequently, sometimes mindsets defy categorization. Furthermore, not all experiences are formative, neither are all insights helpful. Expressions don't always align with mindsets. The way a leader shows up may not have a direct cause-and-effect relationship with individual or corporate results. Despite all these limitations and challenges, mindsets powerfully shape outcomes, and we can know what they are.

Mindsets Are Cumulative

Mindsets are cumulative, resembling how rings in a tree trunk mark the growth of a tree. When a new mindset emerges, we don't discard the old one. Instead, we add the new mindset to the old one, like a tree adds new growth—the tree ring—to its trunk. The old mindset is a foundation, and we retain access to it. Occasionally, we may use an old mindset if it proves helpful in a specific situation. Access to multiple mindsets allows us to make choices, shifting between them as needed. The key is to be self-aware, make intentional choices, and express our mindsets purposefully.

Mindsets Are Malleable

Recognize that we choose mindsets. While created and informed by experiences, values, insights, and environmental influences, we can choose what mindsets we retain or discard. So we can cultivate and modify our mindsets, aiming for better alignment with the evolving challenges we face. In other words, our mindsets are malleable.

Before reshaping our mindsets, we must be aware of alternatives. We can't be aware of different options unless we curiously and consistently reflect on our thoughts and actions. Understanding the malleability of mindsets empowers leaders to take greater control of their mental frameworks and, ultimately, their leadership success.

Mindsets Are Sticky

While mindsets are, indeed, malleable, they are also "sticky." That makes modifying them challenging. As our experiences and insights accumulate, we incorporate cognitive biases and habits that reinforce existing mindsets. These quick cognitive shortcuts help us navigate the bombardment of sensory input that is life. But they also limit our ability to change our mindsets. For example, confirmation bias leads people to seek information supporting their beliefs and ignore information contradicting them, making it challenging to adopt new perspectives. This self-reinforcing nature of mindsets contributes to their stickiness.

Another reason mindsets are sticky is decreased neuroplasticity. Neuroplasticity is the brain's ability to adapt, reorganize, and form new neural connections throughout life. As our brains age, they become less plastic. Aging makes it harder for adults to change ingrained thinking patterns and learn new information. The older we are, the harder it is to develop new mindsets.

It's not that adults can't change; it just takes more intention and effort. Plasticity applies to a 60 year old who wants to start playing the bass guitar or a 45-year-old leader wishing to lead their healthcare organization differently. Our mindsets become sticky because our brains prefer established neural connections. In a way, the "easy button" for us is to keep the familiar and ignore or reject the unfamiliar.

Furthermore, mindsets are tied closely to identity and self-esteem. Shifting a mindset may make us feel like we were wrong or our previous beliefs misguided. That can threaten our self-image. Challenges to our personal or professional identities often stir emotion. It's not unusual for people to shy away from things that stir emotion, another reason for sticky mindsets.

THE IMPORTANCE OF MATCHING
MINDSETS WITH CONTEXT

A last point about mindsets is that the most successful leaders seek to match their mindsets to their context. This approach yields robust and consistent results for their organizations and themselves. Mindset adaptability and keen contextual awareness are vital contributors to successful leadership in complex organizations.

When we talk about matching mindsets to context, we are talking about matching mindsets to systems. In order to do that well, first we must agree on a few systems-related terms and concepts.

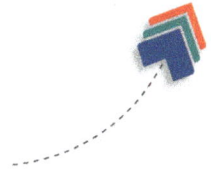

SYSTEMNESS AND WHY IT MATTERS

The System Mindset Shapes the Leader

WHAT SYSTEMS ARE (AND ARE NOT)

All organizations are systems, but not all systems are organizations. This is a critically important point to understand, so I'm going to repeat it: all organizations are systems, but not all systems are organizations. You may be used to thinking of these terms synonymously, but to understand mindsets and how they work, we need to make a distinction between systems and organizations. Let's go deeper and examine the relationship between the idea of a system and the definition of an organization.

What Is a System?

System is a broad concept that refers to a collection of interacting and interrelated parts that form a unified whole.[3] That means toasters, cars, organizations, and rainforests are all systems. Systems can be physical, like the cardiovascular system in the human body, or they can be abstract, like an economic system.

Systems can exist independently of organizations, they can exist coincident with organizations, and they can exist within organizations. In healthcare, it can be confusing to talk about systems because many large healthcare organizations call themselves healthcare "systems." In this book, I am not using the word *system* in the sense of Corporation XYZ's Healthcare System. I am using the word in a broader, more conceptual and abstract sense.

What Is an Organization?

Organizations are structured groups of individuals working toward a common goal or purpose. Humans organize themselves in specific ways to get something done, like creating and running a business or a company. Therefore, healthcare organizations are structurally organized groups of individuals working together to heal people. In most instances, healthcare organizations are companies, businesses, or agencies.

The Relationship Between Healthcare Organizations and the Idea of Systems

Let's look more closely at healthcare organizations. They have many parts: hospitals and clinics, laboratories and surgery centers, physicians, nurses, and more. All the parts of a healthcare organization interact and are interrelated. Combined, they form a unified whole. That means healthcare organizations are, indeed, systems.

However, while every healthcare organization is a system internally, not every system in the healthcare industry is an organization. Individual healthcare organizations operate as self-contained systems; at the same time, the broader healthcare industry represents a systemic interplay of multiple organizations and entities. For instance, a regional multi-hospital organization works as a system. It is also part of a larger city, state, or national healthcare system comprising multiple organizations and entities with diverse functions and goals.

In this book, we explore healthcare organizations as different kinds of systems and try to keep *organizations* and *systems* separate. These terms are not synonymous, even though all organizations are some kind of system. This is a critical distinction, necessary for understanding the importance of mindsets.

FOUR DIFFERENT KINDS OF SYSTEMS

Leaders must understand that there are different kinds of systems and that their organization functions as one or more of those systems. Different kinds of systems require different kinds of leadership. Leadership that works well with one kind of system doesn't work well with another. That is why it is so important for leaders to understand that different kinds of systems exist.

For our purposes, I want to introduce you to four kinds of systems.[4] As you read the various descriptions below, consider your healthcare organization. See if you can discern what kind of system it is most like:

1. *Simple Systems* (also known as *Obvious Systems*): Simple systems are the most straightforward systems, characterized by a few parts which interact in predictable ways. Examples of simple systems include basic mechanical devices like teeter-totters or light switches. Importantly, the unified whole of a simple system is the sum of its parts. The check-in process at a clinic is an example in healthcare. Only a few steps are involved, one step proceeds predictably to the next, and it has a clearly defined beginning and end.

2. *Complicated Systems*: Complicated systems have many interacting parts, but the interactions are still predictable if the system works as designed. Examples include toasters and cars. Like

simple systems, complicated systems are also reducible. That is, the unified whole of a complicated system is the sum of its parts. If we disassemble a toaster or a car into its component parts and then rebuild it, it will work as it should. Many in the industry have traditionally viewed healthcare organizations as large complicated systems.

3. *Complex Systems*: As I described in the Introduction, complex systems have numerous interconnected parts interacting in nonlinear ways. The combined effect of the innumerable parts interacting unpredictably is *emergence*. Emergence occurs when a group of things come together and create something new and unexpected, something you would not see by looking at each thing individually. In other words, the whole is greater than the sum of its parts. Importantly, emergence renders complex systems irreducible. I will have more to say about emergence in the chapters on Complexity (Mindset One) and Change (Mindset Six). Examples of complex systems include ecosystems like rainforests, where the many interactions between species create surprising dynamics; and the economy, where the interactions of countless independent factors shape its overall behavior. One of the foundational arguments of this book is that today's healthcare organizations are complex rather than merely complicated, (i.e., they are more like the economy than like a car).

4. *Chaotic Systems*: Chaotic systems also consist of many interconnected parts interacting nonlinearly, demonstrating emergence. However, the defining characteristic of chaotic systems isn't emergence. It is their extreme sensitivity to initial conditions. Think of initial conditions as the starting point or the first set of circumstances present when the system begins to operate. This sensitivity leads to the "butterfly effect," a concept suggesting that a small event,

like a butterfly flapping its wings in Brazil, could eventually cause a tornado in Texas.[5] The butterfly effect makes chaotic systems highly unpredictable and irreducible. While purely chaotic systems are rare, weather patterns are a classic example. Small changes in things that influence weather can lead to vastly different outcomes, making accurate long-term predictions challenging.

DISCERNING KINDS OF SYSTEMS

Leaders need to know which kind of system they are dealing with, because approaches that work well with one kind of system don't work well with other kinds of systems. Two ways of discerning kinds of systems are (a) observing the way the system functions and (b) identifying the degree of orderliness of the system.

Recognizing Systems by the Way They Function

One way leaders can determine the kind of system they are working with is by paying attention to how the system functions. There are four key functional characteristics that help define systems:

1. *The number of elements involved.* Simple and complicated systems have fewer elements. Complex and chaotic systems have more. While simple and complicated systems tend to have fewer elements, the complexity of a system is not solely decided by the number of elements but also by how these elements interact. In healthcare organizations, elements are divisions, departments, hospitals, clinics, people, processes, etc. Anything involved in how things get done is an element.

2. *The interaction between elements.* In both simple and complicated systems, elements interact in predictable, direct, linear,

cause-and-effect ways, producing expected results and outcomes. Think of simple and complicated systems as "predictable world" systems. In complex and chaotic systems, the elements interact in unpredictable, indirect, nonlinear ways, producing unexpected results and outcomes. Think of complex and chaotic systems as "unpredictable world" systems. Remember that even systems with relatively few elements can exhibit complex behavior. It all depends on how the elements interact.

3. *The boundaries of the unified whole.* With both simple and complicated systems (like toasters), the unified whole has clearly defined boundaries. However, complex and chaotic systems interact extensively with their environment, which can blur the lines between the system and its surroundings. A toaster is essentially a self-contained entity, making it easy to tell what it is and is not. But with a rainforest, a complex system, it is much more difficult to tell where the system ends. Is it where there are no longer any trees? What about the earth or the atmosphere? Complex and chaotic systems have fuzzy boundaries. Their unified whole is less defined.

4. *The interactions with the environment.* As we saw above, simple and complicated systems have limited interdependent interactions with elements outside their boundaries. But complex and chaotic systems have many, even to the point where you can't always tell where the system ends. For example, healthcare organizations interact with government agencies, payers, employers, and community-based services, all "outside" the boundaries of the organization. Complex and chaotic systems are often "open systems," constantly exchanging information, energy, or materials with their environment, contributing to their complexity.

Recognizing Systems by the Degree of Orderliness

Each of the four functional characteristics described previously helps determine the kind of system a leader's organization is most like. Another helpful approach is to take all those functional characteristics and consider them together. If you do that, you can understand how ordered an organization is or is not.

Different kinds of systems have different degrees of order. In short, simple systems are more orderly than complicated systems, and complicated systems are more orderly than complex systems, which are more orderly than chaotic ones (Figure 2). Gaining a general sense of organizational order or disorder can help you decide what kind of system your healthcare organization resembles.

Predictable World				Unpredictable World			
⟶	⟶	Decreasing Order			⟶	⟶	
Simple Systems		Complicated Systems		Complex Systems		Chaotic Systems	
Examples[1]							
Teeter Totter	Light Switch	Toaster	Car	Healthcare[2]	Rainforest	Pandemic	Weather

FIGURE 2. *Four Types of Systems and Orderliness.* Notes: (1) These examples are oversimplified to demonstrate the most prominent inclinations of various kinds of systems. "Car," for example, is comprised of simple and complicated systems; overall demonstrating mostly complicated system inclinations. (2) Healthcare organizations have traditionally been viewed as complicated systems. However, it is more accurate to describe modern healthcare organizations as exhibiting characteristics of complex (less predictable), rather than complicated (more predictable), systems. (Source: Michael Hein, 2025. Adapted from Dave Snowden and Zhen Goh, *Cynefin—Weaving Sense-Making into the Fabric of Our World* (Cognitive Edge—The Cynefin Co, 2020).)

Orderliness is a handy way to understand how organizations function, giving leaders a clue about the kind of system their organization is. However, one must be careful. Orderliness is determined based on how the system *actually* functions, not on the way we think it *ought* to function. To be your most effective self, leaders need to assess their organization through an "orderliness" lens; keeping an eye on the functional characteristics they observe or experience. That approach helps leaders know what kind of systems they are dealing with.

By now, you probably have a clearer understanding of the kind of system that your healthcare organization most resembles. Healthcare organizations are not simple systems, though they contain simple systems. Nor are they entirely chaotic systems, though they may become chaotic for brief periods. Overall, they function most like complicated or complex systems; one kind of system is from the predictable world (complicated), and the other is from the unpredictable world (complex).

The remainder of the book compares these two kinds of systems and the mindsets that define them, keeping in mind that orthodox mindsets are often well-suited to complicated systems, and unorthodox mindsets are usually more well-suited to complex systems. Let's look at the foundational concepts that inform leadership approaches to these two kinds of systems.

THINKING ABOUT SYSTEMS (SYSTEMS THINKING)

Systems thinking is an approach to understanding and solving problems that emphasizes the interconnectivity and dynamic interactions among a system's components. In other words, it is a way of thinking and acknowledging that things happen (or events occur, or phenomena take place—however you want to frame it) within the context of a system.

For example, say a patient develops a Central Line-Associated Bloodstream Infection (CLABSI), a healthcare-associated infection (HAI).[6] Suppose a leader approaches that event with a systems-thinking perspective. They might think, "This HAI happened in the context of a system. To decrease future HAIs, I need to look at the system to determine how and why the infection happened."

However, it is one thing to acknowledge that events occur within the context of a system. It is another thing entirely to view events through a mindset that is biased toward *a specific kind* of system. A key point to understand here is that the science of systems thinking has changed. Historically, systems thinking focused on complicated systems. Today, systems thinking focuses on the existence and characteristics of complex systems. For all practical purposes, all healthcare organizations today are complex systems.

Systems Thinking and Complicated Systems

The mindset underlying historical systems thinking is reductionism. Reductionism is the belief in understanding the entirety of a system by dissecting its constituent parts. In other words, it presupposes that human systems (such as organizations) are complicated, machine-like systems.

Reductionism finds its roots in classical Newtonian physics, where cause-and-effect relationships are clear, and systems behave in predictable, deterministic ways. This approach, foundational in management theory, was prevalent throughout the 20th and early 21st century. This machine-like perspective still influences many areas, notably in healthcare, where systems are often seen as intricate versions of simpler mechanical devices or factory production lines.

A healthcare leader adhering to historical systems thinking, perceiving the organization as a complicated system, might confront an HAI using methodologies like Root Cause Analysis (RCA) or Lean Manufacturing Principles to "find and fix" the problem. They would scrutinize the events leading to the HAI by reducing or breaking down what transpired into individual decisions, process steps, or actions taken. These leaders would look to identify variation from standard protocols or procedures, considered "errors" or "waste." Once identified, leaders would implement new protocols or methods to eliminate the errors or waste (inefficiency). The goal would be to address the HAI's "root causes" by reducing the problem to tangible, identifiable elements gone awry.

Once the identified issue is "fixed," the system is expected to function as designed.

Systems Thinking and Complex Systems

Systems thinking evolved, however, as global complexities and uncertainties grew, and scientific fields unlocked new ways of making sense of the universe and its workings. Now, systems thinking increasingly focuses on understanding systems through the mindsets of holism and emergentism rather than reductionism. This shift moves away from traditional, machine-like complicated systems, making complexity the dominant approach in systems thinking today.

Holism emphasizes that a system must be viewed as a whole, considering all the interactions and relationships among its components. Emergentism underscores the notion that unique, unexpected properties or behaviors naturally emerge within a system, occurring for reasons that cannot be explained by examining individual components. These contemporary perspectives are especially beneficial for leaders when dealing with the unpredictable world, where complex and chaotic systems are prevalent.

A leader whose mindset about systems is grounded in holism and emergentism (better aligned with the complex nature of today's systems) might take a different approach to the HAI incident. Rather than a "find and fix" approach, this leader adopts a "notice and nudge" strategy. These leaders emphasize the importance of understanding emergent patterns and system dynamics over pinpointing and correcting isolated errors. Instead of reducing a problem into individual components, they engage a broad spectrum of stakeholders to grasp what might be called the system's "holistic narrative"—a gathering of as much information, knowledge, and insight as possible about what transpired without reducing the HAI incident into individual components.[7] Rather than looking to find fault and blame, these leaders' primary aim is to listen and learn from those who were involved in witnessing the system's inclination to create an HAI.

Any interventions taken to alter the inclination of the system to create another HAI are subtle and iterative. Leaders deploy interventions in critical leverage points, or "soft spots," (i.e., functional places, situations, or contexts considered most likely to influence the system in favorable ways). Each intervention is cautiously intended to nudge the system toward healthier patterns. Sometimes described as "experiments" or "placing bets," the interventions are handled cautiously because these leaders recognize the unpredictable nature of complex systems. Nudges—these small experiments or bets—may have disproportionate impacts, some favorable, others not. So caution is warranted.

These leaders also expect and prepare for new HAIs to emerge in unforeseen ways. After they deploy their nudges, they don't believe the system is fixed, merely influenced. So these leaders focus on flexibility and resilience rather than eliminating errors, staying hypervigilant for emerging incidents and marshaling a rapid adaptive response when another occurs.

I am not saying a complexity-fit leader would always choose this specific strategy; I am simply trying to illustrate that a leader with a complexity mindset has other approaches to choose from when addressing the problems that emerge in complex systems.

However, it is essential to note a critical challenge inherent in systems thinking when dealing with complex systems: the potential for overwhelming complexity and the difficulty of identifying effective leverage points for intervention. This challenge underscores the importance of robust methodologies and suitable tools for analyzing complex systems. Complex systems require tools that can help identify patterns, simplify complexity without losing essential insights, and guide effective action.[8] In short, a leader cannot rely on the methods and tools of the past (i.e., RCA or Lean) to effectively address the challenges of complex systems.

The crux of the matter is that the healthcare industry has not kept up with the evolving understanding of systems thinking.[9] Consequently, and importantly, when the healthcare industry promotes systems thinking today, it promotes conventional approaches that match complicated, not complex, systems.

Because a leader's mindset about systems determines how they lead, the ongoing retention of outdated mindsets and the promotion of outdated systems thinking is more than an academic exercise. It promotes ways of leading that don't match complexity. The mismatch has profound implications for leadership and significantly affects how the healthcare industry makes sense of "systemness."

SYSTEMS THINKING AND SYSTEMNESS

A practical application of systems thinking is the pursuit of *systemness*. The concept of systemness has gained considerable traction in the industry. In casual usage, systemness means acting more like a system.

If only one kind of system existed, that definition would make sense. But since there are different kinds of systems, a question arises: "What kind of system are we trying to act more like?" For example, acting like a complicated system differs from acting like a complex one. Toasters don't act anything like rainforests.

Systemness in Complicated Systems

The conventional, orthodox definition of systemness is consistent with complicated systems. For example, "systemness describes a desired state of integration and coordination through greater centralized control using conventional corporate management methods."[10]

This kind of systemness is one where individual parts of an organization work well. They function with cost-effective efficiency using consistent and standard processes. The individual parts work similarly to all the other parts of the organization. The entire system works well together in a centrally controlled and coordinated fashion.

There are a couple of things to notice about this version of systemness. First, the function of the whole depends on the parts; the system only functions well if all the individual components do—the sum of the parts equals the whole. Second, how the parts work together is centrally coordinated and managed. The aim is to create predictable, linear cause-and-effect interactions between elements across the organization.

Those two things help us understand what kind of system is presumed and promoted by the conventional appeal for greater systemness. They describe complicated systems—the sum of the parts equals the whole, and the components interact in orderly, linearly predictable, and planned ways. But this kind of systemness does not coincide with today's systems thinking.

Systemness in Complex Systems

Today's systems thinking recognizes that complex systems, like healthcare organizations, are more than just the sum of their parts. They have interactions that are not always predictable and can lead to unexpected results. Those qualities describe emergence. That means with today's systems thinking, "acting more like a system" describes emergence. Plainly stated, *systemness is emergence.* Therefore, complex systems and genuine systemness are inseparable. You cannot have one without the other. If you aspire to and desire systemness, you must aspire to and desire complex systems. It's hard to overstate the importance of that point.

Healthcare organizations often merge with each other, hoping that by combining forces, they'll achieve better outcomes than would be possible individually. That is the pursuit of emergence—achieving more as a collective than as the sum of individual parts. However, simply merging hospitals doesn't guarantee this, especially if the resulting organization is structured and operated as a complicated system. Exceeding the sum of the parts arises when the organization is structured and operated as a complex system, not simply a larger, more complicated one.

Understanding and embracing complexity is key to realizing systemness. Sticking with conventional systems thinking, imagining organizations as merely complicated, and leading them that way, cannot generate genuine systemness. Approaching your organization as if it is complicated creates a false systemness: merely the whole functioning as the sum of the parts. That isn't systemness.

Systemness requires emergence: the whole functioning greater than the sum of the parts. Emergence, which is only present in complex systems, is the source of genuine systemness. Leading organizations as if they are complicated destroys emergence and precludes the organization from ever achieving genuine systemness.

Shifting Mindsets to Pursue Genuine Systemness

Even though hospital-based healthcare organizations function like complex systems today, they are organized, led, and operated as if they were merely complicated systems. That problematic dynamic creates a form (complicated system) and function (complex system) mismatch that is difficult to navigate. Furthermore, genuine systemness will remain unachievable without a paradigmatic shift away from orthodox approaches, which is only possible if leaders think differently about systems. Leaders cannot think differently about systems without shifting their mindsets from orthodoxy to unorthodoxy. That is why a clear understanding of what I mean by shifting is so essential.

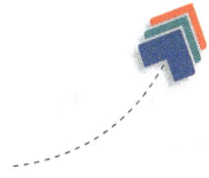

SHIFTING AND WHY
IT MATTERS

Abiding by the Law of Requisite Complexity

WHAT MINDSET SHIFTING IS

Shifting Your Mindset is Moving Your Cognitive Balance

By shifting, I don't mean altogether abandoning one mindset for another. Instead, envision standing with both feet on the ground, your weight mainly, but not wholly, on your right foot. If I asked you to shift your weight to the left while keeping your right foot grounded, you'd sway your center of gravity without lifting either foot. Likewise, the shift I'm referring to doesn't mean altogether abandoning one mindset for another but rather swaying your cognitive center of gravity away from the complicated toward the complex. It's a transfer of your cognitive base of operation from your previous stance toward a new one, retaining some relationship with your previous one while assuming an entirely new posture. You don't throw the orthodox mindsets away or disregard them altogether. They can still be helpful for you in specific contexts—those that aren't complex—which are increasingly rare.

Shifting Your Mindset is Growth

Shifting is primarily about growing, which is personal change at a fundamental level. When we make a shift in our mindsets, we change and grow. Whether we are growing from adolescence to young adulthood or developing our leadership, a shift in mindsets must take place before any behavior change occurs. Of course, we all want to be the most effective leaders we can be, and that aspiration in and of itself implies an understanding that change is required. Change only comes after mindsets have changed.

Shifting Your Mindset is Uncomfortable

Leading in today's complex context is uncomfortable, and that tells us something valuable. Discomfort is often an indicator of where our most significant opportunity for growth lies. This is called a *growth edge*. A growth edge is an area where you have the potential to grow but are not yet an expert. It is where you are challenged and stretched and can learn and develop new skills. In this case, the discomfort we all feel with complexity informs us that there's a growth edge at play. If we pay attention to that, it positions us to change for the better. Shifting mindsets happens after we notice a growth edge but before we take our first action or step.

WHY A MINDSET SHIFT IS REQUIRED

Because Healthcare Organizations are Complex

Healthcare organizations have evolved into complex systems. Healthcare leaders must embrace and appreciate this complexity to lead these organizations effectively. By adopting a complexity-fit mindset, leaders are better equipped to navigate the challenges of a rapidly changing environment, make sound decisions, build strong relationships, and foster a positive work environment.

A complexity-fit mindset enables leaders to focus on the bigger picture and appreciate a complex system's unpredictable and uncontrollable interactions. Complexity-fit leaders demonstrate adaptability, flexibility in decision-making, and responsiveness to change. Moreover, complexity-fit leaders cultivate strong stakeholder relationships and foster a collaborative, positive, and productive work environment.

Because a Complexity Mindset is Required

The way of leading described above is not simply a preference or a style choice. One of the most important things to understand about leading complex systems well is that complexity fitness is not optional. Without complexity-fit mindsets, the leader will struggle, and the organization will operate sub optimally or fail.

We know a lot about complex systems, how they function, and how to influence them. As our understanding of complexity grew, the Law of Requisite Complexity emerged. Think of it like the law of gravity regarding complex systems. It applies to every complex system, regardless of whether the system is naturally occurring or created by people.

First coined as the Law of Requisite Variety, this law derives from the field of cybernetics, a transdisciplinary science concerned with how complex biological, social, managerial, and technical systems adapt, self-organize, and function efficiently.[11] It was later reconceptualized as the Law of Requisite Complexity, which states that a "control system" must be at least as complex as the system it controls.[12] A control system that is too simple will not be able to respond to the changing conditions of the complex system it is designed to influence.

For our purposes, control systems are leadership approaches designed and deployed to influence an organization's outcomes—things like strategic planning, budgeting, performance management, and risk management. Whatever approaches we devise must suit complexity, or the organization will become unstable or fail. The challenge for leaders in complex systems is the propensity to lead them as if they are a simpler system (complicated) than they are (complex) using control systems that do not match. When that happens, the organization becomes unstable—poorer working conditions, weakening financial performance, diminishing standards of care—or it fails altogether.

These are not just theoretical considerations. My colleagues and I at MEDI Leadership see this mismatch happening repeatedly across the industry. Healthcare organizations led as if they were merely complicated rather than complex systems fall short of their promise and become increasingly unpleasant workplaces, churning through providers and leaders while deteriorating financially.

Leading complex systems requires leaders to follow the Law of Requisite Complexity, deriving solutions that fit complexity. To derive solutions—approaches, actions, and behaviors—that are complexity-fit, leaders must think in complexity-fit ways. To think in those ways, leaders must have mindsets that match complexity. If leaders aren't yet complexity-fit, then they must shift their mindsets. That is what this book is all about.

MAKING A MINDSET SHIFT

A Nudge Toward Unorthodoxy Is More Valuable Than a Road Map

I've structured this book to help leaders see and begin their mindset shifts toward complexity. Each chapter in Parts Two and Three ends with a brief discussion about making a shift. These sections should serve as a nudge rather than a road map.

A road map would tell you what to do and how to do it. That approach works about as well as telling your partner how they ought to grow. It would be a disservice if I tried to do that with you. Instead, the "Making the Shift" sections at the end of each chapter are directional, offering nudges rather than a map. I'm supremely confident in your ability to figure out what you need to do and test things out as you learn what works for you in your context. You are already a successful and intelligent leader. You've long ago learned how to reap maximum value from advice about how to do your work. So you do not need my advice about *what* to do. An encouraging nudge to consider a few new mindsets will do much better. Besides, you know your context, your team, and yourself better than anyone else, and those things have a big part to play in whatever you decide to do in response to a new mindset you adopt. I don't have access to specific knowledge about your context, your team, or you as a person, so any advice about actions to take would presume too much on my part to be useful for you.

Curiosity and Self-Awareness are Essential to Making a Shift

Nothing new happens for a leader unless they are first curious about and able to notice themselves in action. Deploying curiosity and self-awareness are particularly helpful if you can practice them during your daily activities, paying close attention to your behaviors as they are happening. While noticing how we act or behave is necessary, it is insufficient. Leaders must also remain curious about why they are showing up the way they do. Behind the *why* is the way you think, and behind the way you think are your mindsets. If you can find your mindset, you will be able to consider it and decide if you want or need to make a shift. In each chapter, you will repeatedly find references to curiosity and self-awareness, underscoring their critical necessity to growth and development as a leader.

Now that we have examined mindsets, systems, and shifting, we're ready for a close look at ten unorthodox mindsets that will help you be more successful with complexity.

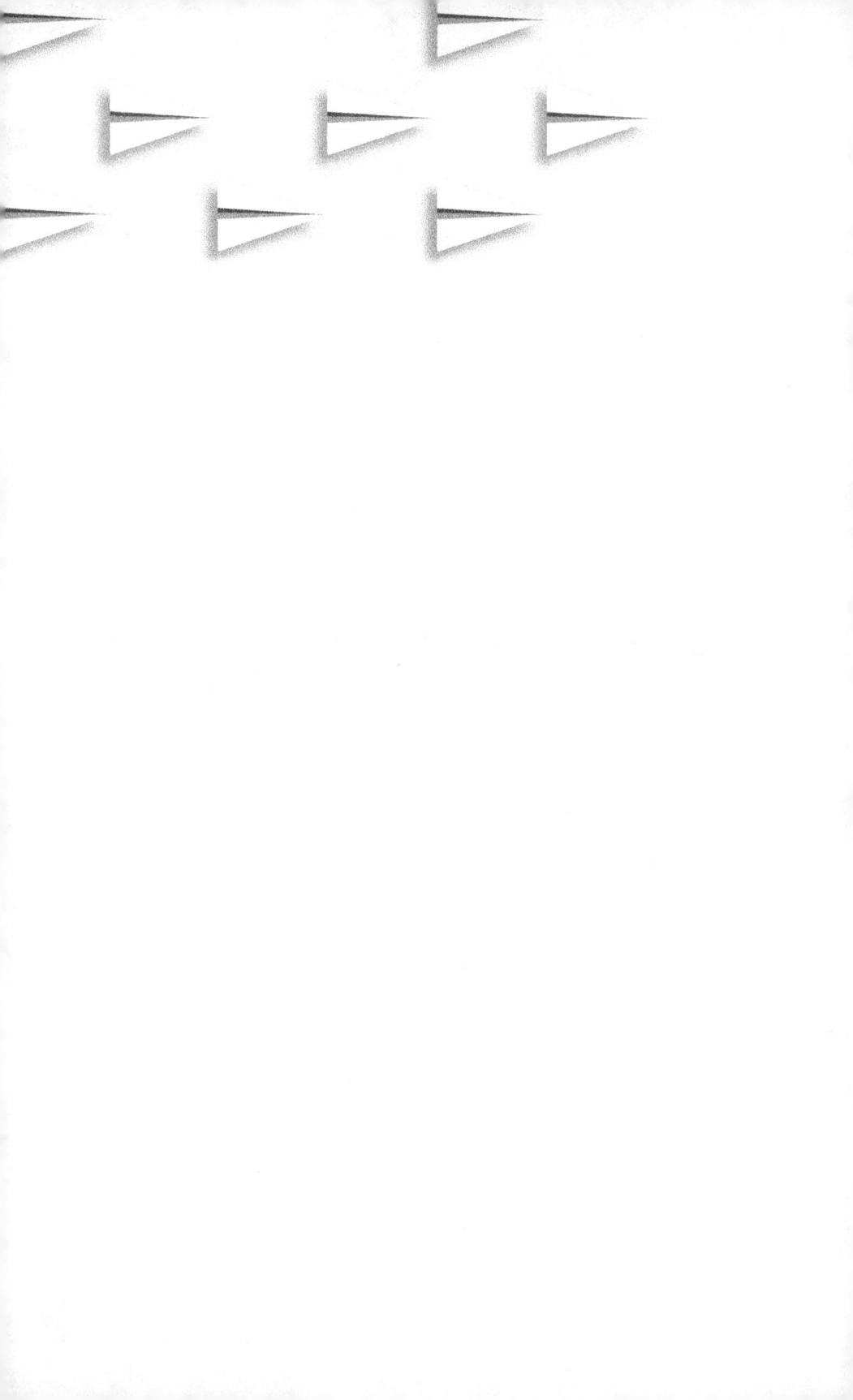

PART TWO

MINDSETS ABOUT SYSTEMS

MINDSET ONE—COMPLEXITY

AN UNORTHODOX MINDSET ABOUT SYSTEMS

Healthcare Organizations Are Complex, Not Just Complicated

ILLUSTRATION 1. *Complex Is Different Than Complicated.*

UNDERSTANDING COMPLEXITY

As I noted in Part One, the two systems most at play in healthcare are complicated and complex. It is often difficult to tell one from the other. The main goal of this chapter is to help you figure out which one your healthcare organization is most like. Accurately figuring out the kind of system you are working with is about making good sense of the system *as it is*, not as you think it *ought to be*. This is essential because strategies that are effective in complicated systems are often ineffective—to the point of being destructive—in complex systems. Understanding how complexity changes things for leaders begins with understanding the differences between complicated and complex systems.

I will begin by examining complicated systems, since complicated systems are the basis of the traditional or orthodox view. After that, I examine complex systems, pointing out how they differ from complicated systems and defy some of our assumptions about how "good" systems work.

UNDERSTANDING COMPLICATED SYSTEMS

There are several ways to know if you're dealing with a complicated system. The following are a few:

Complicated System Elements Interact in Knowable Ways

The first way to tell complicated systems apart from others is by paying attention to how many elements or parts are involved. Organizations that are complicated systems may have few or many elements, but all the elements are known or knowable. For example, you can know all the parts of a car. If your organization is a complicated system, you know or can know all the parts involved in the organization's workings: people, processes, departments, and more.

In addition, all the elements relate to each other in ways that are easy to understand. One thing leads directly to another. This relationship is called "direct cause-and-effect" or "linear interaction." Simple machines like gearboxes work this way. Every element works together in knowable, predictable, and directly connected ways.

Morning lab draws are a good example of a complicated system. Physicians place orders for morning labs. The orders start a known response, sending phlebotomists to round early, drawing blood. Lab technicians take the blood and run the ordered tests. The results of the tests create an expected response: physicians who do their morning rounds see results and order more tests or modify treatments accordingly. The system of daily labs is a complicated system. It has knowable interactions among a limited, well-known set of elements.

Complicated Systems Are Predictable

Another way to tell if you're working with a complicated system is by noticing how predictable it is. Complicated systems function as expected because the elements interact with each other in known and direct ways.

Leaders can increase the predictability of a complicated system by standardizing the interactions between elements. This approach makes the system stable, generating predictable results over long periods.

For example, a healthcare organization standardized its medical and administrative procedures. Over many years, this ensured uniform and predictable patient care and experience, no matter the professionals involved. The highly structured and coordinated interactions between specialists improved predictability in patient outcomes. The efforts to standardize reinforced the stability and predictability of the organizational results and outcomes.

Complicated Systems Are Reducible

Another way to tell if your organization is a complicated system is whether it is reducible. Reducible means you can fully know how the entire system works by understanding how the parts work. For example, you can know how a car works based on your complete understanding of how each part works and how they work together.

When an organization is reducible, leaders can have a correct and in-depth understanding of all the organization's processes. They can fully understand the company culture. They know how the organization is structured and know the people working there. Leaders can completely know how each department functions and how they interrelate. They retain this understanding even if things change.

Reducibility also requires unquestionable operational data. The data must be current and robust enough for thorough and accurate analysis. Accurate analysis aids a leader's critical thinking skills, which suffice to deconstruct problems into smaller, more manageable parts. Leaders can then find and effectively address underlying problems.

Suppose you're the business manager of a private, stand-alone, modest-sized specialty clinic. You can readily understand the clinic's financial performance by understanding each clinician's clinical and ancillary production. If you add the revenue from each clinician, the sum matches the revenue of the whole clinic. In other words, the sum of the parts equals the unified whole. The clinic is reducible. All complicated systems are reducible.

Complicated Systems Are Stable

Another defining characteristic of complicated systems is that they don't change quickly or easily, and yet they endure. They are stable entities designed for stable times. There are many reasons for their stability: one of those reasons results from standardization, as described above.

Another reason is the clarity of roles and responsibilities. Each system part has a clearly defined function, often ordered hierarchically. Changes follow a well-established, structured decision-making process. This minimizes the risk of unexpected outcomes by ensuring an ordered approach to change.

Consider a traditional hospital as an example. The hospital's various departments, such as radiology, surgery, and cardiology, adhere to well-defined protocols and procedures. These procedures ensure that patients receive consistent care at a high standard. Changes are typically slow, following a structured pathway of approval and implementation. This methodical approach to change, grounded in established protocols and clear organizational hierarchies, contributes significantly to the stability of the hospital as a complicated system.

Complicated Systems Are Controllable

Complicated systems thrive when they are well managed. Management is a form of control, creating clearly defined roles and responsibilities and proven, efficient work processes. Because control helps these systems function at their best, they have a robust and bureaucratic management hierarchy. The management hierarchy necessary for control creates organizational stability, which makes change difficult.

Medication administration is an example of a complicated system excelling under tight control. This process is tightly managed and highly structured, with multiple checks for safety. Pharmacists dispense medication based on precise prescriptions. Nurses administer doses at scheduled times. Doctors prescribe medications and then monitor patient reactions. This highly controlled environment, with clear roles and protocols, ensures predictable, efficient, and safe medication delivery.

The Defining Characteristics of Complicated Systems Are Stability and Predictability

The main defining characteristics of complicated systems are stability and predictability. Leaders often characterize their experience with stability in complicated systems as "inertia" or a "resistance to change." That's because complicated systems are stable and designed to be so. Stability enhances these organizations' ability to generate predictable results and outcomes. If stability and predictability are key elements of how your organization *actually* functions (not how you think it *should* function), it's likely a complicated system.

UNDERSTANDING COMPLEX SYSTEMS

Now that we have a clearer understanding of how complicated systems function, let's turn our focus to complex systems and see how they work differently.[13]

Complexity in a system results from the interactions between many interconnected parts. The interactions between those parts are often challenging to figure out, and they create unpredictable outcomes. That makes it hard for leaders to tell which parts of an organization or situation contributed to the results they see. A leader's mindset about systems helps leaders better understand their complex organizations and why they function in such unpredictable ways.

Complex systems are all around us. They include ecological systems such as coral reefs and rainforests, as well as social systems such as economies and social networks. Complex systems can also be human organizations.

There are several ways to know if you're dealing with a complex system. Here are a few:

Complex System Elements Interact in Obscure Ways

Like complicated systems, the first way to tell complex systems apart from others is by observing how many elements are involved. Complex organizations have many parts or elements. Sometimes, they have more elements than can be fully known, often including elements outside of the formal boundaries of the organization. Furthermore, the number of elements changes constantly, increasing uncertainty about how many are involved.

The elements of complex systems interact in intricate, often obscure ways. The interactions between elements are unpredictable because they are nonlinear.

The spread of a pandemic highlights nonlinearity in complex systems. It is a clear example of how innumerable elements—individual behaviors, public health strategies, virus mutations—interact unpredictably. Results and outcomes vary significantly from one region to another, despite regions sharing similar government and public health responses. The interactions of interdependent but indirectly related elements lead to variations in a pandemic's spread, exemplifying the nonlinearity inherent in complex systems.

The same pattern of behavior arises in complex healthcare organizations. Nonlinearity is a clue about the kind of system you may be working with.

Complex Systems Are Unpredictable

Another way to know if you are dealing with a complex system is by its unpredictability. Due to all the nonlinear interactions, complex systems routinely create surprises, some favorable, some not. The interconnected and dynamic nature of the interactions between elements is a primary reason for this unpredictability.

Unlike complicated systems, leaders can't reduce the unpredictability of complex systems through standardization and management. There are two reasons why: first, unpredictability is inherent in the system itself. Attempts to reduce the degree of unpredictability through control "breaks" the system. You can't "fix" what's inherent without destroying the system you're trying to fix. Second, unpredictability is a valuable asset, not a flaw or mistake. Unexpected results are opportunities to demonstrate adaptability in action, a valuable aspect of complex systems.

Consider how an influx of trauma cases in the emergency department (ED) creates an unexpected ripple effect throughout a hospital facility. The sudden surge requires immediate reallocation of resources and staff, impacting surgery and intensive care, and affecting other units in unpredictable ways. This highlights the nonlinear, interconnected nature of hospital functions. Trying to control these surprising surges is impossible. Doing so would disrupt the system's ability to find a dynamic equilibrium. You can't manage these surges, but you *can* build adaptive capabilities to deal with them.

Adept leaders use situations like this to improve organizational adaptability, employing strategies like surge-capacity planning and cross-departmental coordination. This approach enables the hospital to maintain operational flexibility and deal effectively with unpredictable patient-care demands.

Complex Systems Are Irreducible

To determine if your organization is a complex system, consider how breaking it down into smaller parts affects your understanding of how it works. If breaking the organization into smaller components doesn't clarify how the entire system produces its outcomes, it's likely a complex system. It means your organization is irreducible. It's irreducible because something about how the whole organization accomplishes what it does can't be explained by looking at the parts.

Irreducibility is an inherent trait of complex systems. An inability to fully understand how the whole system works isn't due to a lack of leadership abilities, knowledge, or traits. And it's not about a lack of information or data, either. Even the most skilled and well-informed leaders cannot understand or predict every aspect of complex systems.

When organizations are complex, leaders can't know all the processes or fully understand how the organization functions. Too many simultaneous changes are occurring too quickly to accurately understand what is happening. Consequently, information such as operational data, financial reports, and other feedback is incomplete and outdated. That makes a thorough analysis of what is happening now or may happen soon impossible to know with certainty.

Leaders may still try to break down complex problems into smaller parts and look for patterns, but this approach is flawed. It inevitably simplifies what's happening, ignoring the whole for the sake of the parts. It leads to greater misunderstanding, not improved understanding.

Consider a network of hospitals in a city during an influenza outbreak. Each hospital's response varies significantly, influenced by its unique patient demographics, staff availability, and resources. This variation in response affects the network in unpredictable ways.

For example, a patient surge at one hospital might cause resource shortages at another. An admission-policy change in one hospital could unexpectedly impact operations at another. These complex interconnections mean the overall network's response is more than just the sum of individual hospital actions.

Despite having comprehensive data from each hospital, leaders would find it challenging, if not impossible, to predict or fully understand the collective response of the network. This scenario illustrates the irreducibility of complex systems: the whole system's behavior cannot be understood simply by analyzing its parts.

Complex Systems Are Adaptable

An important defining characteristic of complex systems is their innate adaptability. They are inclined to change quickly and unpredictably. It's one of the main ways leaders can tell if they are dealing with a complex system.

The inherently unpredictable nature of complex systems is what makes them adaptable. Some variations—unexpected events—that occur are positive. Those favorable variations advance the system's capabilities, helping the organization adapt quickly. Dynamic environments require that kind of adaptability; the ability to respond quickly to unforeseen events. Complex systems excel in dynamic and uncertain contexts, because their nonlinear interactions cause unpredictable and sometimes favorable variations.

During the COVID-19 pandemic, many healthcare organizations realized the adaptive power of complex systems. By necessity, leaders jettisoned their attempts to manage and control everything. Rules and protocols were relaxed. Decisions were decentralized, with individual departments making swift, autonomous decisions about patient care, resource allocation, and staff deployment. Leaders encouraged creative sourcing for scarce resources. As a result, historically ponderous organizations moved *fast,* changing almost daily, discovering novel approaches that worked well. The pandemic exacerbated the complexity of the larger healthcare ecosystem, leaving leaders with no choice but to respond with approaches, actions, and behaviors that aligned better with the complexity of their own healthcare organizations.

Complex Systems Are Not Controllable

A defining trait of complex systems is their response to control. In these systems, attempts at greater control often fail, leading to a decline in long-term performance. Essentially, complex systems resist control, and this resistance manifests in various measurable ways.

Control fails in complex systems because there are too many fast-moving, interconnected parts to manage. In addition, efforts to standardize for increased predictability reduce adaptability. Diminished adaptability matters because that's how complex systems respond to unpredictable changes effectively. In short, increased management impairs a complex system's long-term performance by undermining adaptability.

For instance, in a healthcare organization with ambulatory clinics and telemedicine services, consider the impact of a new online service that unexpectedly increases patient volumes. Suppose leaders respond with strict rules such as limiting consultation times or enforcing rigid appointment scheduling. This may hinder the organization's natural adaptability and lead to inefficiencies, such as longer wait times and reduced patient satisfaction, since it fails to account for the need for flexibility in response to sudden changes. This scenario highlights how excessive control can constrain a complex system's inherent capacity to evolve and adapt to new circumstances.

The Defining Characteristics of Complex Systems Are Emergence and Adaptability

The main defining characteristics of complex systems are emergence and adaptability. Emergence is the hallmark of complex systems, while adaptability arises from and out of emergence. Therefore, emergence is the generative force behind adaptability.

If these two characteristics aptly describe how your organization *actually* functions (not how you think it *should* function), it's likely a complex system.

COMPLEX IS DIFFERENT FROM COMPLICATED

Table 1 illustrates that *complicated* and *complex* are not interchangeable terms, despite the common misconception that they are synonymous. In system analysis, the differences between these terms are not just semantic; they indicate significant functional disparities. Essentially, complicated and complex refer to fundamentally distinct types of systems.

CHARACTERISTICS	COMPLICATED SYSTEMS	COMPLEX SYSTEMS
General Description	The Predictable World	The Unpredictable World
Elements (Parts)	Few to Many	Many
Interactions	Linear, knowable	Nonlinear, not fully knowable
Predictability	Predictable	Unpredictable
Reducibility	Reducible	Not Entirely Reducible
Change	Stable	Adaptable
Control	Need Control	Resist Control
Defining Characteristic	Predictability	Emergence

TABLE 1. *Complicated and Complex.* The defining functional characteristics of complicated and complex systems. (Source: Michael Hein, 2025.)

THE ORTHODOX MINDSET ABOUT SYSTEMS: Healthcare Organizations Are Complicated Systems

The orthodox mindset about systems is that healthcare organizations are mostly complicated systems. The ideal organization works efficiently, relying on standardized processes and procedures. The aim is minimal variation and redundancy. Management perfects each process step or part of the organization for cost-effectiveness. The goal is for each aspect of the organization to function at its best, at the lowest cost, aiming for cohesiveness and consistency across the enterprise. Experts understand the system by examining the parts, because the system is reducible, the whole organization being no more than the sum of its components.

We are remarkably familiar with this mindset. It dominates the current healthcare leadership and management landscape, underpinning most day-to-day operational decisions. It infuses clinical- and process-improvement efforts, defines strategic planning, and is responsible for the way healthcare organizations are structured and operated. Because this mindset is ubiquitous, it is often assumed and rarely questioned.

EXPRESSIONS OF THE ORTHODOX MINDSET

You can identify the orthodox mindset in yourself or others by noticing the common expressions of this mindset: trusting expertise, embracing standard work, and managing by reduction.

Trusting Expertise

Expert managers are essential in complicated systems. They control the system by keeping order and ensuring it functions as designed. The more complicated the system is, the more control is needed. That's part of why there's been a remarkable proliferation of management oversight in the healthcare industry.

Managers find errors, which are variations, and fix them, restoring system operation to the standard. Since complicated systems are ordered and predictable, "right answers" and "best practices" exist. Expert managers know those answers and practices, or they can find them. Because cause-and-effect relationships are knowable, managers can trace interactions backward to the starting point of a problem, address it, and predict the results. Therefore, leaders fix issues through best practices or standard work, leading to predictable and expected improvements.

Orthodox-minded leaders highly value expertise. They believe organizational results depend on how expert the leader is; therefore a leader can be held accountable for organizational performance. Part of this rationale is that experts should know how to fix things, aligning the organization with the desired goals. If there are unexpected or unwanted variations in performance, it's because a leader isn't expert enough to eliminate them.

As leaders advance to higher levels of responsibility, the pressures to "perform" this way are profound. Pressure becomes a powerful behavioral driver, amplifying a leader's attempts to control the system. Notably, leaders reinforce an orthodox mindset by prioritizing and promoting those who have proven "success" through individual expertise. In short, the quarterback wins the game, the president handles the economy, and leaders are solely accountable for the success or failure of a healthcare organization.

Embracing Standard Work

Leaders express an orthodox mindset by embracing standard work. Standard work clearly defines, documents, and creates consistency in work processes and procedures, improving efficiency while reducing errors. Standard work is essential for controlling and perfecting a complicated system.

Standard work also serves as a foundation for process improvement. It shows a best practice baseline, allowing leaders and team members to find variations. It serves as a means of measuring performance and tracking progress. Progress, to a degree, is gauged by eliminating variation around standard work, as such anomalies show system flaws. The fewer the anomalies the better, and a complete absence of anomalies is ideal.

With standard work as a foundation, organizations can systematically analyze each component's contribution and effect on the system. That reductive approach helps find targeted intervention opportunities to drive improvement. Notice the assumptions behind standard work: the whole equals the sum of the parts—the system is reducible. Stability and predictability are preeminently important.

Furthermore, standard work fosters a shared understanding among team members. It ensures everyone is aligned and working the same way toward a predicted outcome. This harmonization strips away conflict and encourages compliance. It reduces variability, simplifies work, and decreases opportunities for miscommunication. Standard work controls how things get done and is necessary for managing and perfecting complicated systems.

Managing by Reduction

The orthodox mindset presumes reducibility, something noticeable even in the typical description of a healthcare organization. "We are Healthcare West, with thirteen hospitals, including one academic medical center, ten community hospitals, and two critical access hospitals." The unified whole is Healthcare West. The parts are separate hospitals, and enumerating the parts is believed to describe the whole organization adequately. Whenever we define a whole by its parts, we reflect an orthodox mindset about systems.

Suppose Healthcare West is underperforming financially. Improvement begins by reducing the organization to its hospital parts. The belief is that as the hospitals identified as "underperforming" improve, the whole will improve proportionally to the sum improvement of each struggling hospital. This is an example of the unified whole being the sum of the member hospitals—a defining characteristic of complicated systems.

Cost containment efforts often reflect this mindset. If the system falls short of a desired Earnings Before Interest, Taxes, Depreciation, and Amortization (EBITDA) margin (a measure of profitability), some will think that a workforce reduction is necessary. Management assigns each hospital a specific number of employees to let go in order to reduce the workforce. They arrive at the number based on the proportional "opportunity" at each facility. Notice the assumptions: if each hospital reduces the workforce as assigned, a proportionate improvement in profitability will result for the whole organization. This "sum of the parts equals the whole" approach and the proportional response to interventions reflects an orthodox mindset.

Reductionist management controls the system in several ways. The cost-containment example elucidates a few. EBITDA is a quantitative control mechanism directing members toward a specific financial performance target. It drives individual efforts, which is a means of controlling what a leader pays attention to. The result is controlling leaders' approaches, actions, and behaviors. Proportional "opportunity" is another means of control. It assumes two things: first, it assumes a linear cause and effect relationship between the performance of the whole and the parts. Second, it assumes the sum of the parts equals the whole. A reductionist management approach imposes corrective action to align broader leadership behaviors to achieve the desired performance.

THE UNORTHODOX MINDSET ABOUT COMPLEXITY:
Healthcare Organizations Are Complex

The unorthodox system mindset is that healthcare organizations are predominantly complex. The ideal organization is highly adaptable and flexible, successfully responding to the unprecedentedly dynamic nature of the industry. The goal is to maximize the organization to function at its best, generating novel, transformative opportunities quickly. Complex systems, being more adaptable than their complicated counterparts, are not hindered by the liabilities of complicated systems (stability and predictability) in fast-changing contexts.

EXPRESSIONS OF THE UNORTHODOX MINDSET

Expressions of the unorthodox mindset are actions intended to work with the system to maximize its adaptability and cultivate emergence. You can identify the unorthodox mindset in yourself or others by noticing the common expressions of this mindset: trusting distributed leadership, embracing ambiguity, and managing by inclusion.

Trusting Distributed Leadership

The relationship complex systems have with control challenges the very bedrock of our historical understanding of leadership. Traditionally, leaders worked to gain and keep some semblance of organizational control. However, in response to control efforts, complex systems "resist" by shifting toward states of decreased order. When that happens, organizations become less predictable and more challenging to lead. This unique response requires thinking about leadership in an unorthodox way.

The unorthodox way to think about leadership is that it doesn't reside within a specific individual, position, role, or title. It is not something that leaders do. Instead, leadership is an *entity*. It emerges between people in a relationship, as a *co-creative* process.[14] Trust fuels this co-creative process, catalyzing the emergence of leadership. Because people co-create leadership, it only comes to life when two or more gather around a shared purpose. No one can impose leadership on others, as it arises between individuals who freely respond to it. Leadership coordinates actions that spark an organizational movement. Since it isn't a personified quality, it isn't limited to the C-suite or management. Hence, genuine leadership is distributed, and leaders are anyone adept at co-creating leadership between people. The result is a phenomenon called *distributed leadership*.[15]

Distributed leadership isn't a leadership style preference; it is a necessary, co-created entity for complex system survival and function. Certain leadership styles can amplify or diminish distributed leadership, but distributed leadership is not a style and must not be confused with one. Leaders who use complexity-fit approaches, actions, and behaviors tend to generate distributed leadership among many.

Without distributed leadership, complex systems perform poorly or fail. The task for complexity-fit healthcare executives involves learning how to create and trust distributed leadership. Trusting in distributed leadership is a hallmark expression of leaders with a complex-system mindset. It is a necessary first step before leaders can relax control, which is essential for effectively leading complex organizations.

Embracing Ambiguity

Ambiguity is an inescapable part of complex systems because multiple interpretations of what happened or will happen are equally valid, even if paradoxical. The way a complex system's elements interact creates vagueness. There's no one "right" way to explain what happened or predict what will come. There are no "right" solutions—only many possibly useful ones. Therefore, predicting outcomes and making wholly informed decisions is difficult, if not impossible. Efforts to find the right solution or answers delay action. No one knows how any solution or idea will work until they have tried it. All these challenges create an ambiguous environment.

Leaders with an unorthodox mindset embrace the ambiguity. They consider proffered solutions "experiments" and their predictions "hypotheses." They deploy experiments and carefully watch how things happen, seeing whether their hypotheses have merit.

For example, a senior executive team's slow decision-making imperils its effectiveness. These leaders feel trapped and frustrated, because they repeatedly discuss the same issues without resolution. They cannot discern the best answer or approach, which leads to indecision. With a better understanding of the ambiguous nature of complex systems, the team could relax their preferences for finding the "right" or "best" answers. They could gain comfort with several reasonable solutions to experiment with. Greater comfort with ambiguity would allow this team to move faster by making quicker decisions.

Most people are not well-equipped to deal with ambiguity. Our brains prefer certainty; if we cannot have that to some degree, it makes us uncomfortable. We try to avoid or end the discomfort of ambiguity in several ways, and those instincts are often the opposite of how to lead well in complex systems.

What does work well is embracing ambiguity, a telltale sign of leaders who express a complex-system mindset. Four ways leaders embrace ambiguity include absorbing uncertainty (Mindset Five), acknowledging that their "story" is always incomplete (Mindset Nine), being curious (Mindset Ten), and managing by inclusion (below).

Managing by Inclusion

Leaders express an unorthodox mindset about systems through their relationship with other perspectives. Because cause-and-effect relationships are obscure in complex systems, certainty is absent, and no one can have the right or best answers. Therefore, the story a leader creates to make sense of what is happening around them is, by necessity, always incomplete. The only way to gain a more complete story is by taking on and including multiple perspectives.

This differs from merely understanding other perspectives, which is cognitive assent, (i.e., acknowledging that another perspective exists and is understood). Taking on multiple perspectives demands much more. It's like dressing up in another's attire, shoes and all, temporarily setting aside our own. It requires genuine curiosity and humility. Leaders must be curious, because the other person sees and knows what they cannot; leaders must be humble, because they must admit that they don't know enough, become students, and let another teach them.

Taking on multiple perspectives also requires holding all of them simultaneously, even if those perspectives are paradoxical. Leaders who take on multiple perspectives draw upon all the available perspectives, synthesizing novel solutions. The goal is to do that as often as possible.

Most leaders are *aware* of other perspectives, and many *understand* other perspectives, but very few *take on* multiple perspectives. The ability to take on multiple perspectives is rare and beautifully expresses a complex-system mindset.

MAKING THE SHIFT

Before the Shift

I have asserted that you are leading a complex healthcare organization. But you have to decide if my assertion is valid. Before any mindset shift, you must determine what kind of problem, situation, or system you're dealing with. You must decide whether your healthcare organization is predominantly a complex or complicated system. The descriptions and examples above can help you with your assessment.

If the mindset you hold matches the system you have, there's no need to shift. On the other hand, if your mindset doesn't match, a shift is recommended. Below are three things to consider if you find yourself in need of shifting.

Be Prepared to Relax Control

As I pointed out earlier, notice the critical difference: orthodoxy aims to control and force the system to follow a complicated mindset. Unorthodoxy aims to be in harmony with a complex system. This has nothing to do with control. Complex systems can be influenced but not controlled (see Mindset Four—Power). If you try to control a complex system, it unravels.

Orthodoxy assumes that leaders are outside or independent of the system, as observers or actors upon it. They act by controlling the system. Conversely, unorthodoxy acknowledges that the leader is just one element of the system, inescapably entangled in it, influenced by the system just as much as they influence it. There's no way to control what happens with you and the system. Unorthodox expressions intentionally relax control, a necessary precondition for emergence, adaptability, and distributed leadership.

For most leaders, relaxing control is not a trivial endeavor. Control is a hardwired management response honed through years of training, education, and experience. These controlling approaches are both obvious and subtle. The least obvious are the most difficult to relax. For example, leaders subtly express control in how they talk—their tone, the words they use. Nearly every action, approach, or behavior a leader has used with success has some component of controlling intention behind it. That's how pervasive and ingrained is the notion and need to control systems.

Moreover, the orthodox mindset predominates, leading to widespread expectations that leaders deploy control, forcing the system to comply and function as a complicated system. Before leaders can shift, they must grapple with leading in ways that relax control while navigating expectations for imposing it. Relaxing control can be exceedingly uncomfortable for leaders. You can begin shifting away from the familiar by simply noticing how you try to control yourself, others, and the organization you lead.

Be Prepared for the Costs and Benefits of Shifting

How a leader relates to control is just one part of a larger issue. Shifting from an orthodox mindset to one that fits complexity entails costs and benefits. On the one hand, it requires unlearning established patterns while accepting the discomfort of unfamiliar territory. On the other hand, it presents an innovative leadership approach and a fresh lens through which to perceive the world.

It's noteworthy, however, that shifting places you in the minority among healthcare leaders. Most healthcare leaders keep to a conventional approach, often due to a limited understanding of the implications of complex systems, even when they acknowledge that complex systems exist. As a result, their behaviors rarely reflect the complexity of the healthcare organizations they lead, especially under stressful circumstances. Embracing an unorthodox mindset puts you at the forefront of healthcare leadership, albeit with the potential discomfort of being an outlier.

Be Patient with Yourself

Expect this shift to be a journey requiring patience, acceptance of unfamiliarity, and a commitment to enduring change. It is a transformative process that can take time to realize fully, but it is undeniably worth undertaking. It takes time, because most of us have interwoven conventional system thinking with our understanding of the world. Those ways of thinking are deeply rooted, so it takes considerable introspection to notice and disentangle from them. Even as your mindset embraces the unorthodox, old habits will persist, causing behaviors to lag behind your thinking. This lag is natural and should not deter your progress. Over time, and with persistent effort, your actions will eventually align with your evolved mindset.

So be patient with yourself and others on this transformative journey. It is a remarkable odyssey that offers a rewarding and refreshing approach to leadership and understanding of the world.

WHY SHIFT

Because the Orthodox Mindset Is Less Useful Today

Despite a growing realization that a complicated system mindset is less useful than it was, many continue with it. Compelling evidence suggests that an orthodox mindset and its derived management practices offer limited prospects for long-term success in today's contexts. The evidence that it's not working as well as we'd like is widely apparent. Despite exceptionally talented and expert managers, healthcare organizations still grapple with sustainable transformation. Notably, the common expressions of an orthodox mindset diminish the likelihood of achieving genuine systemness. That seems counterproductive to the intent behind the development of large healthcare organizations. These persistent challenges and the need for authentic systemness underscore the necessity of shifting.

Because Increased Control Deteriorates Performance in Complex Systems

Even though most healthcare organizations are structured, managed, and led as complicated systems, they don't function that way. Healthcare organizations are complex systems. The more complex these organizations become, the more leaders with an orthodox mindset apply increasing degrees of control through management. They keep trying to force the organization to "behave" as it "should," but increased control of complex systems usually worsens things.

The relationship between control and complex systems is a defining and crucial characteristic of these two mindsets. Imposing excessive control upon a complex system leads to unintended consequences. Most notably, decreased, not increased, order. Decreased order is a diminished alignment between actions and expected outcomes, increasing uncertainty and reducing system stability. Those results are the opposite of what leaders intend. It is a paradoxical response to our natural inclinations to reach for greater control when things feel chaotic. The key principle is that increased control of complex systems usually worsens things.

Ignoring or being unaware of this principle can lead leaders into a dangerous organizational feedback loop: the leader notices decreased order and tries to impose greater control, which leads to less order, which compels the leader to apply greater control. If the loop persists, either the leader or the system will reach a breaking point. The leader may leave the organization or suffer emotional or physical health issues. The organization can stagnate and irreparably harm its marketplace position. Organizational culture can become toxic, driving away workforce talent. Leaders who express a complicated mindset in a complex system can get trapped in this negative loop. It's something to avoid and another reason to shift.

The last point is the Law of Requisite Complexity: leading complex systems well requires complexity-fit leadership. Our systems underperform and sometimes fail when we don't lead that way. You and your organization's success depend on your ability to make the shift.

Because Systemness Is Unachievable in Complicated Systems

Recall that genuine systemness is a product of complex, not complicated, systems. To have systemness, you must have emergence. Emergence is a quality of complex systems, not complicated ones. If systemness is a goal, then leading complex systems well is necessary. Attempting to lead complex systems with an orthodox mindset results in worse system function. To achieve genuine systemness, leaders must shift to unorthodoxy.

HOW TO SHIFT

Sense the System

Leaders must have a solid understanding of complex systems and how they function differently from complicated systems. A conceptual understanding comes before experiential awareness and recognition—we can only see what we believe. So first, we must have some cognitive understanding of complexity before we can see and make sense of it in the world around us. Curiosity and education lay the foundation for shifting from a complicated-system mindset toward one anchored in complexity.

However, education alone is insufficient. We will need others who are or have been on a similar journey. Interacting with and learning with or from them is essential and valuable. Making good sense of complex systems is difficult, but it is often easier and more complete when done as a team. Once these things are in place, a leader can more readily sense the system they are dealing with.

Match Your Expressions to Your Mindset

Having access to multiple system mindsets is a critical first step. The second is matching your leadership to the system you are dealing with. An entire portfolio of complexity-fit expressions is available to you in the following chapters. All of them may be important for your success. You can begin by being curious and self-aware of your current expressions and considering whether they align with the kind of system your organization is.

Practice the Shift

You will find that there are systems within systems in your organization. The organization is likely a complex system, but there will be complicated, or even simple problems, situations, and systems nested in the unified whole. As you interact with these various systems, you'll need to shift your cognitive weight from complicated to complex and back again. The practice of shifting demands quite a lot from us. We need to be self-aware, noticing how we are showing up. We need to notice and sense the system we are dealing with. These demands require turning off our autopilot—our patterned approaches, actions, and behaviors—then pausing and being curious about what is happening around us. In the pause, we must notice how we make sense of things. All this takes practice. Practicing the shift can begin at once. There's plenty of opportunity in your day-to-day work.

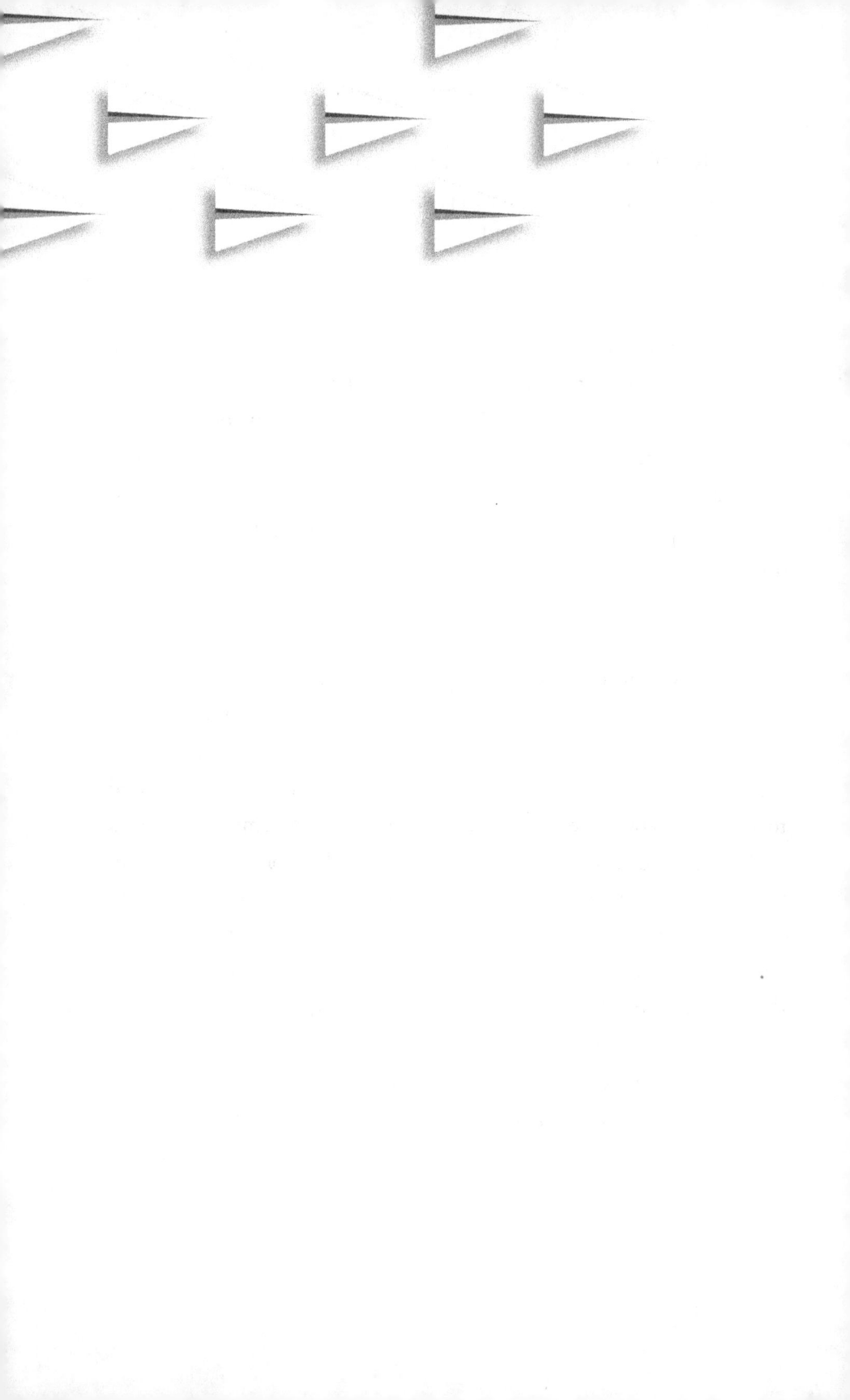

MINDSET TWO—POLARITY

AN UNORTHODOX MINDSET ABOUT PROBLEMS

Polarities Are Opportunities, Not Problems to Resolve

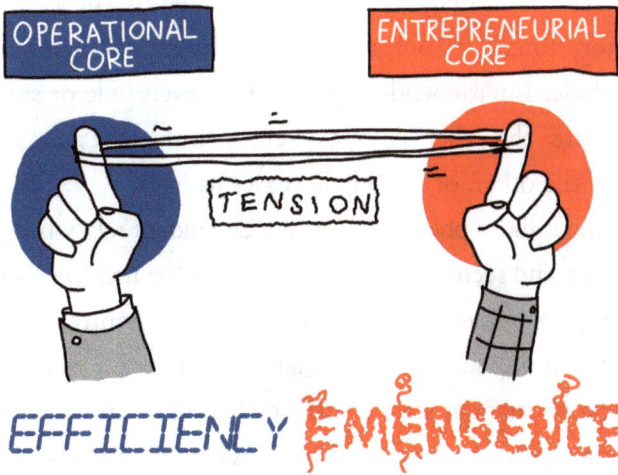

ILLUSTRATION 2. *Polarity: The Operational Core::Entrepreneurial Core.*

UNDERSTANDING POLARITY

Distinguishing polarities from problems is crucial for the effective leadership of complex healthcare organizations. When leaders mistake polarities for problems, they make choices that undermine organizational performance. Polarity increases as healthcare organizations become more complex, raising the likelihood of adverse choices. When polarity is accurately identified, leaders can work with it to advance opportunities rather than try to resolve polarity as if it were a problem.

POLARITY DEFINED

Polarity describes the dynamic interplay between two or more seemingly contradictory forces or "poles." Together those poles form an interdependent whole. Interdependent means that each pole or side depends on and requires the other for its existence. Both sides need the healthy existence of the other, or the whole ceases to exist.

Breathing is like a polarity. There is a dependent relationship between two necessary and seemingly contradictory poles: inspiring air, expanding our lungs to extract oxygen; and expiring air, contracting our lungs to expel carbon dioxide. You wouldn't last too long if you only tried to breathe in (a permanent state of inflated lungs) or only tried to breathe out (a permanent state of deflated lungs). We need both to survive, which means we need to find harmony between these two states.

Harmony in Polarity

By *harmony in polarity* I mean a dynamic, adaptive relationship between the poles of a polarity, the whole of the system, and the environment or context the system is in. The ways that the poles of polarity interact are unpredictable and ever-changing in response to dynamic contexts. For example, the harmony we need as we breathe varies depending on what we ask our bodies to do. Suppose you're exercising. You breathe faster and deeper. If you are asleep, you breathe more slowly, even briefly pausing your breath. The relationship between the two poles is dynamic and harmonized to match what is needed. When the harmony between the poles doesn't fit with what the body needs, in a physiological sense, that is disease. If there's a severe mismatch between what the body needs and how the poles harmonize, the whole system is at risk, possibly resulting in death.

The same is true of the polarities found in complex systems. If we favor one pole at the expense of the other, then it's like deciding that you will only breathe in. In addition, if there's a mismatch between a harmonized polarity and the context, the system becomes "ill" and at risk of demise. The ability to see and harmonize polarity to match organizational context is critical for the successful leadership of complex healthcare organizations.

Pressure and Tension in Polarity

Importantly, there is tension in polarity. It creates a form of pressure that compels action. Once again, breathing is an apt metaphor. Notice the tension that increases as you breathe out. The closer to the end of your breath, the more pressure you feel to breathe in. The tension between the poles of inhalation and exhalation generates the pressure we feel to take action and breathe. Breathing exists in constant tension between inhalation and exhalation.

Leading complex organizations, where polarities abound, also creates tension, a kind of organizational pressure that compels us to act. The approaches, actions, and behaviors leaders adopt in response to this pressure depend on their mindset about problems. It's important to understand that unlike solving a problem, harmonizing polarity doesn't resolve the tension or the pressure it creates.

Polarities Are Not Pendulums

Breathing is a useful example of polarity, because it shows how two seemingly opposite states are both essential to our survival. Yet it would be a mistake to characterize polarity as a pendulum swinging between two different states: polarity is not a pendulum. In other words, polarity is not about a simple back-and-forth, cause-and-effect dynamic between two opposing extremes. Polarity is about existing in a state of dynamic harmony between two seemingly contradictory states that are both essential to an organization's survival.

Finding the best ways to represent this harmonized interaction is difficult given English-language conventions that favor cause-and-effect relationships. To avoid implying such a relationship in how I present polarities, I'll use the punctuation convention of a double colon. For example, the polarity of breathing is inhale::exhale.

Examples of Common Polarities in Healthcare

Some common examples of polarity in healthcare are Quality of Clinical Care::Cost-Effectiveness, Personalized Care::Standardization, and Access::Excellence. The first example, Quality of Clinical Care::Cost-Effectiveness, often plays out in tensions between medical staff and administration, with one accusing the other of being overly or inadequately focused on finances. "No Margin, No Mission" is a statement that reflects this common polarity. The second example, Personalized Care::Standardization, often generates tension between advocates and adversaries of clinical protocols. The third example, Access::Excellence, exemplifies the tension between supplying good care to all and the best care to whoever can afford it.

These three examples are just a few of the many instances of polarity that can be found throughout healthcare organizations.

THE INTRINSIC POLARITY OF COMPLEX SYSTEMS

Beyond these examples, there is also a polarity intrinsic to complex systems, (i.e., a systemic polarity). As with all polarity, one cannot resolve, avoid, or end the tension and pressure a systemic polarity causes in organizations. To lead complex healthcare organizations well, leaders must recognize this systemic polarity, relate to it advantageously, and avoid the temptation to resolve it.

Systemic Polarity: The Entrepreneurial Core

To some degree, all healthcare organizations must embody an entrepreneurial spirit. To do this, they must foster a culture that promotes some bottom-up decision-making, local flexibility, and a degree of autonomy. These characteristics are the lifeblood of organizational adaptability.

Every organization must adapt or risk being left behind in an ever-changing environment. Greater adaptability requires relaxing centralized control, allowing local leaders to address local contextual realities. The capabilities that foster rapid organizational adaptability represent a pole of the systemic polarity inherent in complex systems that I refer to as the "Entrepreneurial Core."[16]

Systemic Polarity: The Operational Core

Complex healthcare organizations must also constantly produce, harnessing the efficiencies of a well-managed Operational Core, adopting a more centralized, formal, and top-down approach. To do this, they must foster a culture that promotes central decision-making, systemic standardization, and greater control through skilled management. These characteristics are the lifeblood of organizational efficiency.

Every organization must be efficient or risk being left behind, unable to consistently deliver high-quality service while maximizing financial returns for investment capital and growth, impairing their ability to compete. The capabilities that foster organizational efficiency and effectiveness represent a pole of the systemic polarity inherent in complex systems that I refer to as the "Operational Core."[17]

The Entrepreneurial Core and the Operational Core Are Both Essential

The Entrepreneurial Core yields innovation. Innovation, in turn, requires capital. Capital is a product of the Operational Core. The efficiency created by the Operational Core also requires an adaptable workforce and the ability to find better, faster, and less expensive ways of doing things. Those capabilities are products of the Entrepreneurial Core. It's clear that one core cannot exist without the other. They are in tension with each other and reflect the inherent polarity of complex systems. Figure 3 depicts the relationship between the Entrepreneurial Core and the Operational Core.

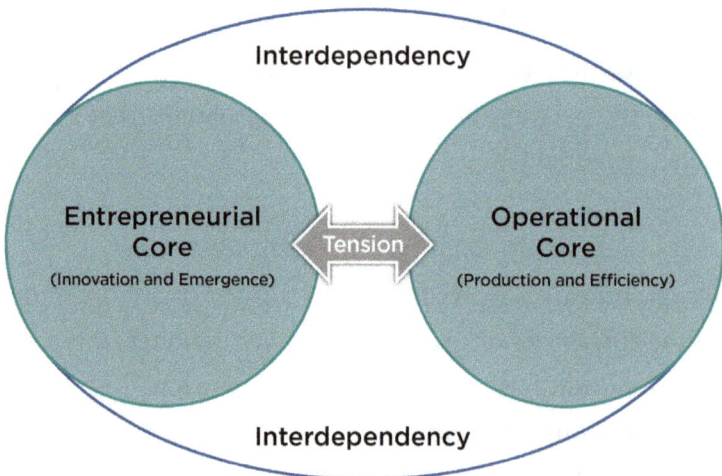

FIGURE 3. *The Systemic Polarity of Complex Systems.* The Entrepreneurial Core and the Operational Core are two seemingly opposing forces that are both interdependent and intrinsic to the system. (Source: Michael Hein, 2025. Modified from: Mary Uhl-Bien and Michael Arena, "Leadership for Organizational Adaptability: A Theoretical Synthesis and Integrative Framework," *The Leadership Quarterly* 29, no. 1 (2018): 89–104, https://doi.org /10.1016/j.leaqua.2017.12.009.)

Like all polarities, the polarity of complex systems is inescapable and unresolvable. If you prefer one pole, you imperil the other, threatening the whole. Complex systems are polarities. The tension and pressure leaders feel when leading them does not represent a problem to solve, a dilemma, or an organization to fix. It represents a polarity to harmonize.

DISCERNING POLARITIES FROM PROBLEMS

Polarities and problems are commonly confused with each other, but polarities and problems are not the same. Problems are situations that cause conflict, contradiction, or inconsistency and require resolution. They can be solved through analysis and decision-making. In other words, problems are amenable to an answer or solution, but polarities are not.

For example, Mission::Margin is a classic polarity in nonprofit healthcare. Mission is a commitment to supply the best possible patient care, regardless of the ability to pay. Margin is the ability to maintain financial viability and sustainability. The margin depends on how the organization meets its mission. The mission depends on how the organization meets its margin. Mission::Margin is not a problem. It's a polarity.

On the other hand, reducing hospital readmission rates is a complex problem: it can be solved. Steps an organization might take to reduce hospital readmission rates include first improving inpatient care, including better discharge planning. Then, working closely with the clinic, leaders could improve the coordination of follow-up care. The final focus might be working within the community to address social determinants of health. If the hospital has a problem with high readmissions, it is a problem that can be resolved.

Polarities and Problems Feel the Same

As leaders, we may pride ourselves in our dispassionate, rational reasoning. But people are emotional creatures, and leaders are no exception.

We make decisions and interact in the world through our hearts as much as our heads. This plays out for us with polarities and problems, which leaders often confuse because they feel the same.

As mentioned earlier, both polarity and problems generate pressure and tension, a sense of unease that compels us to act. Leaders facing problems or polarities describe the pressure and tension they feel as anxiety, stress, fear, excitement, thrill, opportunity, hope, or enthusiasm. All of those are powerful motivators for human action. Notably, the pressure and tension of problems and polarities not only compel individuals to act, but also compel entire organizations to change. This pressure and tension are an immensely potent organizational force.

What leads to confusion between polarities and problems is that most leaders are habitually inclined to assume the pressure they feel is a problem to be solved. This is especially true if they have an orthodox mindset about systems where "find and fix" is equated with effective leadership. To avoid an "autopilot" behavioral response to the pressure, leaders must be aware that polarities are not problems, though they feel the same. It is hard to overstate the importance of that last point.

Certain Kinds of Problems Mimic Polarities

Simple problems can be easy to distinguish from polarities: if the resolution to a situation is straightforward and clear, it is likely you are dealing with a problem. But senior healthcare executives typically deal with more difficult problems. These types of problems are not simple to resolve, and that's often why they are escalated to senior leadership.

Some kinds of difficult problems mimic polarities, making it hard for leaders to distinguish between the two. Two kinds of problems that mimic polarity are *dilemmas* and *impasses*.

Problems that are dilemmas. Dilemmas are problems that require a difficult choice between two or more options. Each of the options in a dilemma has benefits and adverse consequences. But dilemmas are resolvable, even if the benefits and risks of either option offer no clear best choice.

Resolving a dilemma doesn't always mean finding a perfect solution; rather, it often means making a choice that's considered the best under the circumstances despite the trade-offs involved. Sometimes, the resolution of a dilemma may still leave residual challenges or create new problems.

Dilemmas often involve moral or ethical considerations that challenge a leader's values or principles or those of others. Sometimes, the options are mutually exclusive, and the leader cannot return to the decision if things go awry. The no-going-back aspect of dilemmas increases the pressure to make the "right" choice. However, the options of a dilemma are not dependent on each other, differentiating a dilemma from a polarity.

An example of a dilemma in the healthcare context is the donation of a scarce organ. A younger patient may gain more years of life from the transplant and is likely healthier, increasing survivability. On the other hand, the older patient might have been on the waiting list longer or be in more immediate danger. Organ donation is a dilemma because each choice has significant moral and ethical implications. Making one choice means the loss of the other possibility. There is no universally correct answer. The decision can depend heavily on the unique circumstances of a situation and the ethical framework used to guide the decision.

Problems that are impasses. Given the challenges of a dilemma, it's not unusual to arrive at a place where a resolution seems impossible. Leaders can get stuck in a dilemma due to entrenched disagreement over the choices to be made—an impasse. In these tricky situations, stakeholders become entrenched in their respective positions. The longer they stay rooted to their position, the more resistant they are to compromise. When that happens the goal shifts from finding a solution to winning a battle. An unresolved impasse harms relationships and erodes trust. Ultimately, impasses destabilize an organization.

Impasses mimic polarity because they seem unresolvable, like polarities. But an impasse and a polarity are not the same. Impasses are problems, having devolved from dilemmas.

Suppose a community hospital has been struggling financially for many years, and its nurse-to-patient ratios are slightly below the industry average—there are fewer nurses available to care for patients at that hospital than the national average. The nurses believe the staffing ratios are too low, contributing to nurse burnout, lower-quality care, and increased harm. They want more nurses. However, hospital administration thinks nursing deployed an outdated and inefficient staffing model, causing the burnout, harm, and care quality issues. The financial implications of hiring more nurses are untenable, especially in an environment of tight budgets and financial pressures. The administration wants the same number or even fewer nurses.

For several years, the dilemma remains unresolved. The hospital administration makes minor adjustments but does not fundamentally address the low staffing ratio. The situation becomes entrenched, and the nursing staff grows increasingly frustrated.

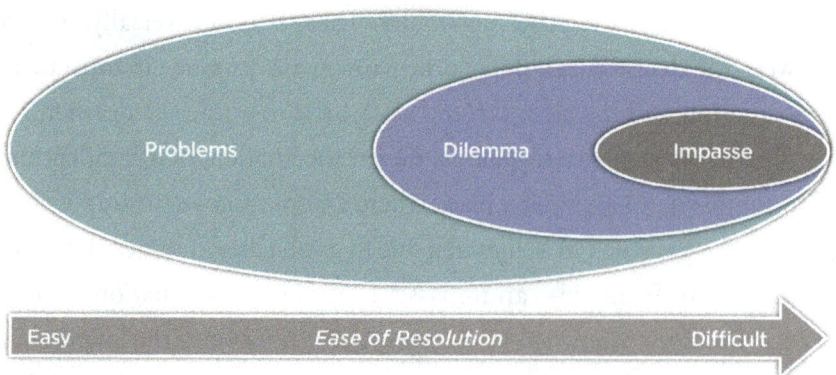

FIGURE 4. *Types of Problem*. Problems are situations that create conflict, contradiction, or inconsistency and require resolution—they are obstacles to overcome. A dilemma is a subset of a problem, and an impasse is a subset of a dilemma. Problems, including dilemmas and impasses, are not polarities. (Source: Michael Hein, 2025.)

To break through the impasse, the nurses unionize. They leverage collective bargaining to achieve better working conditions, including increased staffing ratios. In this case, the long-standing, unresolved dilemma between enhancing staffing ratios and maintaining operational costs became an impasse, with both sides fighting to win their position. Unionization became the strategy the nurses used to resolve the impasse.

An impasse is a problem born out of an unresolved dilemma. A dilemma is a problem that poses tough choices that are not interdependent. Dilemmas and impasses are both problems, and neither are polarities (Figure 4).

Polarities, Problems, Dilemmas, and Impasses

In complex systems, polarities and problems coexist. Polarities fuel problems and are often confused with problems, especially dilemmas and impasses. It isn't easy to keep them separate in our minds. It is easy to confuse them with each other. Table 2 summarizes how polarities, problems, dilemmas, and impasses relate.

CONCEPT	SYSTEMS THINKING DEFINITION	EXAMPLE	SOLUTION	RELATIONSHIP
Polarity	An interdependent pair that need each other to function effectively. The apparent opposition and subsequent tension or pressure that's felt do not reflect a problem to be solved but seeming opposites to harmonize. Not a Problem.	Mission::Margin	Continual harmonization of both poles while simultaneously harmonizing the polarity to context. Favoring one pole over the other risks the whole.	Polarity can amplify or spin off problems associated with one of the poles. In that manner, polarity can "cause" problems. Polarities are not problems.
Problem	A **situation** regarded as unwelcome or harmful; one that must be dealt with and overcome. Not a Polarity.	Increased hospital readmission rates.	Define the problem and possible contributions, generate potential solutions, select the best one, implement it, and review its effectiveness. Adjust as necessary.	A problem can be or lead to a dilemma if multiple potential solutions exist, and the system must choose. Problems can form from spin-off issues related to a polarity. Problems are not polarities but may be polarity "in disguise."
Dilemma	A **situation** that is a problem where a difficult choice must be made between two or more alternatives, often equally undesirable or beneficial ones. A subset of Problem.	Hiring more nurses to reduce nursing ratios versus reducing operational costs to meet financial and strategic demands.	A thorough analysis of options, stakeholder consultation, and decision-making, seeking a compromise or alternative solution; looking for shared interests between opposing positions, building on what's in common between opposing positions.	Unresolved dilemma becomes an impasse. Polarity can contribute to the problems involved in dilemma. Dilemma may be polarity "in disguise."
Impasse	A situation that is a problem in which no progress seems possible, usually because of disagreement; a deadlock or a stalemate between two opposing positions. Born out of Dilemma, a subset of Dilemma.	Physicians demand full ownership of an outpatient surgical center; hospital administration demands full ownership of an outpatient surgical center.	Facilitation, negotiation, or possibly mediation or arbitration to identify legitimate interests behind both positions and find a way forward. Picking a side, agreeing to revisit or adjust after a trial period, if possible.	Impasse emerges from a dilemma. Polarity can fuel problems related to one side of an impasse. An impasse may be a polarity "in disguise."

TABLE 2. *Polarity, Problem, Dilemma, and Impasse.* Each concept has different implications and requires different strategies in a systems context. Systems thinking is about understanding how these elements interact and influence each other, rather than looking at them in isolation. (Source: Michael Hein, 2025.)

WHY POLARITIES ARE SO HARD TO SEE

By now it should be clear how polarities differ from problems, yet many leaders struggle with differentiating between the two. There are several reasons why leaders may not recognize polarities when they encounter them.

Lack of Awareness

Leaders won't see polarity if they don't know they exist or what they are. A mindset that accounts for polarity helps leaders see polarity—we only see what we believe. Awareness includes naming the polarities we meet, naming their poles, and describing their interdependency. The practice of finding and naming the polarity and discerning how the poles interact builds the mental discipline necessary to recognize polarity quickly.

Our Brain's Preference for Certainty

Even though polarities are common in complex environments, they can be challenging to see because our brains prefer a problem to be solved over a polarity to harmonize. Choosing a side supplies the certainty our brains crave, leading to mischaracterizing a polarity as a problem. To see polarities, we must resist our brain's preferences for certainty.

Moving Too Fast

We won't see polarity if we move too quickly from task to task, reacting to the tension we feel, assuming it stems from an unresolved problem. To avoid polarity blindness, we must pause and consider whether the tension arises from a problem or a polarity. One way to discern between the two is by looking for the characteristic interdependencies in polarity, which don't exist with problems.

Personal Preferences

Personal preferences alter how perceptive of polarity we are. Our motivations and core values often pull us toward the pole with which we affiliate more closely. As we do, our appreciation for the other side diminishes, creating a kind of blindness. This increases the likelihood that we will see polarity as a problem in search of a "right" answer—that answer being the one that fits best with our motivations, core values, and preferred pole.

Leaders who are unable to discern the differences between polarities and problems risk wasting time and resources trying to "solve problems" when they should instead be focusing on harmonizing polarity.

THE ORTHODOX MINDSET ABOUT PROBLEMS:
Polarities Are Problems to Resolve

The orthodox mindset about problems does not recognize polarity, only problems. Healthcare leaders, indeed, have many genuine problems to deal with. They experience the pressure and tension related to problems as they navigate the myriad challenges associated with leading healthcare organizations.

Problems that arise must be addressed and make up the day-to-day dealings of leadership. Senior executives are skilled problem solvers, having a history of successfully navigating problems and finding reasonable solutions. Addressing dilemmas and navigating through impasses are particularly potent and valuable leadership skills. Exceptional orthodox leaders are adept at dealing with any kind of *problem*.

EXPRESSIONS OF THE ORTHODOX MINDSET

Expressions of this mindset are related to how leaders find and address problems. The most notable expressions aim to achieve efficient and effective problem resolution, including resolution of the pressure and tension that problems cause.

You can identify an orthodox mindset in yourself or others by noticing its common expressions: pursuing the right answer, relying on analytical problem-solving, and adopting best practices.

Pursuing the Right Answer

Pursuing the "best" or "right" answer or solution expresses the orthodox mindset. Leaders naturally pursue right answers due to the brain's preference for certainty and predictability. Because orthodox-minded leaders trust in direct, cause-and-effect relationships, they believe they know what will happen after deploying a solution. They project the past into the future to anticipate results. The combined effect of a preference for predictability and trust in linear, direct, cause-and-effect relationships is the belief that best or right answers exist and can be known. The orthodox mindset holds that a leader's job is to solve problems by finding the right answers.

Right answers are also attractive because they are amenable to objective criteria. Objective criteria give us a measuring stick for determining if something is best or right. Efficiency, cost-effectiveness, reliability, and safety are measurable, so what's best or right is knowable. In addition to being measurable, objective criteria also allow for comparison, a means of knowing when a problem has been solved.

This is why healthcare leaders with an orthodox mindset about problems are inclined to pay attention to what is measurable. What is measurable is far more likely to define what the problem is and what is or is not success. Success is finding the best way or being right about something. In the end, the availability of objective criteria defines and decides what situations are problems and whether a particular solution was right or best.

In addition, in healthcare, getting something right is often a matter of life or death. That adds to the pressure leaders feel to find the right answers.

Relying on Analytical Problem-Solving

Leaders express an orthodox mindset about problems when they break problems down into smaller components. Smaller components are more understandable and are often easier to measure with objective criteria than larger components. With smaller, objectively-defined components, leaders can deploy a structured process to analyze problems. Notice the reductionist approach to analysis, an underpinning element of the orthodox mindset about problems.

This expression defines a problem by first figuring out the key components or variables involved. Leaders then gather relevant data and employ structured analysis techniques to examine the relationships, patterns, and potential causes of the problem. These processes may include tools such as SWOT analysis (strengths, weaknesses, opportunities, threats), root cause analysis (RCA), or other problem-solving frameworks to find the underlying contributing factors. This approach prioritizes objectivity and evidence-based decision-making, including expert opinions and expertise. This reductionist, analytical approach helps decision-makers understand the problem better.

Beyond reductionism, analytical problem-solving reflects orthodoxy in several other ways. A logical analysis scrutinizing relationships, patterns, and potential causes shows a belief in linear, cause-and-effect relationships. This scrutiny involves experts, who are often needed to see the connections, and the goal is a "best" solution, implying a belief that the correct answer exists.

Adopting Best Practices

Searching for and applying established frameworks expresses an orthodox mindset about problems. Established frameworks are best practices, evidence-based protocols, or preexisting frameworks deployed to solve problems. These frameworks appear to have utility because they previously demonstrated success elsewhere. Perhaps the best practices have been affirmed by experts, proving that they work and have merit. One example of the best practice approach in healthcare comes from Quint Studer and his company. The Studer Group's Rounding for Outcomes is a widely known and implemented portfolio of best practices for improving patient experience and outcomes.[18]

Leaders with an orthodox mindset about problems trust and rely on these frameworks and believe they and their organization will achieve their desired results by following them. They avoid reinventing the wheel and benefit from the lessons and successes of others. Sometimes it's an efficient and effective way to lead and realize success.

This approach underscores healthcare's value of and confidence in consultants with broad access to industry best practices, multiple frameworks, and shared learning from many organizations. It also explains healthcare's value of and trust in clinical protocols, solutions for clinical problems created to provide best-practice guidance, and shared learning from other scientists and clinicians.

THE UNORTHODOX MINDSET ABOUT PROBLEMS:
Polarities Are Opportunities, Not Problems to Resolve

The unorthodox mindset about problems accounts for and works with polarities when they are encountered. Unorthodox leaders harness the inherent pressure and tension of polarity as a powerful generative source of creative energy. The discomfort caused by the pressure and tension still exists, but it is held differently than by leaders with an orthodox mindset.

Unorthodox leaders don't use the discomfort as motivation to resolve the inherent tension and pressure of polarity. Instead, they use the discomfort to help others find useful and novel approaches that may advance the organization. They know and embrace the fact that they can't resolve the discomfort of polarity, or the polarity itself.

EXPRESSIONS OF THE UNORTHODOX MINDSET

Expressions of this unorthodox mindset are approaches, actions, and behaviors related to how leaders recognize and work with polarity. The unorthodox mindset aids leaders in discerning problems, especially dilemmas and impasses, from polarity.

The most notable expressions aim at leveraging polarity to maximize opportunities and generate innovation so that the system is appropriately responsive. You can identify the unorthodox mindset in yourself or others by noticing its common expressions: pursuing the many possibles, relying on harmonized polarities, and adopting systems thinking.

Pursuing the Many Possibles

One of the ways leaders express an unorthodox mindset about polarity is by embracing the pursuit of plurality—the many possibles—rather than seeking rightness. They do that by actively looking for and *simultaneously* exploring multiple potentially reasonable solutions, (i.e., plurality).

They approach leading their organization in this way because they understand that the complex relationships within their organization are nonlinear and not fully knowable. That makes it impossible to predict which solutions will work, so they try out many. They know that their past experiences and solutions have limited utility. Every situation is new, no matter how familiar it seems to be.

These leaders view their organization's results and outcomes as "inclinations" resulting from complex interactions and feedback loops. Inclinations of a complex system are the organization's inherent patterns and preferences, including the results and outcomes the organization produces. This perspective aligns with the notion that the organization is perfectly designed to produce the results it does. Complexity-fit leaders navigate and influence organizational inclinations by understanding and working with them, not trying to eliminate or fix them.

Relying on Harmonized Polarities

Leaders with an unorthodox mindset recognize polarity and seek to integrate the strengths and benefits of opposing poles rather than favoring or choosing one over the other. Some have described this as "finding a third way." However, that language can be misleading, implying an alternative and singular choice, a third one, from multiple possibilities.

In polarity, harmonization isn't choosing or crafting one best possible way from among numerous options. There's no one best or better way to go. What differentiates harmony from finding a third way is that harmonization is dynamic and changeable. It reflects continuous adaptability to the variabilities of complex organizations. This means finding not just a third, but also a fourth, and even a hundred ways to go. Leaders work on various possibilities simultaneously, embracing and managing the poles together without trying to resolve the tension by choosing a specific "third way." In other words, unorthodox leaders trust in the necessity of harmonized polarities as they lead organizations that are complex systems.

They are leading those organizations in a relationship with a contextual reality that matters. The point of harmonizing polarity is not just to pay attention to the poles, although that is important. More pressing is harmonizing the polarity in a maximally beneficial way in relationship with contextual reality.

For example, suppose the external organizational environment is stable and predictable, with minimal competitive threats. In that case, the organization is best served by harmonizing the systemic polarity to maximize the benefits of the Operational Core. This takes full advantage of the organization's ability to thrive in stable contexts, create maximum value, and deliver on its mission and purpose. That doesn't mean the Entrepreneurial Core is ignored, dismantled, or neglected. It just means that, for a time, the Operational Core is amplified, but not at the expense of the Entrepreneurial Core.

On the other hand, if the external environment is unpredictable, dynamic, uncertain, and volatile, the organization is best served by harmonizing the systemic polarity with an emphasis on the Entrepreneurial Core. This approach uses the organization's agility and adaptability to better align with the dynamic environment. That doesn't mean the Operational Core is ignored, dismantled, or neglected. The organization can't survive without two healthy poles.

As you can see, there is no right or wrong way to harmonize. It all depends on what maximizes system performance, given the contextual reality. System performance requires both poles. The best way to harmonize the poles is decided by whatever the context calls for, not by a leadership preference or style.

Surfing provides an apt metaphor for this concept. A surfer works with their surfboard to ride a wave, drawing upon the energy of the ocean and the direction of the wave. The rider does not and cannot control the ocean (the world at large) or the wave (the organizational context). The surfer does not have complete control over the board (the polarity), either. The board has inclinations of its own, depending upon what type of surfboard it is and how it was constructed. A successful rider uses harmony with the board and the board with the wave to go as far as they can (and have fun doing it!).

There is no right way to surf a wave and no map to follow. At the beginning of the ride, you have no idea how long it will last or where you will end up. You have theories, hypotheses, and aspirations but no specific plan. If you have a plan, it goes out the window in the first few seconds! Ultimately, successful surfing is about harmonizing with the ocean's energy and seeing where it takes you rather than fighting it. Fighting it, in fact, only ends in wiping out.

Harmonization encourages adaptive responses, iterative experimentation, and ongoing system adjustments to navigate the evolving dynamics of the polarity and the complex contexts in which healthcare organizations find themselves. Complexity-fit leaders are a lot like surfers.

Adopting Systems Thinking

Leaders with an unorthodox mindset understand and adopt contemporary systems thinking. They must examine and be aware of the system's structure, dynamics, and feedback loops to gain insights into how the whole functions and evolves. That approach aids their ability to nudge the system successfully. Analysis leads to insights into a system's elements and interactions, enabling a better—yet incomplete—understanding of the underlying system patterns. Sometimes called "sensing," this approach helps leaders notice the forces driving the system's inclinations. When leaders take this approach, they need to keep in mind that the whole is not merely the sum of its parts.

Systems thinking encourages a shift from linear, cause-and-effect thinking toward recognizing complex, nonlinear relationships. It acknowledges that events and outcomes often result from multiple and never fully knowable factors that work together in intricate and unpredictable ways. Contemporary systems thinking helps leaders expect and uncover the emergence of hidden connections and unintended consequences arising from seemingly isolated actions. By understanding these hidden, complex, and dynamic connections, leaders can make better decisions with a more complete awareness of the potential impacts of their choices on the entire system.

MAKING THE SHIFT

Before the Shift

Be Prepared to Pause Your Problem Solving

Keep in mind that you're likely very good at problem solving. You're so good at it that you may not notice when you're in problem-solving mode. In that case, before you can shift, you must be able to observe yourself solving problems, then pause. Paying attention to the common expressions of the orthodox mindset will help you catch those behaviors. When you see yourself trying to solve problems—especially in situations involving seemingly unsolvable problems—and pause, you will be in a better position to make a shift.

Be Prepared to Embrace Discomfort

Remember that you are not trying to eliminate pressure or tension like you would when solving a problem. You're trying to tap into that tension and use it to energize creative and collaborative action from yourself and others. When the pressure is on, your natural inclinations will be to decide, pick a side, and move on, but that is the least helpful approach to polarity.

Instead, embrace the discomfort and take advantage of it. Don't try to eliminate the pressure. Even after finding harmony in the polarity, the discomfort will not resolve. The unresolvable nature of the pressure and tension of polarity is one of the reasons why complex systems are so taxing on us. Be prepared for that, and help others be prepared too (see Mindset Seven–First Work). Hold yourself and others with compassion as they deal with the relentless daily pressure polarity brings.

Be Prepared to Hold Both Poles with Equanimity

Do your best to hold both poles with equanimity. By that, I mean holding both poles as equally necessary, valuable, and interdependent—but not necessarily holding both poles equally. Your goal is to harmonize those two (and sometimes more) poles to fit the context, situation, and organizational needs. Which may mean, for a time, that one pole is amplified, but not at the expense of the other. Remember, the more you favor one pole, the easier it is to ignore or diminish the other. If that happens, you risk "breaking" the polarity. If the polarity is systemic, you risk breaking the system.

WHY SHIFT

Because Polarity Flourishes in Complex Systems

Polarity flourishes in complex systems. This is an inescapable reality. Being adept at recognizing and harmonizing polarity is a fundamental prerequisite for successful healthcare leadership in the 21st century.

Because Treating Polarity as a Problem Breaks Polarity

If you treat polarity as a problem, you'll break the polarity, and whatever is entangled in that polarity breaks with it. That reality has consequences for your leadership, those you work with, and the organization. If you pick a side in polarity, you may think you are "winning" or being decisive and making the right or hard choices. Instead, you're dismantling the system.

Recall our earlier example, Entrepreneurial Core::Operational Core, the inherent polarity of complex systems. Maximizing cost-effectiveness and efficiency through central control and standardization—the Operational Core—often comes at the cost of local autonomy, adaptation, and innovation—the Entrepreneurial Core. It's a true polarity, where an overfocus on one comes at the expense of the other. There is no right side to this equation, no best way. The most useful harmony for this polarity is whatever is in the organization's best interest, which is constantly changing and not fully knowable, especially by a handful of executive leaders.

I suspect the first place your mind goes is, "How do you do that?" I'll suggest an approach in next chapter—but notice how inclined we are to draw upon either/or thinking here, wondering how you can amplify the Entrepreneurial Core without disregarding the Operational Core. We are inclined to think that increasing one must come at the expense of the other—either/or. But, in polarity, we cannot afford to think that way, so we must find ways to amplify the one and keep the other—both/

and. It's not easy, but that is what is called for in complex systems, and it is the reason you must shift.

HOW TO SHIFT

Notice Polarity

You begin by being curious about and then noticing polarity. A telltale sign of polarity is a lack of straightforward solutions, and the resurfacing of issues already dealt with. Polarities are tenacious. They seem to recur or cycle. On the other hand, problems come and go. They are more likely one-off situations or isolated incidents.

Recall that polarities have interdependent poles and problems don't. You must be looking for, and curious about, situations where things seem to be in opposition. When you notice opposing positions, views, or perspectives, be curious about each and examine them closely to see if they depend on each other. It takes practice to see interdependencies, because we are naturally inclined to see problems to solve instead.

Lastly, recall that polarities are not easy to see. You will need to work on seeing them, especially at first.

Practice Both/And Thinking

Harmonizing polarity demands "both/and" thinking, whereas "either/or" thinking is suitable for solving problems. Either/or thinking is our natural inclination, so both/and thinking requires persistent effort and intention. One way you can tell which thinking mode you're in is by noticing the language you use to describe your situation. If it includes absolutes like *right, wrong, good, bad,* or *should,* you're likely operating out of either/or thinking. If you find yourself using those words to describe a situation or explain your solution, pay attention! You may be using either/or thinking, and you want to be sure that's the most useful way to be thinking.

Learn to Harmonize

I've avoided using the word *manage* to describe how we work with polarity. Management is about control. We don't control polarities. We work with and make use of them as we find the proper relationship between the poles. It's also important to keep in mind that polarities are dynamic. Harmonizing them is ongoing work, not a once-and-done project or initiative—it's not about finding a third-way solution. The Learn More section at the back of this book offers resources that provide practical frameworks for dealing with polarity.[19]

MINDSET THREE—ADAPTABILITY

AN UNORTHODOX MINDSET ABOUT CREATING VALUE

Maximize Adaptability, Not Just Efficiency

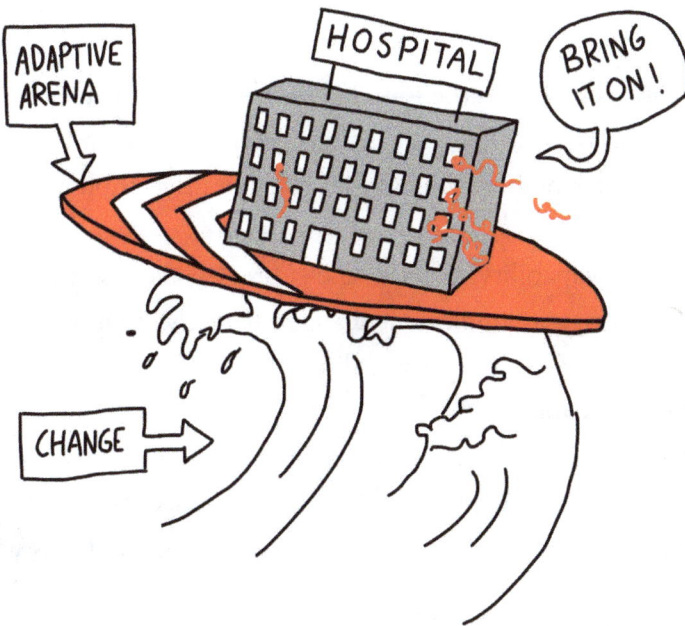

ILLUSTRATION 3. *Adaptability and the Role of the Adaptive Arena.*

UNDERSTANDING ADAPTABILITY

Adaptation is the process of responding to changes in one's environment. The fact that we and our organizations exist proves we all adapt. At issue is the escalating inadequacy of our adaptive response to the challenges we face. Healthcare tends to lag behind the pace of change, leading to underperformance and failure. As a result, adaptability is a fundamental challenge in the healthcare industry.

ADAPTABILITY DEFINED

Adaptability is the effective response to change. It is essential for thriving in a changeable world. To adapt, we need adaptive *capacity*, *capability*, and *suitability*.

Adaptive capacity is the foundation of adaptability. It includes the resources needed to adapt, such as time, money, people, and technology. Capacity for adaptation comes from resources that support or enable change.

Adaptive capability refers to the strategies, tactics, and essential qualities necessary to implement change effectively. Adaptive capability is the action component of adaptability. It is how we enact organizational and personal change.

Adaptive suitability is the evaluative component of adaptability. It tells us whether the adaptation fits with the changes that prompted it. Adaptive suitability is how we know whether an adaptation is working or not.

Insufficient Adaptability Is Maladaptation

When our adaptive efforts fall short in capacity, capability, or suitability, maladaptation ensues. Maladaptation is insufficient, detrimental, or counterproductive adaptation.

For example, a clinic needed to increase revenue and decrease operating expenses. They elected to implement an electronic health record (EHR) to help address their challenges. However, they did so without adequate training. The implementation permanently decreased productivity by 15 percent, reducing revenue. The subsequent hiring of scribes (documentation assistants) helped regain some lost productivity but increased labor expenses. The clinic was never able to exceed preimplementation productivity because of inherent limitations in the EHR itself, which permanently hindered clinician efficiency.

In this case, there was a shortfall in adaptive *capacity*, due to the selection of an EHR that limited the organization's ability to increase productivity or lower cost. There was a shortfall in adaptive *capability*, because the poorly trained workforce could not use the EHR in ways that increased productivity. Lastly, there was a shortfall in adaptive *suitability*, because the adaptation failed to align with what prompted the change: the need for increased revenue and decreased expenses. The EHR implementation proved to be a maladaptive response.

Adaptability Is About Thriving, Not Just Surviving

Adaptability goes beyond survival. It aims to position an organization or individual to thrive, resulting in changes that precisely align with new challenges or contexts. Adaptability is fitting optimally to what has changed.

Optimal fitness isn't an unrealistic ideal—it's what enables an organization to perform at its best. Any adaptation that falls short of this optimal state is maladaptive, creating gaps that, over time, undermine effectiveness and threaten long-term viability. This is why adaptability isn't optional; it's essential. Adaptability is the continuous ability to adjust in ways that close these gaps, ensuring the organization doesn't just survive but thrives in a constantly changing environment.

ADAPTABILITY AND VALUE CREATION

Value Defined

Optimal performance is a function of creating value. Healthcare organizations that create value excel at improving a population's health while achieving high-quality care. Their patients consistently experience services as accessible, equitable, empathetic, and dignified. Patients and those purchasing care on their behalf spend less than they would with a competitor. In these organizations, harm to patients is rare or does not happen. Successful organizations create value in unique ways that match their market. As a result, they become the provider of choice and are financially sound.

In other words, healthcare creates and increases value through improved health, quality, and experience. Likewise, increased cost (spend) or harm to patients decreases value. Written as a value equation, it might look like this:

$$\text{Value} = [(\text{Health} + \text{Quality} + \text{Experience}) \, / \, \text{Spend}] - \text{Harm}$$

Any one of the variables in the equation can change. When they do, organizations must adapt to that change. If they don't, the value they create decreases. When organizations don't create enough value, they lose ground to competitors who do.

Adaptability and the Healthcare Value Gap

The value equation changes so quickly that most are not keeping up. Even those that have done well in the past are falling behind. The pace of change is too fast, and it creates an adaptability gap. The adaptability gap results from maladaptation.

The underpinning cause of maladaptation is complexity. Complexity demands a pace of change that exceeds the adaptive capacity of most organizations, requiring more resources than are available. Because healthcare leaders tend to approach organizations as if they were complicated systems—relying on incremental adaptive mechanisms to create value—the rate of change also outstrips adaptive capability. The combined impact of complexity, changeability, and outdated organizational constructs results in a shortfall of adaptive suitability. In other words, complexity challenges healthcare organizations across all dimensions of adaptability—capacity, capability, and suitability. Consequently, most healthcare organizations end up in a maladaptive state. Healthcare leaders must deploy skills, practices, and approaches that nurture and expand organizational adaptability in order to avoid maladaptive responses. That begins by creating an adaptive "space," where adaptability thrives.[20]

ADAPTABILITY AND THE ADAPTIVE ARENA

The Adaptive Arena Defined

The Adaptive Arena is an organization's adaptive space. It is conceptual, cultural, and often structural. As described in the previous chapter, complex systems have an intrinsic polarity between the Operational Core (focused on efficiency) and the Entrepreneurial Core (focused on innovation). Conceptually, the Adaptive Arena is an organizational "neutral zone," resulting from a continuously negotiated "ceasefire" between the Entrepreneurial and Operational Core (Figure 5).

Notably, both the Entrepreneurial and Operational Cores contribute to the Adaptive Arena, while restraining inclinations to seize or cede territory from the other. The Adaptive Arena, therefore, is a tension-filled neutral zone with constant border skirmishes between poles, where both sides protect and cultivate their preferred approaches.

An Adaptive Arena emerges in organizations in response to specific leadership approaches, actions, and behaviors. These leadership expressions become cultural and relational norms that drive organizational expectations and practices, influencing organizational structure. Some activities and actions expand the Adaptive Arena, while others contract it. The larger the arena grows, the more adaptable the organization becomes. Conversely, the more the arena shrinks, the less adaptable it becomes.

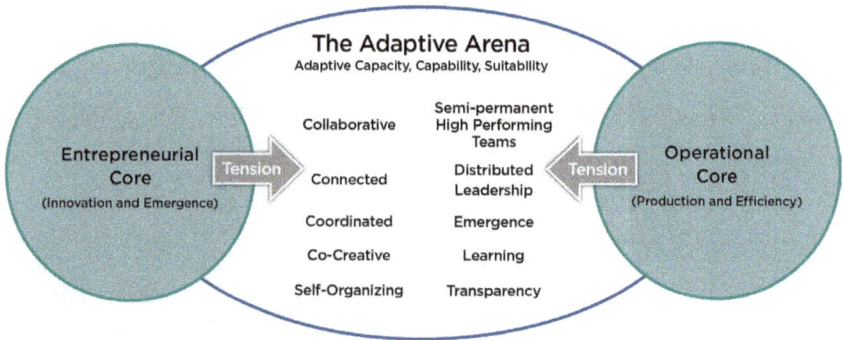

FIGURE 5. *Common Characteristics of the Adaptive Arena.* The Adaptive Arena is a tenuous territory within the polarity of a complex system. A handful of the most common organizational characteristics of a robust Adaptive Arena are listed. (Source: Michael Hein, 2025. Modified from: Mary Uhl-Bien and Michael Arena, "Leadership for Organizational Adaptability: A Theoretical Synthesis and Integrative Framework," The Leadership Quarterly 29, no. 1 (2018): 89–104, https://doi.org/10.1016/j.leaqua.2017.12.009.)

The Adaptive Arena Requires Efficiency and Innovation

Organizations source adaptation from both poles of complex systems. On the one hand, the Operational Core drives adaptation through management practices that focus on efficient production. Management practices are methodologies that maximize production efficiency. Well-known examples include Scientific Management (Taylorism), Lean Manufacturing and the Toyota Management System, Total Quality Management (TQM), and Six Sigma. These and others like them are effective in tightly structured, hierarchical, and bureaucratic organizations.

In stable environments with predictable conditions, these practices work well, advancing adaptability incrementally.

On the other hand, the Entrepreneurial Core drives adaptation through practices that foster innovation and emergence. These approaches are far less common in healthcare. For example, the Agile Manifesto (formally known as the *Manifesto for Agile Software Development*) outlines guiding values and principles that prioritize individuals and interactions, working solutions, customer collaboration, and responsiveness to change over rigid processes and tools.[21] Agile and similar management practices include experimentation, connectivity, and transparency. They also rely on self-organizing teams that are semipermanent, collaborative, co-creative, cross-functional, and high performing. Learning happens by "failing forward" fast in psychologically safe environments. This adaptive approach works exceptionally well in fast-changing and unpredictable contexts, allowing organizations to keep pace.

The Adaptive Arena Gains Speed from the Entrepreneurial Core

Both poles and their approaches advance adaptation and are necessary for closing the adaptability gap. However, optimal adaptability requires speed, which comes from the Entrepreneurial Core alone.

An analogy from the years I coached competitive swimming is the front crawl (or freestyle stroke). Freestyle is usually the fastest stroke, with speed coming from two components: the kick (legs) and the pull (arms). The kick is essential for forward movement but adds little to overall speed. The arms are much more powerful, pulling the body forward faster than the kick can push.

Like the pull, the Entrepreneurial Core supplies swift adaptability. The Operational Core supplies slow adaptability, like the kick—effective if speed does not matter. If you are in a race—which you are if you are leading a healthcare organization—Operational Core adaptability matters, but Entrepreneurial Core adaptability matters more.

The Adaptive Arena is Ambidextrous

There is abundant academic and popular business literature about organizations that take full advantage of their "pull" and "kick," generating adaptability from both poles of the polarity in complex systems. These are called ambidextrous organizations.[22]

An ambidextrous organization harmonizes two seemingly contradictory goals: rapid adaptation through experimentation (innovative ideas, technologies, and products) on the one hand while focusing on refining and maximizing their current services on the other. These organizations respond to fast-paced and unpredictable environments more effectively than those focusing on a single pole.

Ambidextrous organizations are as difficult to sustain as polarities are to harmonize. They require constant vigilance against either pole encroaching on the neutral zone of the Adaptive Arena. If one side gains the upper hand, it impairs the other, collapsing the Adaptive Arena and decreasing adaptability.

The Adaptive Arena's Tenuous Existence

Advocates of the Entrepreneurial Core encroach on the neutral zone when they promote unrestrained autonomy and innovation, undermining the efficiencies gained from adaptations by the Operational Core. A decrease in central constraint allows the development and funding of local experiments in the pursuit of innovative ideas. However, those innovations may not align with the organization's strategic goals. The consequent proliferation of entrepreneurial endeavors siphons energy, focus, and capital away from other organization-wide opportunities.

For example, consider a healthcare organization that allows member hospitals to operate independently. Those hospitals move quickly to take advantage of strategic opportunities, adapting swiftly to local changes. That results in divergent strategies and operations, making it difficult to take advantage of economies of scale, undermining one of an integrated healthcare organization's most potent competitive advantages. Unrestrained innovation collapses the Adaptive Arena by jettisoning large-scale, incremental adaptations that increase efficiency.

Likewise, advocates of the Operational Core encroach on the neutral zone when they promote excessive standardization, undermining the adaptive behaviors necessary for innovations by the Entrepreneurial Core. Management approaches that increase standardized work cultivate a workforce that adheres to policy and procedure. This approach is designed to reduce variation and cost, but it also risks eliminating potentially positive deviations and discouraging innovative practices.

Note that I use the term *variation* to refer to the expected range of differences in any process or outcome. The term *deviation*, on the other hand, refers to differences that fall outside this expected range—whether positive or negative—in relation to processes and outcomes.

The advancement of standardization impedes the creative energy, drive, and abilities the organization requires to be innovative. For example, consider a healthcare organization that centralizes most functions and eliminates local hospital CEOs and executive leaders. Instead, they put in place a lead administrator who oversees centrally deployed strategies and processes. This results in slower responses to local changes and strategic opportunities because of the requirement for central evaluation and decision. In today's fast-paced reality, opportunities come and go quickly, often awarded to faster and more nimble organizations. A centralized organization may be more efficient, but it is slower. Centralization collapses the Adaptive Arena by jettisoning the ability to make quick, local, innovative adaptations.

Each pole of the Adaptive Arena requires specific support and conditions to succeed. Advocates for each pole are justified in pursuing the adaptability each engenders. However, the pursuit of one undermines the ability of the other, creating tension and conflict. Consequently, the Adaptive Arena is tenuous, requiring constant defense and nurturing from advocates of both poles.

Healthcare organizations cannot rely on either core alone for adaptability. Production efficiency is a slow train to nowhere. Unrestrained innovation is wasteful and often directionless. Successful organizations need ambidexterity, even though it is challenging.

Given the current industry preference for production efficiency, most leaders must relax their Operational Core and amplify their Entrepreneurial Core to create an Adaptive Arena. That means becoming less efficient in production to gain greater adaptive speed, which may seem heretical to some.

AN EXAMPLE OF THE ADAPTIVE ARENA

For many, the U.S. Veterans Health Administration (VHA) epitomizes the bureaucratic healthcare organization. It is the largest integrated healthcare organization in the United States.[23]

In the early 1990s, the VHA sorely needed reform. The VHA was mired in its vast bureaucracy, and its poor performance reflected systemic issues that drew national attention.[24] In 1994, President Clinton appointed Dr. Kenneth Kizer to lead the VHA. Kizer initiated sweeping changes that improved performance.[25]

Kizer broke the VHA into 22 regional Veterans Integrated Service Networks (VISNs) entities, relaxing centralized control.[26] Each VISN had its own administrative and clinical leadership that was granted autonomy in decision-making, allowing tailored adaptations to improve care for local Veterans. Kizer imposed stringent performance metrics, motivating VISN leaders to meet or exceed care quality and efficiency standards. Collaboration and shared learning were encouraged between

VISNs and facilitated through regular communication and knowledge exchange. The interactions were self-organized and led to the wide dissemination of successful strategies and innovations.

Service Lines as Entrepreneurial Core

In VISN 23, the leadership team established regional service lines, intentionally creating a meshed interconnection of leadership and management across eight medical centers (hospitals) and roughly sixty ambulatory centers (clinics) in a five-state upper-Midwest region.[27] The service lines were responsible for the VISNs' strategic direction, innovation, and programmatic oversight. The medical centers were accountable for VISN business operations and clinical performance. The service line and medical center directors reported directly to the VISN Executive Director but not to each other.[28]

Strategic Initiatives Nurture Innovation

One of the tactical approaches that encouraged innovation within VISN 23 was the VISN-wide implementation of a competitive program to solicit and support strategic initiatives. Anyone in the organization could develop and propose strategic initiatives; local teams submitted most proposals. Service lines supported and facilitated the process.

The Executive Director took a personal interest in the projects. Successful proposals were supported with funding, personnel, and recognition and were deployed VISN-wide. Applicants were held accountable for their initiatives and supported by the service lines. They provided quarterly progress updates in person before the VISN board of directors.

Deployment of the supported strategic initiatives required interaction and transparency across all medical centers, connecting people with resources and information they would not otherwise have had access to. Success required collaboration, semipermanent, high-performing teams, and diversity of thought—since each medical center tended to do things differently. The successful implementation of the initiatives depended on distributed leadership (one of the hallmarks of the Adaptive Arena). The competitive process and subsequent deployment of successful strategic initiative proposals helped participants learn and expand their appreciation for VISN processes and efficiencies.

The strategic initiatives drove rapid organizational adaptation. Some were spectacular successes, propelling VISN 23 into national prominence. Some were promoted and deployed in other VISNs or integrated into national efforts. Other initiatives were unsuccessful. All provided valuable learning and innovation.

How the VHA's Approach Expanded the Adaptive Arena

When Kizer decentralized the VHA, decision-making shifted to regional leaders. That positioned VISN 23 leaders to increase adaptive capacity by using local resources to create service lines. VISN leaders increased adaptive capability by taking ownership of performance standards and self-organizing for greater connectivity, improving the flow of information and ideas. The strategic initiatives added to that capability by fostering the knowledge, skills, and experiences necessary for innovative ideas and practices. Leaders addressed adaptive suitability through quarterly updates and the free flow of information afforded by a matrixed structure, facilitating the continuous sensing of the system's response to the initiatives.

The service lines were the Entrepreneurial Core, and the medical centers were the Operational Core. This fundamental differentiation between the service lines and the medical centers is what created the Adaptive Arena within the organization. The Adaptive Arena was programmatic, cultural, and real. Service lines were not responsible for improved financial, operational, or clinical performance—the medical centers were. There would have been no Adaptive Arena if service lines and medical centers had combined to advance production efficiency through clinical and operational standardization. Instead, the service lines were dependent upon and in supportive opposition to the Operational Core. The service lines were primarily focused on promoting innovation, not standardization.

There was tension between the service lines and the medical centers. Medical center leaders complained that the service lines were interfering with their chain of command and siphoning off the resources and focus they needed to run and support their operations efficiently. Service line leadership complained that the medical centers were resistant and slow to change, self-interested, and overly focused on their fiscal performance. However, the tension rarely became personal, with leaders generally respecting the roles of each pole, trusting in the shared purpose and commitment each had to the mission and vision of the whole. The trust in shared purpose was something the executive director was particularly good at promoting.

There were intentional efforts to keep the Adaptive Arena safe from encroachment by either pole. The clearly defined service line role was most notable: identifying and promoting the organization's strategic direction, fostering innovation, and developing programs to implement that strategy. Efficient operations and improved clinical performance were the responsibility of the medical centers. Their fiscal and clinical performance accountability made that clear. Likewise, there was a repeated emphasis on the duty of the service lines to support medical center efforts and the medical centers' duty to support the service lines. VISN leadership intentionally set up ambidexterity, and the leaders of each pole helped the other keep the neutral zone safe so that the Adaptive Arena could thrive.

Dr. Kizer's reforms received wide praise for improving healthcare delivery to Veterans, and they had a lasting impact. The VHA still faces challenges today, but that does not mean that Dr. Kizer's reforms fell short—quite the opposite. Kizer's reforms excelled for a specific time, place, and context, (i.e., they demonstrated adaptive *suitability*). The key takeaway is that organizations can never consider adaptation a completed task. They must continuously evolve to meet the demands of an ever-changing context. Thus, adaptability—the nurturing of an Adaptive Arena—must be the focus of healthcare organizations that want to continue to thrive rather than rest on the achievements of reforms that used to work.

Some leadership mindsets amplify adaptability, expanding the Adaptive Arena. Other mindsets contract the Adaptive Arena. By noticing these mindsets in yourself and others, you can better understand and take the approaches, actions, and behaviors that serve adaptability.

THE ORTHODOX MINDSET ABOUT ADAPTABILITY:
Adapt Through Efficiency

The orthodox mindset holds that adaptation comes by improving production efficiency, thereby creating value. Efficiency is primarily about reducing unit costs and focusing on controlling expenses. Reduced cost means reduced spend, the value equation variable to which these leaders pay the closest attention. Managers rely primarily upon various production management tactics to achieve that efficiency. As a result, adaptation occurs incrementally. Focusing on efficiency is a familiar and successful means of creating value.

EXPRESSIONS OF THE ORTHODOX MINDSET

You can identify the orthodox mindset in yourself or others by noticing the common expressions of this mindset: improving processes, increasing consistency, and looking to blame.

Improving Processes
Leaders with this mindset believe that every organizational output results from a process or a combination of processes with component steps that

function best when ordered rationally and predictably. If the contributing processes are obscure, they can still be known, usually with the help of experts. When each step works as designed, it produces a predictable result. If the outcome of a step in the process varies from standard, the outcome of the entire process changes proportionally. All variations get scrutinized because they represent inefficiencies, which are considered wasteful and add to production costs.

Importantly, processes are separate from people who act on the process in compliance with an assigned practice or procedure. If something goes "wrong," it is because someone did not do something "right." Noncompliance by people causes variation, creating inefficiency. It is like a factory worker on an assembly line: the product will be flawed if the worker does not do their job correctly. This assembly-line mental model, a lingering legacy of the industrial age, is profoundly ingrained in our collective subconscious, informing us about how things function.

Variation represents a mistake because each assembly line step has a predictable and tightly managed output that relies on people's compliance. Management's primary function is improving efficiency by error reduction through enhanced compliance, the elimination of unnecessary process steps, or both. That is how organizations adapt; it is a slow, steady, predictable, and highly effective approach.

Increasing Consistency

Inconsistency is nettlesome, hindering organizational success because it wastes time, money, and people. The best organizations are consistent, demonstrating minimal variation in processes, procedures, and outputs across the enterprise. For example, the ideal organization has the same position descriptions, electronic health records, and single suppliers at each hospital. Leaders strive to operate similarly, producing consistent results through standard processes and procedures. Sameness is value creation—like McDonald's, serving the same hamburger no matter where you are.

Deploying best practices is one common approach for creating consistency. The orthodox mindset holds that outcomes are process based and replicable. Since people are separable from processes, successful best practice deployment is the transference of a process from one site to another. After the appropriate education takes place, compliance with the new process should lead to the expected improvements. If the transferred best practice does not yield similar outcomes, it is likely due to noncompliance caused by inadequate training or resistance, not because of limitations in the best practice itself.

Best practice serves two purposes: it improves performance and spreads consistency. It is an attractive approach because leaders with this mindset believe that systemness equates to consistency. If variations occur, then people, departments, or hospitals are "not acting like a system." The best systems act together in pursuit of consistency across the entire enterprise, and best practices are a valuable tool for accomplishing that.

Looking to Blame

A good process fails because someone makes a mistake. Variation exists because people do not follow the rules, policies, procedures, or best practices. There are right and wrong ways of doing things. Therefore, variation is someone's fault. If leaders believe that to be true, they look to blame someone for doing something wrong. An efficient workforce is accountable, and good managers are adept at imposing accountability. In doing so, leaders contribute to developing and sustaining a blame-based culture.

Being held accountable is uncomfortable, and most people would rather avoid it. We tend to scurry away from blame, deploying a whole battalion of behaviors to escape. Some leaders hold others accountable because it helps them hide from their own accountability! People pass blame like a hot potato until someone dares to own it. In a blame-based culture, these avoidant behaviors become normative and ingrained, resulting in decreased transparency and low psychological safety.

Adaptation proceeds slowly and incrementally, because managers train the workforce to avoid variation and expect blame. Adaptation is risky where blame abounds. People do not speak up, advance innovative ideas, or eagerly participate in something new. Adaptation in those environments requires active, persistent prompting through encouragement or compulsion. Leaders commonly interpret the effort needed to overcome the fear of blame and its consequences as resistance to change.

THE UNORTHODOX MINDSET ABOUT ADAPTABILITY: Adapt Through Innovation

The unorthodox mindset is that adaptation occurs through rapid innovation. Efficiency derives from novel, reasonably cost-effective solutions and processes that quickly respond to the changeable variables of the value equation. Speed is the paramount element of efficiency, not cost.

EXPRESSIONS OF THE UNORTHODOX MINDSET

Expressions of the unorthodox mindset are the approaches, actions, and behaviors that enable rapid adaptations from emergent innovations. You can identify the unorthodox mindset in yourself or others by noticing the common expressions of this mindset: innovating processes, increasing positive deviation, and looking to learn.

Innovating Processes
Leaders with this mindset believe that processes work best when they can be changed quickly, without central oversight. That allows those working within the process to respond to challenges and feedback

iteratively. Process alterations are experiments that may lead to improvements with unpredictable consequences. The consequences are often disproportionate to the change in the process, necessitating curious scrutiny of what transpires afterward. This approach sometimes results in variations that increase or decrease value, improve efficiency—speed, cost, or both—or have no impact. There is no way to know what will happen until it does.

A critical shift in this mindset is that people and processes are inseparable. People work within the process. They influence the process as much as the process influences them. Therefore, you cannot fully extract the process from people. That is why blame is usually unfounded, and the transference of best practices often does not realize repeatable results.

Variations arise from the changeable intermingling of people and processes, usually resulting in expected outcomes—but not always. Significant variations raise curiosity rather than blame and are embraced, because variations are just as likely to be improvements as detriments.

Best practices are still helpful, because they are educational, illuminating how one group influenced inclinations within a complex system. There may be something transferrable gained from using best practices, albeit requiring modification. Leaders know that best practices are not entirely scalable or transferable, because they result from unique individuals working within processes derived from and deployed in an irreproducible system. To replicate best practice results from one setting to another requires copying everything, including the people, which is impossible.

Adaptability increases by cultivating a culture that favors continuous experimentation—tinkering with processes without central oversight or control. Consistently creating value across an enterprise is what's relevant, not creating consistent processes. The unorthodox mindset, in essence, relaxes the conviction or belief in a direct cause-and-effect relationship between process and outcome. Just because a process is consistent does not mean the outcome will be.

Increasing Positive Deviation

The unorthodox mindset is curious about variation, because it may lead to positive deviation, a primary source of adaptive success. A good process is inherently variable and occurs because people, processes, and contexts interact in complex ways—which means variation is unavoidable and potentially beneficial. Therefore, leaders with an unorthodox mindset tolerate and encourage variation, monitoring results—closely and with curiosity—and looking for deviations.

Deviations are statistical outliers, variations that go beyond the expected. They may hinder, improve, or have no impact on performance. Harmful deviations and whatever adaptation led to them get shut down quickly, while positive deviations are promoted. Positive deviations are those that move the inclinations of the system closer to the purpose of the organization.

Suppose a healthcare organization designed a position description for an important strategic role that exists at each of the organization's hospitals. Local leaders adjusted the position at one facility to align with their existing workforce. They expanded the role to include a unique constellation of responsibilities, changing the title to match. The combined responsibilities improved the results for the strategic initiative. Unlike most organizations, leaders at the highest organizational level allowed the variation in the position and noticed the positive deviation in results. Consequently, the organizational leaders worked with other local leaders to redefine their position descriptions, incorporating similar responsibilities. The change accelerated the strategic initiative's overall success.

Finding and deploying resources to locations primed for innovation is the primary mechanism for setting up positive deviation. Leaders with this mindset have high trust that others will adhere to the organizational purpose and mission and find innovations that align strategically. Local leaders are intimately connected with organization-wide information, data, and resources, so they can effectively sense shifts in performance resulting from their local interventions. They are as concerned about organization-wide performance as local performance and are sometimes willing to put the needs of the many (the whole organization) ahead of the needs of the few (the local organization). Central leadership spends considerable time, effort, and energy supporting and facilitating innovative local responses to emerging challenges, believing it to be their primary leadership purpose.

Leaders with this mindset believe that systemness comes from emergent and innovative inconsistencies arising from the highly interconnected parts of an organization, ultimately generating the positive performance of the whole. It is like the chemistry of a high-performing team that pursues a shared vision and goal; it can't be explained by looking at the team members in isolation.

Looking to Learn

Curiosity—looking to learn—is the management response to deviations, driving a learning-based culture. Leaders looking to learn carefully monitor process outputs, sort variation (expected) from deviation (unexpected), and investigate. The careful study of positive deviation leads to insights into organizational performance inclinations, possibly replicable elsewhere, supporting efforts to scale innovation. Likewise, learning from unfavorable deviations supports efforts to suppress the spread of unfavorable inclinations.

Looking to learn is a co-creative activity between leaders and those who work within the process. Together, they learn about deviations, their causes and consequences, and then co-create adaptive responses to the challenges or opportunities deviations bring. By maintaining a vigilant curiosity regarding deviations, teams can continuously sense system tendencies, allowing them to adjust processes quickly and collaboratively to maximize performance.

When leaders look to learn rather than to blame, individuals within the processes become the experts, teaching those leaders, flipping the usual hierarchy. In that environment, it is easier for the workforce to own their work and to hold themselves accountable for the outputs. In other words, an Adaptive Arena workforce is accountable to themselves, (i.e., they take ownership). Leaders suited to the Adaptive Arena are adept at fostering a learning-based culture and creating ownership. There is little need for managers or leaders to hold others accountable.

In learning-based cultures, adaptation is fast, because psychological safety is high. It is easier to take risks, voice different perspectives, and offer unconventional yet potentially remarkable suggestions. Consequently, people are more likely to speak up, advance innovative ideas, and eagerly participate in something new. They do not resist change, they embrace it.

MAKING THE SHIFT
Before the Shift

Be Prepared by Understanding Adaptability

Adaptability is about continuously achieving an optimally fit performance. Anything that falls short is maladaptive. There are degrees of maladaptation, but the longer an organization persists in a maladaptive state, the more perilous its survival. The choices you make either unlock or constrain the full adaptive potential of a complex system. Orthodox strategies and tactics in healthcare work to constrain adaptability by staying focused on the Operational Core, positioning organizations in a maladaptive state.

Adaptability requires collective interdependence, promoting variation, and monitoring for deviation. The organization's focus should be on capturing positive deviations and suppressing unfavorable ones.

The more you attempt to decrease variability through greater standardization, the more you constrain adaptability. Dynamic, unpredictable environments demand greater and faster adaptability, making demands on you and how you lead. Most likely, those demands go against your natural inclinations, let alone the industry standard, so be prepared for that. If you want to lead successfully in a complex environment, you must be willing to embrace the discomfort that prioritizing adaptability may bring.

Be Prepared for Tenuous Ambidexterity

Protecting the Adaptive Arena is challenging. Your present mindsets and experiences likely lean heavily toward the Operational Core, where you and your team are comfortable, and where your trust and confidence lie. However, today's complex healthcare context requires a preferential lean toward the Entrepreneurial Core. This likely pulls you and your team further away from your comfort zone, skillsets, and experience.

The temptation to reach for what you know in times of duress is powerful. It is not easy to be ambidextrous, mainly because it is not easy for leaders to deal with a complex system's polarity. We are all hardwired to choose a side and tend to do that when stressed. If we lead from our preference, we tend to encroach upon the neutral zone, imperiling the Adaptive Arena.

Before the shift, leaders must be clear-minded and committed to creating and sustaining the Adaptive Arena. For most leaders, that results from amplifying the Entrepreneurial Core and restraining the Operational Core. That approach can counter our natural inclination for greater control, favoring the Operational Core. Protecting the "neutral zone" includes the approaches, behaviors, and action choices you make. These include how you interact with and depend on teams and your structural and operational choices, as VISN 23 leaders did with service lines.

Be Prepared to Keep Adaptability Paramount

Organizations continuously create value by adapting. They cannot survive, let alone thrive, unless they do. To thrive, your organization must adapt in ways that match the complex environments you are in—the Law of Requisite Complexity. For most, that means more adaptability through the Entrepreneurial Core because it brings speed. While your team must continue adapting through the familiar, incremental efficiency of the Operational Core, sufficient adaptability is impossible without the Entrepreneurial Core adding quickness.

Remember that the Adaptive Arena requires both means of adaptability. Proponents of each core must restrain themselves from encroaching into the neutral zone, simultaneously maximizing their adaptive capacity, capability, and suitability.

WHY SHIFT

Because Adaptable Organizations Win

Starkly put, in complex environments, reaching for the Operational Core alone to create a sustainable and thriving path forward is a leadership error of epic proportions. That approach violates the Law of Requisite Complexity. The organizations that "win" today have adapted to match their context, which is complex.

Suitable adaptability is not achievable through the Operational Core alone. Because it reflects a polarity, you must harmonize the operational and Entrepreneurial Core to generate the adaptability you need—creating an ambidextrous organization. The tension between the cores opens an Adaptive Arena. If you nurture the tension with intention, conviction, and clarity, the Adaptive Arena can generate the adaptive capabilities a complexity-fit organization needs to thrive.

Creating and sustaining an ambidextrous organization requires different leadership, which focuses on more than effectively leading the Operational Core; it must also support the Entrepreneurial Core and defend the Adaptive Arena.

HOW TO SHIFT

Relax Control

Control constrains innovation, so shifting requires relaxing your sense of and need for control. Control is derived from various sources of power. Relaxing control means decreasing our use of certain forms of power while increasing the use of others. We will go into detail about this in the next chapter.

Relaxing control is not easy, because we take comfort from and have confidence in our abilities to manage operations and people, ensuring predictable outcomes. Furthermore, the Operational Core thrives under control.

The only way to succeed in complex environments is to adapt quickly. The only way to adapt quickly is by relinquishing control. That means fostering distributed leadership: relying upon and trusting in those closer to the work to do what is in the organization's best interest. You must increase your trust in the capabilities of others and their ability to take the organization where it needs to go. If your team is not trustworthy enough for you to relinquish control, that is a separate set of issues that imperils your organization's success in complex environments. A substantial part of your leadership work is creating an organization that can thrive with only as much central control as is minimally necessary.

Rely on High-Performing Teams

You cannot relax control if you do not trust your team's ability to perform at an elevated level. Creating high-performing teams is not rocket science, but being able to create and sustain them repeatedly is decidedly tricky work. High-performing teams are interdependent, self-organizing, and trustworthy. They have chemistry. They deal well with conflict, stick to their commitments, hold each other accountable, and deliver results.

In the context of complexity and an Adaptive Arena, high-performing teams are semipermanent and composed of diverse individuals from, near, or on the frontline. They pull themselves together without central control or permission, coalescing around opportunities and challenges that they identify. These teams sense favorable and unfavorable deviations and respond to them appropriately. They are highly motivated to address the challenges they encounter, because they own the process and the outcomes. Teams anchor the adaptive response in a complex system.

Beginning a successful shift toward unorthodox mindsets includes increasing the importance of and reliance on high-performing teams. Establishing and supporting high-performing teams within your organization is essential to successfully making this shift.[29]

Trust Adaptability

To trust adaptability, you must first let go of the idea that people and your organization resist change. While it is a profoundly ingrained belief that people resist change, they do not, especially if we think of change as adaptation (For this unorthodox view of change, see Mindset Six—Change).

Instead, be curious about adaptive capacity, capability, and suitability. "Resistance" is most likely some limitation in one or more of these areas. In other words, something is getting in the way of change, limiting adaptability. That something is not resistance.

People and organizations can, do, and want to adapt—trust in that. The issue is the escalating inadequacy of our adaptability. Your work is to unlock and catalyze the adaptive potential in you and your organization. It is not only possible but necessary. It is not only necessary but an awful lot of leadership fun.

MINDSET FOUR—POWER

AN UNORTHODOX MINDSET ABOUT USING POWER

Use Power to Expand Influence, Not Just to Gain More Control

ILLUSTRATION 4. *Power, Control, and Influence.* Power converts to control and influence, which impacts systems differently. Choose wisely.

UNDERSTANDING POWER

Effective leadership hinges on the judicious use of power. Leaders use power by converting it into control and influence through specific approaches, actions, and behaviors. The choices leaders make about using power depend on their mindset about power. Those choices drive organizational momentum.

Without power, meaningful organizational movement is impossible. However, the term often evokes negative feelings shaped by our experiences of power exploitation and malpractice. Consequently, some people shy away from power, while others look for more. No matter our relationship with power, it is indispensable for effective leadership.

HOW POWER WORKS

Power is the capacity to change our or others' behaviors, attitudes, or outcomes. It is the ability to effect change or make decisions that affect an organization or its members. We may think we have a clear understanding of power, but power works in various and nuanced ways within systems.

Power is Used by "Agents" and Experienced by "Subjects"

An individual, a group, or an organization may use power. For our discussion, I am referring to power used by an individual. The person using power is the *agent*. The person or group of people toward whom the agent directs power is the *subject*. Subjects experience an agent's use of power.

Power Converts to Control and Influence

Power exists only as potential until it is activated. It's bottled up in various sources, waiting to be used. We use power by tapping into those power sources.

Simply having power does not make you an effective leader. For power to have efficacy (potency), leaders must tap into and use those power sources. When leaders do this, power converts from mere potential into control, influence, or both.

In short, agents use power to gain control and influence. That is how leaders are effective at driving organizational momentum. Without power, you cannot lead, and you cannot lead without converting power into control and influence.

THE IMPACT OF CONTROL AND INFLUENCE

The Impact on Change

Control and influence are different. Control is exercising power to guide, regulate, or manage others. It enforces compliance. In contrast, influence is the exercise of power to affect feelings, attitudes, or behaviors through persuasion, inspiration, or modeling. It builds commitment. Influence relies on interdependent relationships, trust, and credibility. Many people mistakenly use control and influence interchangeably; however, they are two separate ways of initiating change in others and organizations.

The Impact on Individual Autonomy

The principal way that control and influence differ is in how they affect the autonomy of subjects. Autonomy is the ability to make independent choices. If you have autonomy, you can make your own decisions, free from external constraints. If you lose autonomy, you lose your freedom of choice. When an agent uses power for control, it always reduces a subject's autonomy. In contrast, power used for influence retains the subject's autonomy.

Autonomy comes in shades of gray; there are degrees of autonomy. Agents using power for control pull autonomy away from subjects; agents using power for influence push autonomy toward subjects. Power use moves autonomy up and down a scale from entirely autonomous to no autonomy. Wherever our autonomy or the autonomy of others resides along that scale is a *locus* or its location on the scale (Figure 6).

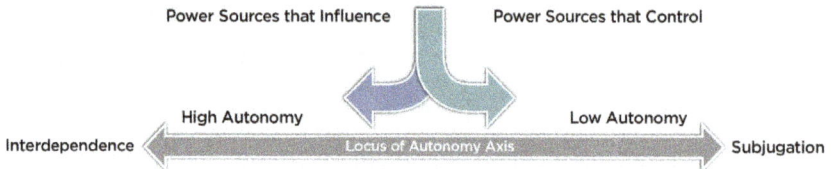

FIGURE 6. *Locus of Autonomy*. The use of power moves the locus of autonomy up and down the locus of autonomy axis. Where the locus of autonomy resides for the subject depends on the mix and persistence of the leader's use of various sources of power. (Source: Michael Hein, 2025.)

The Impact on Organizational Culture

Leaders who consistently use power for greater control rather than influence tend to create organizations characterized by subjugation. Subjugation is the systematic erosion of individual or collective autonomy. When leaders do that, subjects become reliant on the organization and the leader. That's because subjugation is a state of diminished autonomy. It stifles creativity, fostering an environment of dependance and compliance over innovation.

On the other hand, leaders who consistently use power to influence create organizations characterized by interdependence. Interdependence describes a state where individuals or units within an organization are mutually reliant, sharing responsibilities and outcomes. In an interdependent system, exercising influence leads to collective ownership of goals. Influence fosters an environment ripe for commitment, innovation, and adaptability.

It's important to point out that influence creates a culture of interdependence rather than independence. Independence signifies self-reliance and unilateral decision-making. It implies the complete decoupling of influential relationships, where autonomy is so extreme that the individual functions independently of others. This can occur with organizations as much as individuals. For example, individual hospitals in a regional or national system may pine for independence when interdependence would better serve them.

Organizations are, by design, ways of working together. That is why absolute independence is a concept or preference for organizational life and leadership that doesn't work well. Interdependence, however, captures the spirit of collaboration that develops when a leader uses influence rather than control to move others and their organization.

The Impact on Cooperation

At a basic level, leaders use power to gain organizational movement or change through coordinated cooperation. Both control and influence can result in this outcome, (i.e., the cooperation of others). However, the mechanism of cooperation that results from the use of control is fundamentally different from that resulting from the use of influence.

In an organization where leadership prefers control, subjects experience a diminishing sense of autonomy and a culture of subjugation. In this environment, the mechanism of cooperation is compliance. Compliant people follow the rules, policies, and procedures closely. They avoid deviating from the standards while striving for measured or quantifiable excellence. A compliant workforce does steady and predictably excellent work. Under extreme conditions, however, a compliant workforce may resist control. Furthermore, a subjugated workforce struggles to be innovative or adaptable. Innovation and adaptability require interdependence and a high degree of autonomy, which a subjugated workforce cannot access.

Conversely, in an organization where leadership prefers influence over control, subjects experience an enhanced sense of autonomy. That creates a culture of interdependence. In this environment, the mechanism of cooperation is commitment. Commitment is the voluntary, intrinsic alignment of individual and organizational goals. It fuels intentional, long-term contributions to collective goals, which contrasts sharply with compliance.

Committed people do what they are trained for and go beyond it. They strive for excellence as measured by radically improving the outcomes that matter most to key stakeholders. A committed workforce tinkers, finding better ways to get things done faster. They innovate and adapt. An interdependent, committed workforce will bristle at efforts to enforce compliance (Figure 7).

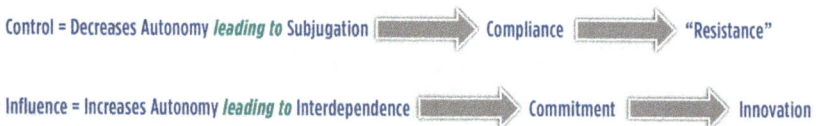

Control = Decreases Autonomy *leading to* Subjugation ⟹ Compliance ⟹ "Resistance"

Influence = Increases Autonomy *leading to* Interdependence ⟹ Commitment ⟹ Innovation

FIGURE 7. *Simplified Relationships of Control and Influence.* Power converts to control and influence. Control decreases autonomy, leading to subjugation, compliance, and resistance. Influence increases autonomy, leading to interdependence, commitment, and innovation. (Source: Michael Hein, 2025.)

Leaders often confuse compliance with commitment because things get done either way. However, the intentions, motivations, and methods that result in compliance and commitment differ. It's valuable for leaders to be aware of these differences and how they impact the workplace and the organization's effectiveness. Effective leaders make choices about control and influence, intentionally shaping organizational culture and fostering either subjugation or interdependence.

DIFFERENT SOURCES OF POWER AND THEIR USE

Power converts to control or influence depending on the source of power used. To recognize and use power appropriately, leaders need to understand the seven primary sources of their power.

To help illustrate and define these various power sources, I will use the example of a client named Jamie. When I worked with Jamie, she was the regional chief nursing officer (CNO) of a system that had recently bought a new hospital. Based on her earlier experience with system integrations, she was concerned about a cultural mismatch between the parent company and the newly acquired hospital. Because she wasn't assigned a formal role in the integration process, she felt powerless to stop the "train crash" she saw coming.

Positional Power

Positional power derives from a person's rank or title and is tied to the role, not the individual. Since the power source is tied to the role—not the person—positional power converts exclusively to control. When positional power is used, the locus of autonomy exists with the leader. While positional power can effectively keep order and ensure compliance, it offers virtually no influence, since influence comes from people, not roles. When a leader uses their role or position as a source of power, it always results in a loss of autonomy for the subject.

In Jamie's case, although she held a key role as regional CNO, she was not assigned a direct role in the integration effort. Because Jamie initially believed that position was her only power source, she felt powerless.

Coercive Power

Coercive power employs force or threat to get others to act. The leverage for coercive power comes from other power sources. So coercive power is always used in combination with other power sources. The degree of leverage available depends on the potency of the other sources. No matter the coupling, coercive power converts everything to control. In essence, coercion trumps whatever power source it is coupled with. The combination nullifies what the coupled source of power typically converts to. This happens because coercion forcibly shifts the subject's autonomy from interdependence toward subjugation.

In Jamie's case, she could use her position as CNO to coerce the integration leaders to change their approach, perhaps by building a coalition of like-minded nursing executives, rallying resistance. The message from her coercive coalition would be, "Change your approach, or we will make it difficult for you."

Informational Power

Informational power comes from knowing something others don't and distributing, withholding, or manipulating that information. Informational power converts to both control and influence. Withholding information—low transparency—results in moderate control by restricting or granting access to information. Conversely, sharing information—high transparency—results in moderate influence by inviting collaboration and co-creative decision-making. In other words, transparency is a "rheostat" for informational power: turn up transparency to gain influence, turn down transparency to gain control.

Because Jamie knew the nursing staff at the acquired hospital, she had information about the integration that other team members did not have. Jamie could withhold that information, allowing the integration to fail, using her power as a means of control. Or she could share the information, using it to influence others, empowering them with added information to reshape the trajectory of the integration effort.

Expert Power

Expert power originates from specialized knowledge or ability in a particular area. Expert power converts into moderate control when used to decide what is right, correct, or best. On the other hand, it converts to moderate influence when used to inform a co-creative process, formulate a hypothesis, or help search for the many possibles. Its usefulness, however, is limited and only powerful in the area of specialized knowledge the expertise represents.

Jamie had led cultural integrations before, so she was an expert in that area. Her expert power was not applicable unless she was involved in the integration effort. If she got involved, how she used her expert power would define whether it was for control or influence. If she decided on her own what the right or best way to integrate was, then told people how to do it, she would be using her expertise for control. If she offered her expertise to others collaboratively, she'd be using her expertise for influence.

Reward Power

Reward power derives from a leader's ability to grant or remove rewards. Like coercive power, reward power relies on other sources of power, which increase or decrease the potency of the reward. For example, praise from the CEO may mean more than praise from a coworker—reward coupled with positional power.

Reward power converts into moderate control when a reward is withheld or withdrawn and moderate influence when a reward is offered or provided. Its use is nuanced and multifaceted, and its effect depends on context and how it combines with other power sources.

In addition, each form of reward may or may not have meaning for the recipient. Reward power might include money, approval, recognition, or the leader's attention. For these reasons, leaders need to handle reward power carefully, paying close attention to the locus of autonomy to discern whether reward power converts to control or influence.

Charismatic Power

Charismatic power stems from shapable personal qualities, including physical appearance. It's composed of character, substance, and style, which comprise executive presence.[30] Like coercive and reward power, charismatic power combines with other sources as an amplifier. Charismatic power raises the degree of control or influence the coupled power source converts to. For example, a leader with high charismatic power using positional and coercive power exerts far greater control than a leader with low charismatic power. We see the potency of charismatic power play out negatively in tyrants and narcissists and positively in our most transformational leaders.

Jamie was a charismatic leader. If she asked to be part of the integration effort, her charisma would increase the likelihood of her involvement. It also would increase the likelihood she'd succeed.

Referent Power

Referent power comes from earning a follower's trust and devotion. Unique to this form of power is its referral—hence "referent"—from one individual to another. Referent power works exclusively through influence.

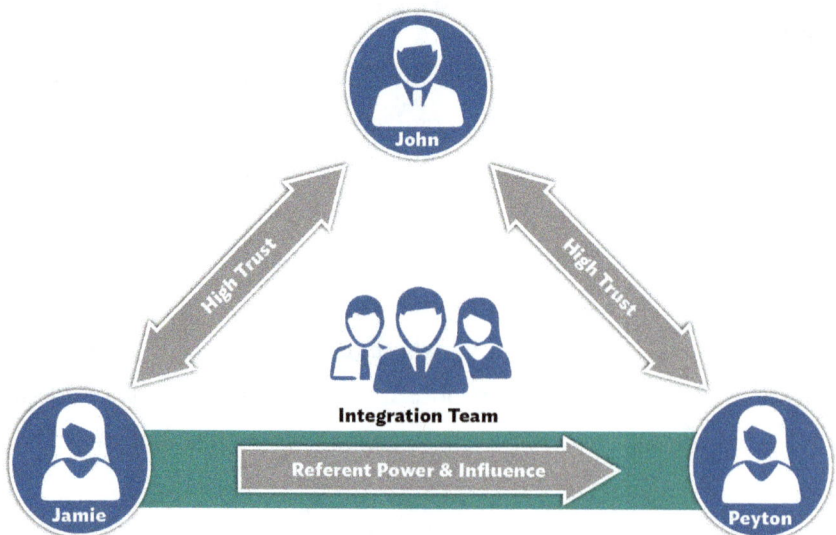

FIGURE 8. *Referent Power.* John has referent power with Peyton. Jamie's request greatly influences Peyton because of the high trust they both share with John. Peyton has high trust in Jamie because John does, even though Peyton and Jamie don't know each other. The result is that Jamie has referent power (influence) with Peyton. (Source: Michael Hein, 2025.)

Referent power turned out to be the key to Jamie's situation. Jamie reported to John in the organizational hierarchy, and she had a strong, trust-based relationship with him—John had referent power with Jamie. Peyton, the integration team leader, also had a strong, trust-based relationship with John, even though she did not report to him—John had referent power with Peyton.

If Jamie asked John for a referral to Peyton, tapping into referent power and requesting to join the integration team, Peyton would likely agree. Not because Peyton knew Jamie (she didn't) but because Peyton knew John. In this case, Jamie had power (influence) over Peyton's decisions because of John (Figure 8).

Combining Sources of Power

After reviewing her seven power sources, Jamie realized she was much more powerful than she thought. While she had minimal positional power, she could use coercion if she chose to, leveraging other power sources to force Peyton to include her. She didn't.

Jamie had access to information about the cultural clash that others did not (informational power). She had earlier experience with integrations gone wrong and knew what a failed integration might cost (expert power). She brought considerable charisma to the table (charismatic power) and, most notably, had a strong relationship with John, who was highly influential with Peyton (referent power).

After considering her options, Jamie ultimately chose to approach John. She explained her experience with integration and her concern for the organization. She asked John if she could oversee cultural integration. John passed her request to Peyton, vouching for Jamie. Peyton readily agreed to include Jamie, whose work led to what Jamie called "our most successful integration of a newly acquired hospital." Jamie found that understanding and using all her power sources was the difference between feeling powerless and being effective.

USING POWER EFFECTIVELY IN DIFFERENT KINDS OF SYSTEMS

Matching the use of power to the context is critical for leadership effectiveness. There are situations or systems where control will be more effective than influence, or vice versa. For example, the onset of a pandemic temporarily shifts a complex system into a chaotic state. When that happens, influence is not as effective as control. In other words, influence is less potent in chaotic systems than control. In fact, using power for greater control is potent in most systems. That is part of why we are so familiar with control and adept at using it. However, familiarity and potency do not mean control is always the best approach.

Effective Power Use in Simple Systems

Simple systems require control because there is a best or right way to do things. We create processes, procedures, and training programs designed to avoid deviation. Simple systems function best when people do what they are supposed to and nothing more. There's no need for autonomy—in fact, the introduction of autonomy often makes the system function poorly.

Effective Power Use in Complicated Systems

Complicated systems do well with control. They are designed to be controlled and merely tolerate influence. Control works well because these systems are the sum of several simple systems. Complicated systems function best in predictable, stable environments where standard work drives efficiency and adaptation occurs incrementally. There is little room for autonomy, because it decreases compliance, impeding system performance.

Effective Power Use in Chaotic Systems

Chaotic systems demand control. Leaders must increase order and stabilize the system quickly before it unravels. A leader may have autonomy within a chaotic system, but there is little room for the autonomy of others. Shifting an organizational culture away from control-based mechanisms, and building greater adaptability in the workforce, takes time. In chaotic situations, there's simply not enough time to do that sort of work. Leaders must act quickly, relying on power sources that result in control.

Effective Power Use in Complex Systems

Complex systems are unique. They do well with influence and are intolerant of control. They are the only systems wherein influence is more potent than control. The heartbeat of a complex system is the Adaptive Arena, and because of that, the power that garners the most adaptability is the most potent. Influence drives innovation and commitment, accelerating adaptability. Therefore, influence is more potent in complex systems than control.

Table 3 summarizes the different sources of power, whether they convert to control or influence, and their potency in different kinds of systems.

SOURCE OF POWER	DEPENDENT ON:	CONVERTS TO:	LOCUS OF AUTONOMY	RELATIONSHIP			
				Simple	Complicated	Complex	Chaotic
Position	Title or Rank	High Control	Toward Subjugation	●	●	○	●
Coercion	Other Power Sources	High Control	Toward Subjugation	●	●	○	●
Information	Transparency	Moderate Control Moderate Influence	Low Transparency: Toward Subjugation. High Transparency: Toward Interdependence	○	◐	◐	○
Expertise	Area of Expertise	Moderate Control Moderate Influence	Imposing Standards: Toward Subjugation, Otherwise Toward Interdependence	○	◐	◐	○
Reward	Other Power Sources, Given or Withdrawn	Moderate Control Moderate Influence	Withdrawal, Toward Subjugation. Promote, Toward Interdependence	○	◐	◐	○
Charisma	Other Power Sources, Personal Qualities	Depends on Other Sources	Depends on Other Sources	○	○	●	○
Referent	Relationship	High Influence	Toward Interdependence	○	○	●	○

● Highly Effective ◐ Moderately Effective ○ Ineffective

TABLE 3. *Summary of Power.* Summary table of the power sources, relevant dependencies, what they convert to, their locus of autonomy, and potency in complicated or complex systems. (Source: Michael Hein, 2025.)

THE ORTHODOX MINDSET ABOUT POWER:
Use Power to Increase Control

The orthodox mindset uses power for greater control. This mindset suits complicated systems, which by design need control. Power sources potent for control drive compliance and are the primary sources of power used in management practices. (Figure 9).

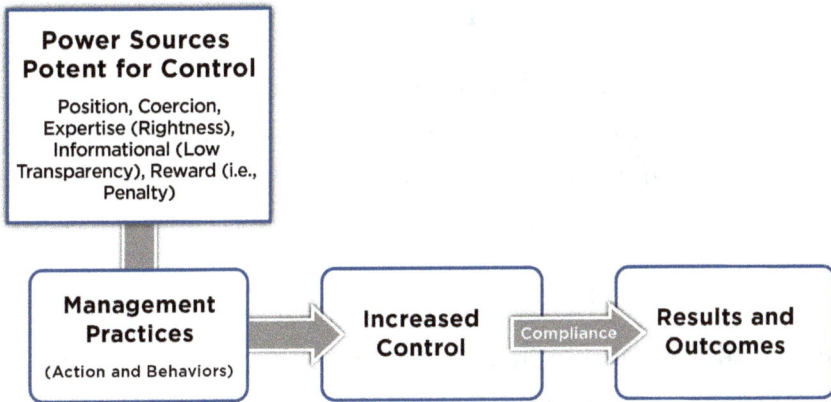

FIGURE 9. *Control Advances Management.* The orthodox mindset is expressed through management approaches, actions, and behaviors—practices—that convert power sources to increase control, deriving results and outcomes through compliance. (Source: Michael Hein, 2025.)

Management practices are essential for ensuring organizational resource use is efficient and effective and that tasks align with objectives.[31] In this sense, management derives from converting power sources to increase control, leading to compliance from others. Approaches, actions, and behaviors that convert power to control are not necessarily micromanagement or restrictive practices. They include setting up proper systems, guidelines, and performance measurements that help achieve consistency and order in operations. All those are essential capabilities of complicated systems.

Some may argue that modern management has transcended control, focusing on collaboration, empathy, and shared decision-making.

However, when leadership operates out of an orthodox mindset, even these approaches intend to compel compliance with established plans and processes; thus, control remains. That's often what's meant when leaders seek to gain "buy-in" to ideas, plans, or processes. The means of gaining buy-in may be more enlightened, but the locus of autonomy moves away from interdependence toward greater compliance.

EXPRESSIONS OF THE ORTHODOX MINDSET

The expressions of the orthodox mindset convert power sources potent for control into compliance, which are reflected in management practices: relying on positional power, using coercion for compliance, and deferring to centralized expertise.

Relying on Positional Power

Positional power derives from the division of labor from management. The definition of two distinct classes of workers—labor as opposed to management—is a foundational construct created in the Industrial Age. This concept ties power to organizational hierarchy, consolidating it at the top, usually in the hands of a CEO or president.

Positional power is the most familiar power reference for us all—so much so that many equate leadership to position. No wonder, then, that leaders with the orthodox mindset focus on positional power, often manifesting concerns about reporting structures or frustration over a lack of control. Positional power converts to control, but this control has its limits. The limits are especially relevant in today's complex organizational landscapes, where control loses potency.

Using Coercion for Compliance

Coercion is a source of power that only has potency when combined with other sources, for example, positional power. Management practices use coercive power in both subtle and obvious ways. For example, management roles come with hiring and firing responsibilities. So there's inherent coercive power with position. Anytime someone can make decisions that affect your livelihood, they wield coercive power over you. It doesn't matter if it's implicit or explicit, the message is the same: "Do your job this way, or else."

Coercive power is uniquely potent at radically shifting the locus of autonomy away from interdependence, forcing compliant behavior. It is often used for this particularly valuable quality. In that regard, it can be an amazingly effective tool for managers, especially if they have keen insights into what motivates or matters most to the subject. With that insight, managers use coercive power to put at risk what matters most to the subject in order to achieve the desired results. Effectiveness and potency are why coercive power use is so common and tempting.

Coercive power use is not always overt or malicious. Some may not consider it coercive (control) but rather persuasive (influence). Many contemporary strategies draw upon behavioral psychology attuned to human motivation and use that knowledge to influence others. But, if the leader's approaches, actions, and behaviors move the locus of autonomy of the subject away from interdependence, it is control, not influence. No matter how enlightened the strategy, subtle forms of coercive power are still a form of control.

Imagine a situation where administrative leaders craft a change in managing inpatient flow. Furthermore, imagine that implementing this change depends on changing physician behavior. Rather than "bothering" physicians early in the development process, administrative leaders wait to introduce physicians to the new approach while they begin laying the groundwork for it.

Eventually, looking for buy-in and input, the administration sets up a meeting with the physicians. The administrative representatives show that the new process will decrease length-of-stay and increase revenue.

However, this information is not persuasive to the physicians. Instead, they express frustration about being brought into the process late, with no meaningful opportunity to change the approach. The physicians thought the request for their buy-in was disingenuous. What the administration wanted was compliance, not commitment.

The intention was persuasion: the administration tried influencing the physicians by using data and examples while inviting input. However, the result was coercion because the physicians had no alternative other than compliance.

People must have autonomy to commit to and "buy-in" to something. In this example, being brought in late to the development process gave the physicians no meaningful opportunity to change the approach. They couldn't commit; they could only comply. Failure to comply would violate a standard of practice and result in corrective action, threatening their medical staff privileges and, thus, their livelihood. In other words, it was coercion.

Deferring to Centralized Expertise

The orthodox mindset defers to centralized expertise because it highly values an expert's ability to know or discern what's right, what's wrong, and what's next. This meritocracy of expertise concentrates expert power in the executive suite.

Leaders with an orthodox mindset value and hoard specialized knowledge—a significant power source—using low-transparency informational power to increase control. Experts tend to dominate discussions, confident in their experience, leading to decide-and-tell decision-making. These leaders often set narrow performance and operational boundaries, focusing on technical metrics, like financials, rather than qualitative ones, like quality or safety.

By holding specialized knowledge close and emphasizing their unique skills, they maintain dependency on their expertise, further centralizing control within the organization.

THE UNORTHODOX MINDSET ABOUT POWER:
Use Power to Increase Influence

The unorthodox mindset uses power for greater influence. Power sources potent for *influence* drive commitment and are the primary sources of power used in *leadership* practices, as opposed to the power sources potent for *control* that characterize *management* practices. (Figure 10).

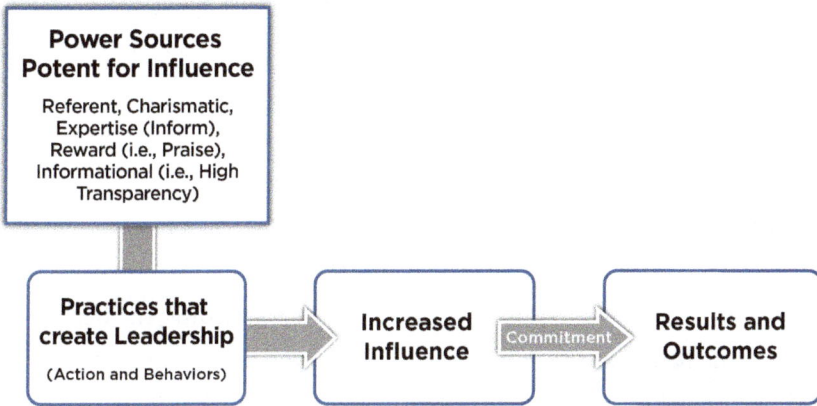

FIGURE 10. *Influence Advances Leadership.* The unorthodox mindset is expressed through approaches, actions, and behaviors—practices—that create leadership. Leadership results from power sources that increase influence, deriving results and outcomes through commitment. (Source: Michael Hein, 2025.)

Leadership practices are approaches, actions, and behaviors that generate the co-creation of coordinated movement through trust-based relationships, which is the basis of effective leadership. Unlike management, which primarily seeks stability and order through compliance, leadership practices aim to inspire commitment, challenge existing conventions, and create something new, thereby enhancing adaptability.

Power sources that convert to influence have potency in complex systems because influence drives interdependence, leading to greater adaptability. Therefore, to be effective in complex systems, leaders must lead in ways that create leadership through influence. That requires a preference for sources of power that convert to influence, relaxing the use of sources that convert to control.

EXPRESSIONS OF THE UNORTHODOX MINDSET

Expressions of the unorthodox mindset convert power sources potent for influence into commitment by leadership practices. You can identify the unorthodox mindset in yourself or others by noticing the common expressions of this mindset: relying on referent power, using reward for greater commitment, and deferring to distributed intelligence.

Relying on Referent Power

Leaders who master growing and using referent power are the most effective in complex healthcare organizations.

Referent power is fundamentally relational. Forming the deep trust attendant to these crucial relationships takes persistent, intentional effort, focusing on what fosters or deteriorates one's trustworthiness. Developing and demonstrating trustworthiness is essential for building and using referent power.

In complex environments, people and teams change quickly. We often don't have much time to forge trusting relationships, even though they are crucial for success. So leaders must excel at quickly building trust with and among others.

The critical ingredient to rapidly building trust is a willingness to be vulnerable, which helps people find a connection with each other. Often, that means sharing parts of ourselves that allow others to experience us as human beings. With our clients at MEDI Leadership, we often swap stories about our upbringings, highlighting everyone's resilience and resourcefulness. That exercise helps us see each other as real people, quickly building trust.

Referent power compounds. The more interconnected trust-based relationships we have, the more referent power increases. It increases exponentially. For example, imagine you have three referent relationships, as do I. When we forge a referent relationship, your referent power source is multiplied by three, as is mine. One connection between us results in three times as much referent power. That's one of the reasons why referent power is so potent and why it matters so much.

Referent power is not networking. Networking is building transactional relationships necessary for bridging across social networks. Those relationships are less robust than referent relationships, which must be deeply trusting and transformational.

The influence generated through referent power flows across an interconnected network of trust-based relationships. That flow is vital because it's how referent power influences others far removed from the source (Figure 8). Suppose we both have a friend and colleague named Taylor. She has referent power and uses it. She always seems to know someone you or I should meet. When we connect with the people Taylor refers us to, an immediate bond frequently develops. Taylor seems to know which connections will matter. As a result, Taylor's network of trust-based relationships and her influence grow. Referential connections bear influential fruit over time, as ideas, opportunities, and other relationships flourish through the expanding network.

Referent power is not the "good old boy network." Those networks typically include carefully controlled connections with low diversity. Unlike referent power, good old boy networks constrain flow, decreasing influence while increasing control. They rely heavily on positional power and secrecy (low-transparency informational power), using coercion to keep members "in" or "out." Good old boy networks are the opposite of referent power.

Using Reward for Commitment

Reward powerfully influences people if it acknowledges desirable behaviors and actions. It converts to influence through affirmation and recognition, catalyzing increased commitment, engagement, and innovation. Leaders who use reward power to influence are inclined to celebrate success. They routinely highlight positive outcomes, whether those outcomes reflect incremental progress or significant milestones. The use of reward power is a principal means of nudging complex systems.

Reward power can be converted to influence by offering attention and acknowledgment, such as promotions or pay increases. However, depending on the recipient, both informal and formal praise—whether public or private—along with appreciation and recognition, often supersede the influence of financial rewards.

Reward power extends beyond accolades. Constructive feedback, paired with validation, is powerfully influential if it's devoid of coercive power. Challenges met head-on with support and encouragement deepen trust, thereby building influence. It is an act of kindness to provide prompt, helpful feedback, clarifying expectations and performance gaps when they occur. Acts of kindness are potent extensions of reward power. Most adults are hungry for reward and feedback. If feedback is done well, reward power is converted to influence, moving organizations forward.

Leaders who master the art of reward power do not merely manage their teams; they inspire, motivate, and guide them toward a commitment to excellence, enhancing adaptability in complexity.

Deferring to Distributed Intelligence

The unorthodox mindset holds that everyone in a complex system is an expert at something; this is a form of distributed intelligence. Leaders with this mindset have an almost compulsive need to tap into distributed intelligence, seeking multiple perspectives. They know their understanding of the system is and will always be incomplete, partly because it's changing so quickly and unpredictably.

In their efforts to make good sense of the system, these leaders cast a wide net. They ask for many stakeholder perspectives. They work diligently to connect and be connected. They tend to include too many perspectives, not too few, continually expanding the borders of inclusion. While this may risk cumbersome decision-making, these leaders often mitigate those risks by deploying strategies, such as Agile, that take advantage of many voices while facilitating speedy decisions.[32]

Deference to distributed intelligence leads to structural and technological capabilities that ease the rapid distribution of information flowing across many connections. Leaders tap into these sources to better sense system inclinations by listening to learn from others how they are making sense of what's happening. They don't rely upon data reports alone. Feedback is rampant, open, authentic, quick, abundant, facilitated, and solicited. Transparency is high. For some, the requisite degree of information flow and openness feels "dangerous." If you're getting to that point, you know you're getting close to distributed intelligence.

MAKING THE SHIFT
Before the Shift

Be Clear About the Difference Between Management and Leadership

I encourage you to be clear in your mind about what management and leadership are.[33] They are not synonymous. Separating both from a position, title, or role is critical. Think of it this way: management and leadership are characteristics of the relationships that emerge between people as a result of their interactions.

Whether management or leadership emerges depends on the chosen approaches, actions, and behaviors of the people involved in the relationship. You are not a leader or a manager simply because you have a leadership or management role in the organization. You are a leader or manager because you use approaches, actions, and behaviors in ways that create relationships characterized by leadership or management.

Therefore, leadership and management depend on practices that convert various power sources to influence (leadership) or control (management). This is an essential and critical concept to remember as you use power, especially in predominantly complex organizations.

Be Clear About Your System and What Power to Use

The system or situation you are in determines the power sources to use. Complex systems thrive when influenced and come unwound with control. Complicated systems need control and merely tolerate influence. It can be tempting to rely on your favorite sources of power, those with which you are most familiar or comfortable, but that is not an effective way to lead.

You must be clear about what is needed most—control or influence—in each situation, because control and influence have consequences. A compliant workforce gets things done steadily, efficiently, and predictably but is not creatively innovative or speedy. A committed workforce gets things done with enthusiasm, albeit often unpredictably, offering quick radical transformations and a degree of unsettling messiness. Ideally, you strive for a harmony between compliance and commitment that matches your context. Remember that you're best served in complex situations by leaning toward influence and commitment and away from control and compliance.

Mind the mismatches. When leaders use power for control in systems that demand influence, or influence in systems that demand control, system performance deteriorates. Deteriorated performance manifests itself in many ways: one of those ways is by decreasing the ability of the organization to adapt. The consequences of power mismatches can take years to resolve, placing the organization in a prolonged maladaptive state.

In today's fast-paced, high-pressure environments, systems tolerate power mismatches far less than they used to. There's less time for the system to recover from our errors in judgment. We can't afford the years it takes to redevelop organizational adaptability, and competitors will quickly take advantage of our missteps. So matching your power sources to your context is critical.

WHY SHIFT

Because You Can't Control Complex Systems

The straightforward reason for making a shift is that you can't control complex systems. If you try, it impairs the system's ability to function. Control damages the Adaptive Arena because it fosters compliance, impairing a complex system's ability to rapidly adapt, perform, and thrive.

While complex systems are intolerant of control, they respond to influence. Most notably, influence facilitates distributed leadership, an essential precondition for the Adaptive Arena. In short, distributed leadership is necessary for complex systems to thrive. Distributed leadership happens as more people commit to the organizational mission, purpose, and direction. At the same time, those individuals gain interdependence, working together to nudge the system's inclinations in ways that directionally align.

To build and sustain an adaptive, thriving healthcare organization suitable for the challenges of the twenty-first century, leaders must shift their mindsets about power away from the orthodox preference for greater control toward the unorthodox preference for greater influence.

Because You Are More Powerful Than You Think

Unless you fully appreciate all the sources of power at your disposal, you will feel powerless. There's nothing wrong (or right) about power. It's a neutral source of potential "energy" that only matters if you use it. You cannot do anything as a leader unless you have and use power.

If you don't make a shift, you will rely on sources of power that convert to control. We've covered why that's a problematic choice. It's also an approach that unnecessarily diminishes your full potential.

To be your most successful self, you must use power. If you shift, you are more likely to access all the available power sources. And you are more likely to use power in the contexts where it will be the most potent.

HOW TO SHIFT

Redefine Your Relationship with Control

Because the world and our organizations are increasingly complex, the age of leading by preferentially using power sources that convert to control has ended. Now, the challenge for many is relaxing and redefining their relationship with control and how they make sense of its place in effective leadership. Since effectiveness connects with our livelihoods and professional and personal identities, redefining our relationship with control is often unsettling. That discomfort must not deter us. Shifting is necessary to be an effective healthcare leader.

To shift, a leader must notice their relationship with power and control while being curious about why shifting toward influence seems risky. With that clarity, leaders are better positioned to use control only when necessary, preferring to use power for influence.

Remember, shifting is not about swapping out the orthodox mindset for the unorthodox. It is about adding the unorthodox to the orthodox. That means control still has a place, even with an unorthodox mindset. Your work is to relax your propensity to use power for control while at the same time growing all your sources of power, favoring those that convert to influence.

Lastly, to genuinely shift, one must be clear about control and influence. Much of what we call influence today is still control. The key is paying close attention to what happens with the locus of autonomy. Influence shifts toward interdependence, and control does not.

Notice Power Sources That Cause Discomfort

Be curious about your relationships with each power source. There will be some that stir emotions and memories. Notice what those power sources are drawing out in you that is uncomfortable. Your self-awareness, mindset, and relationship with power will become clearer as you reflect on what you notice. Being mindful and curious about your relationship with the different sources of power is a valuable exercise because, otherwise, it's unlikely you'll tap into sources of power that cause you discomfort. That's a potential problem because leaders need access to all seven power sources to be their most effective selves. Don't render yourself powerless because you avoid unfamiliar or uncomfortable sources of power.

Identify Which Sources You Need to Grow and Use

You shift by growing all your power sources and using them judiciously where they are most potent.

▸ Positional power increases as you take on new roles with greater responsibilities and decreases when you move away from those positions. To grow it, take on new roles with greater positional power.

▸ Coercive power grows as you gain strength in the other six sources of power, providing more leverage should you tap into this power source. It decreases as your other power sources decrease.

▸ Information power grows with greater connection, as information flows across and through your social and organizational network. Boost informational power for greater influence by increasing transparency. Grow your informational power sources by connecting and being connected.

▸ Expert power grows as you become more adept at what you do and gain added experience. Expertise is primarily an issue of depth, not breadth, so qualities like perseverance, loyalty, and duty matter. Your expert power grows with experience and education, but can decrease if you move too quickly, switch industries, quit, or retire.

▸ Reward power grows as you gain more strength in the other six sources of power, providing you with greater rewards to offer or withdraw. Boost reward power for greater influence by generously extending and giving rewards. Boost reward power for greater control by being less generous. Reward power diminishes as your other power sources diminish.

▸ Charismatic power grows by intentionally building your executive presence, including your character, substance, and style. Charismatic power amplifies the potency of other power sources. Inattention or neglect of executive presence decreases charismatic power, undermining the potency of all power sources.

▸ Referent power grows by connecting and being connected in trust-based relationships. It diminishes if those relationships are neglected or harmed. It can become less accessible as systems grow and spread across different geographic regions, making meaningful connections more difficult. Intentionality overcomes that challenge.

Focus on Relationship

Ultimately, power is a relationship. The most influential leaders connect and are connected, intentionally growing the number and quality of their relationships by paying close attention to how they are with others. Powerful leaders are rarely careless in this arena, carefully and authentically shaping perceptions and reality about themselves. They understand that influence is preferred and potent for the systems we lead. They intentionally do what they can to grow all their power sources and preferentially actuate those that convert to influence, which are inevitably relational. Shifting toward the unorthodox embraces this reality.

MINDSET FIVE—UNCERTAINTY

AN UNORTHODOX MINDSET ABOUT
HANDLING THE UNKNOWABLE

Uncertainty Can Be Absorbed, Not Just Reduced

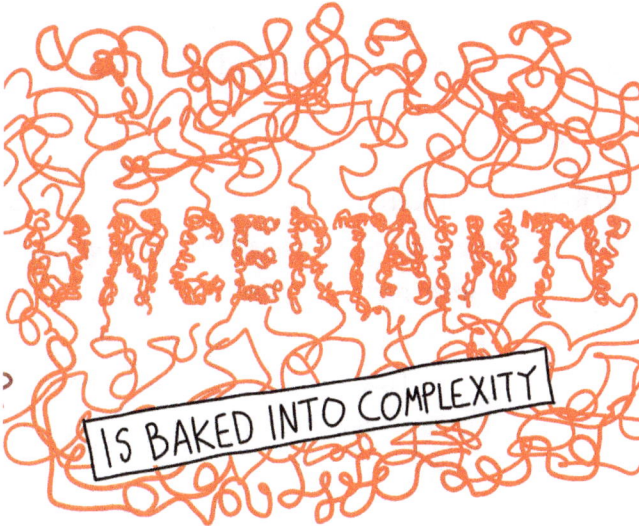

ILLUSTRATION 5. *Uncertainty Is Baked into Complexity.*

UNDERSTANDING UNCERTAINTY

Uncertainty is part of the human condition, which means we relate to it daily. Uncertainty is the condition of being unsure—having doubts or lacking confidence—about something. It's not having enough information to make a clear, definite decision or prediction. It's like when you're trying to guess the outcome of a coin toss—you know it will be either heads or tails, but you can't be sure which one it will be until it happens.

In life and leadership, uncertainty can apply to many things, from small daily choices to major life decisions. It reflects our limited knowledge and the unpredictable nature of the world. In other words, uncertainty is a natural part of life and leadership, because we can't know everything about the future or even the present.

Complex organizations add to the degree of uncertainty we encounter. The inherent polarity, the imperative for adaptability, and the tension between control and influence that characterize complex systems all tend to magnify uncertainty.

We tend to think of uncertainty as all or nothing; we are uncertain, or we are not. But there is more than one kind of uncertainty, and the degree of uncertainty we experience varies in intensity. Understanding the various kinds of uncertainty helps leaders know how to best relate to each kind. Conversely, a lack of understanding of the various kinds of uncertainty creates leadership and organizational difficulties.

FOUR KINDS OF UNCERTAINTY

While scientists who study uncertainty characterize it in many ways, I've chosen to address four specific kinds of uncertainty that healthcare leaders are likely to encounter.

Uncertainty Related to Possible Future Events

Uncertainty arising from potential future events is called *stochastic uncertainty*. Stochastic uncertainty refers to processes or situations that involve random events that impact future results. Take, for example, Emergency Department (ED) staffing decisions. We can't precisely predict how many people will need emergency care tonight. However, we can make an educated estimate based on historical data and other factors like community events or weather conditions. Estimating like this is an informal way of relating to stochastic uncertainty.

Scientists rigorously model stochastic uncertainty through probability distributions, quantifying the range and likelihood of possible outcomes. For example, several groups modeled the anticipated mortality rate of the COVID-19 pandemic. Such models are formalizations of the intuitive calculations we all make. Stochastic uncertainty arises when leaders try to anticipate unpredictable-but-important events that directly impact immediate decision-making.

Uncertainty Related to a Lack of Knowledge

Uncertainty arising from knowable but unknown information is called *epistemic uncertainty*. Epistemic uncertainty pertains to the gaps in our knowledge or understanding that create uncertainty when one could, in theory, fill those gaps. This form of uncertainty can arise from "known unknowns." The known unknowns are situations where one decides to act despite known gaps in essential information. Epistemic uncertainty can also arise from the "unknown unknowns." Unknown unknowns are those instances where one believes they have all the necessary information only to discover later that they didn't.

Consider Catherine, a healthcare CEO who spearheaded the acquisition of an ambulatory surgery center. Drawn by the promise of a favorable profit-sharing arrangement and the need to move quickly, she based her decision on the available financial statements. After the acquisition, a deeper audit revealed a significant miscalculation in the center's operating margin. Had the organization conducted more thorough due diligence, they would have uncovered this error and potentially renegotiated the deal or avoided the acquisition altogether—an unknown unknown.

This was a case of epistemic uncertainty: Catherine based her decision on incomplete but obtainable information. Healthcare leaders routinely navigate epistemic uncertainty—including both known unknowns and unknown unknowns. Decisions affected by epistemic uncertainty often have financial, operational, and clinical ramifications.

Uncertainty Related to Inherent Variability

Uncertainty arising from inherent system variability is called *aleatoric uncertainty*. Aleatoric uncertainty refers to the unpredictable variations that are a natural part of all systems.

Consider the classic example of a dice roll. Each face of a six-sided die represents a probable outcome, much like each patient in a healthcare organization embodies a range of possible responses to treatment. In the same way that six-sided dice exhibit a predictable range of uncertain outcomes, human beings exhibit a wide range of individualized unpredictability—even when undergoing the same treatment. In other words, people are like many-sided dice.

When we roll a die, its faces—or sides—are the visible markers of its inherent variability. The rolling action activates these potential outcomes, creating a spectrum of uncertainty. Similarly, in healthcare, each patient embodies a multitude of variables—genetics, lifestyle, preexisting conditions—that activate differently in response to a treatment, even if that treatment is the same. The action of treatment activates the many potential outcomes, creating a spectrum of uncertainty about how the patient will respond. The uncertainty of patient treatment is generated because every kind of system has inherent variability, just like the dice.

The term *breaking the system* applies when there is an attempt to eliminate this natural and inescapable variability. A loaded die creates a broken system, because someone has removed the inherent variability. The expected degree of unpredictability no longer exists. We call that cheating.

Rigorously standardizing treatment to ensure predictable outcomes, disregarding patient uniqueness, or enforcing one-size-fits-all solutions is like loading the dice. Overly ambitious standardization compromises the system's integrity, ignoring its inherent variability. The consequent increase in predictability reflects suboptimal performance, not improved performance. That seems counterintuitive and contrary to the prevailing view of the healthcare industry. The key point is that reducing the uncertainty caused by the inherent variability of a system does not improve the system; it breaks the system.

Healthcare organizations have a form of "sidedness," because they are systems with inherent variability. Leadership decisions activate this variability, much like the roll of a die. Whether it is a strategic shift, an acquisition, or a change in workflow, the system's unpredictability responds in kind. An attempt by leaders to tightly control every aspect of an organization's operations—akin to loading the dice—risks stifling innovation, lowering morale, and ultimately breaking the system.

Just as we cannot alter the intrinsic uncertainty of a die roll without manipulating the essence of the game, we cannot escape the aleatoric uncertainty inherent in treating a diverse patient population or leading a complex healthcare organization. Attempts to do so would be futile and erode the quality and effectiveness of care and the integrity and adaptability of the organization.

Uncertainty Related to Worldviews

Uncertainty arising from the limitations of our conceptual frameworks or worldviews is called *ontological uncertainty*. These frameworks shape how we understand the nature of existence, reality, or "what there is."

This kind of uncertainty emerges when different people or disciplines have varying interpretations of what is "real" or essential in each situation, often leading to divergent decisions or judgments. In essence, ontological uncertainty pertains to the constraints or limitations inherent in our understanding of reality.

For example, the attending physician's clinical intuition and experience with hundreds of other patients leads her to keep a patient over the weekend. The case manager, a nurse who monitors patient stay suitability, looks at the labs and consultant's notes. In the case manager's mind, the patient should be discharged. The physician has a different conceptual framework for patient care than the case manager, arising from past experiences, insights, and responsibilities. Drawing from their conceptual frameworks, the attending physician and the case manager encountered ontological uncertainty: should the patient be discharged?

The diverse perspectives arising from ontological uncertainty are invaluable for leaders and their organizations, especially when leveraged effectively. The presence of ontological uncertainty grows exponentially with a system's complexity, an inherent byproduct of the system. When a leader ignores or attempts to suppress or eliminate this diversity— whether in thought, experience, or interpretative framework—they risk undermining the system itself. Effective leadership requires the ability to engage with and navigate the inevitable uncertainty that springs from a multitude of conceptual frameworks and worldviews.

REDUCIBLE AND IRREDUCIBLE UNCERTAINTY

Defining What's Reducible or Not

Being uncertain makes us uncomfortable. Most of us will try to do something with that discomfort, such as reducing our uncertainty or eliminating it if we can. The urge to do something about uncertainty is strong. That urgency impacts how leaders show up.

Knowing there are four distinct kinds of uncertainty helps, but leaders are even better off if they know how to work with each kind of uncertainty. To begin, it is important to understand that some kinds of uncertainty are reducible, and some are not. If we can eliminate uncertainty, it is reducible. If we can't, it is irreducible.

Stochastic and epistemic uncertainty are reducible. If we can predict better (stochastic) or know more (epistemic), uncertainty is reduced. Aleatoric and ontological uncertainty are not reducible because to do so would require breaking the system. If variation was eliminated (aleatoric) or diversity suppressed (ontological), the system would cease to function properly.

Reducibility Depends on the Kind of System

The degree of reducible or irreducible uncertainty varies depending on the kind of situation or system you are dealing with. For example, reducible forms of uncertainty are most prevalent in the predictable world of complicated systems, and irreducible forms predominate in the unpredictable world of complex systems. (Figure 11).

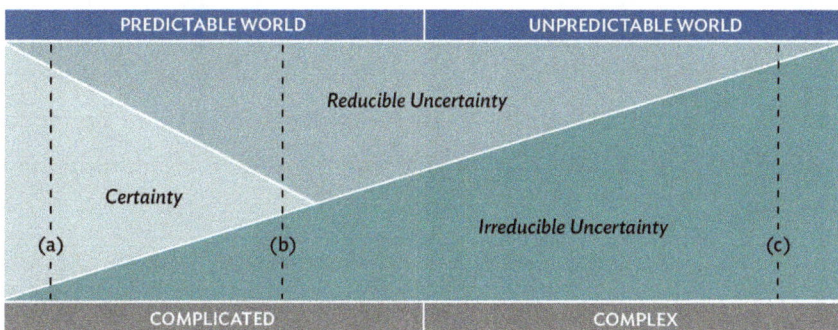

FIGURE 11. *Relative Uncertainty in Complicated and Complex Systems.* System (a): high certainty, low reducible and irreducible uncertainty. System (b): low certainty, high overall uncertainty, some reducible. System (c): high uncertainty, most irreducible. (Source: Michael Hein, 2025.)

Complicated systems are predictable, containing a large degree of certainty and relatively low levels of reducible and irreducible uncertainty. But as complicated systems approach complexity, the degree of certainty decreases, eventually disappearing, while reducible and irreducible uncertainty increase.

Complex systems are unpredictable, with increasing levels of irreducible uncertainty. As irreducible uncertainty increases in complex systems, the degree of reducible uncertainty decreases. In complex systems, total uncertainty—reducible and irreducible—is extremely high. There's virtually no certainty remaining. The high degree of uncertainty, most of which is irreducible, is a significant contributor to the difficulty leaders experience working in complex systems.

Uncertainty Makes Us Uncomfortable

We are uncomfortable with uncertainty because our brains build forecasts of the future, (i.e., they act as prediction machines).[34] Our brains constantly make educated guesses based on what we know, akin to a weather forecaster predicting tomorrow's weather.

Our internal alarm system sounds when something unexpected happens, demanding our attention. This alarm isn't merely cognitive; we experience it emotionally, often as discomfort or unease. This warning system serves us well by heightening our awareness of potential risks, but it takes a toll when we face situations too uncertain for easy prediction.

Imagine living with a perpetually uncertain severe weather forecast, compelling you to continuously consider what's necessary to keep yourself and your family safe, no matter when the severe weather strikes. Over time, the sustained uncertainty would wear us down, perhaps leading to mental illness.[35] Because uncertainty is so troubling, we tend to take actions to try to relieve the discomfort it causes.

RELATING TO UNCERTAINTY

Relating to Reducible Uncertainty

We usually deal with uncertainty by trying to reduce how uncertain we feel, hoping to decrease the associated discomfort. Here are some common ways we do that:

Improving prediction capability. More data or information helps us better understand the past and anticipate the future. Better analytical and forecasting capabilities help us understand and predict. Improved prediction reduces uncertainty.

Relying on experts. We rely upon and trust in our expertise and experience or that of others. That reduces our uncertainty because we trust experts to teach us or show us what will happen.

Gathering with like-minded people. There's a tendency to be drawn to or draw others to us who are like-minded. Seeking social support and reassurance decreases uncertainty about our ideas, thoughts, or convictions.

Relying on management practices. We reduce uncertainty by budgeting, strategic planning, and education. Increased management makes things more predictable, and formal risk assessment helps mitigate what feels risky to us.

Relating to Irreducible Uncertainty

These familiar strategies don't work in the face of irreducible uncertainty—in fact, they can make things worse. Leaders need a different approach, one that adapts to and accommodates uncertainty that is irreducible. This adaptive accommodation is what I call "absorbing" uncertainty.

You likely have already experienced absorption, although you may not have thought about it in those terms. Think of something wholly unexpected and unpleasant that happened to you. Life conspired with the universe. You got caught up in a mess, and multiple forms of uncertainty appeared simultaneously on your doorstep.

Initially, you were likely at a loss for what to do but felt compelled to do something. Your past experiences, however, weren't helpful, because you'd never encountered this kind of situation before. I've heard many seasoned healthcare executives use those exact words—"We've never encountered this before"—to describe what it was like for them to lead their organizations beyond the COVID-19 pandemic.

In your situation, other people—experts—weren't helpful either. Every example they offered didn't quite fit the circumstances you were facing, though you were able to extract some valuable insights from them. Maybe you had to make quick critical decisions, but there were so many pieces in play that you couldn't sort it all out. There was no way of knowing what the right thing to do was.

Eventually, you made sense of that challenging time in an unfamiliar way. You decided to act, because it was better than doing nothing. You stopped seeking advice, because it mostly wasn't helpful. You gave up on getting it "right," because what did that mean? And you made decisions without knowing what would happen, but you watched to see what followed and adjusted.

The moment you recognized that you could never know what was next and acted was absorption. You recognized that some of your uncertainty was reducible, but most of it was not. You ended up "surfing" the moments as they occurred, riding the wave of what was happening, sensing things shift under your feet, adjusting your stance to adapt. You took an adaptive approach, and that approach was absorption.

Clinicians who work with critically ill patients can easily recognize themselves in the surfing metaphor. They interact with patients who respond to interventions in unpredictable ways. They often must make decisions with incomplete information, such as trying this medication, that therapy, or both. Afterward, they carefully watch to see if they nudged the "system" toward a healthier state. Some call being with uncertainty in this way "the art of medicine." A critical care clinician's actions, informed by science and deployed into a sea of uncertainty, beautifully express the absorption of irreducible uncertainty.

Healthcare leaders are more likely to demonstrate absorption during a crisis. A prime example comes from the early days of the COVID-19 pandemic, when there wasn't much information. Few knew what to expect. Leaders stood up incident command centers and quickly made decisions; later retracting many of those decisions, because they didn't work or something changed. They watched and responded to whatever emerged, and as new things happened, leaders tried other things. Like clinicians with critically ill patients, they surfed the sea of irreducible uncertainty, absorbing by accepting what was irreducibly uncertain.

How a leader approaches uncertainty, whether reducible or irreducible, is dependent upon the mindset they have about it. The orthodox mindset approaches uncertainty to reduce it, the unorthodox mindset approaches uncertainty to absorb it. To be clear, absorption is not a reduction strategy. Absorption is a familiarly uncomfortable relationship with the kinds of uncertainty that are irreducible.

THE ORTHODOX MINDSET ABOUT UNCERTAINTY:
All Uncertainty Can Be Reduced

The orthodox mindset about uncertainty does not acknowledge distinct kinds of uncertainty and sees all uncertainty as reducible. Leaders with this mindset believe that uncertainty represents a deficiency. There is no reason to be uncertain if we are smart enough, have enough resources, or know enough people.

The most powerful affirmation of this mindset is that it has worked. Humans have accomplished remarkable things by employing it. As a result, it dominates the business world. Our successes at being right have led to the belief that there is only one kind of uncertainty and that it can, will, and should always be reduced.

EXPRESSIONS OF THE ORTHODOX MINDSET

The expressions of this mindset are approaches, actions, and behaviors intended to reduce uncertainty: having certainty about being right, reaching for greater control, and trusting in simple stories.

Having Certainty about Being Right

We can be right when direct, cause-and-effect relationships exist. We can know the results with enough knowledge about each variable and suitable prediction methods. In essence, all uncertainty is either stochastic or epistemic.

The correct answers are more available to experts, because they have the experience and smarts we don't. So we value experts over nonexperts. When we take steps to increase our knowledge or improve our ability to predict, we are expressing this mindset.

Appealing to experience demonstrates our trust that history—ours, others', and the organization's—informs the present and future. Something like, "I've seen this before. All we need to do is *A*, and *B* will follow."

We admire leaders who consistently demonstrate rightness. We gain comfort from their correctness and often translate that comfort into greater trust and admiration. We may even try to emulate them. Leaders can attain celebrity-like status when they display exceptional talent in decreasing uncertainty by being right.

Examples include Jeff Bezos (revolutionizing retail through the internet), Sheryl Sandberg (shaping the future of technology and social media), and Warren Buffett (mastering the stock market and business performance). If these examples don't resonate, consider your personal favorites and observe the qualities you admire in them. Undoubtedly, their ability to be right will be among the traits you admire the most.

On the other hand, leaders who express uncertainty are considered less effective. This puts leaders in the position of never being able to admit they don't know or that they may have been wrong. In extreme cases, a leader's reluctance to admit to uncertainty can become engrained in the organizational culture. A culture of leadership that never admits uncertainty or mistakes can lead to the downfall of an entire organization.

Being right, growing in knowledge, or anticipating the future (informed by the past) are orthodox ways we relate to uncertainty. The orthodox mindset reduces uncertainty by having certitude about rightness.

Reaching for Greater Control

Yet again, our propensity to reach for a greater sense of control expresses this orthodox mindset about handling the unknowable. In this instance, some leaders shift toward directives and some toward micromanagement. They take this approach because it provides a sense of increased predictive ability. If I tell people what to do precisely and monitor things closely, I'll gain greater certainty about the outcome.

Doing the work themselves, which is time-consuming and exhausting, is another path some leaders move toward. Or leaders may become more driven and determined, pressing too hard on people and the organization to gain movement. Others become more careful, impeding their organization's ability to adapt quickly enough. When uncertainty is high, these are just some ways a leader attempts to gain greater control—working to increase predictability, thereby reducing uncertainty's discomfort.

Organizationally, if leaders decide the system is unwieldy (uncertain), they often seek to gain control by increasing management. One leader shared with me that, after merging two sizeable regional hospital systems, their system felt unmanageable to the leadership team. In response, they created twelve layers of management to deal with the uncertainty they felt. Instead of helping, they found that the new layers of management only slowed down decision-making. They were in the process of unwinding those layers the last time I talked to them.

The initial response to their unwieldy system underscores how management is fundamentally about greater control. Those leaders reached for more management to increase the predictability of achieving the desired outcome.

There are many other ways we reach for control, and we've noticed those with some of the previous mindsets. Some means are apparent, others less so. No matter the means, reaching for greater control expresses an orthodox mindset about uncertainty.

Trusting in Simple Stories

We also express the orthodox mindset about uncertainty by creating simple stories. If a cause-and-effect relationship isn't readily available to us, we make one up (our brains being prediction machines). I join others in calling these "simple stories."[36] What makes them simple is that they have a clear, direct, cause-and-effect relationship, a hero (often us), a villain (often them), a beginning, an end, and they help us anticipate the future.

Simple stories are convenient because they make us right. We create them quickly and are geniuses at it. We do this because our brains need cause-and-effect, and our simple stories meet that need nicely. Whether our stories are true is not what matters. We believe them to be true, making it easier for us to reduce uncertainty. We can readily see this propensity for simple stories in the conspiracy theories that routinely swirl around social media. Conspiracy theories are, by and large, simple stories created to reduce uncertainty.

Simple stories touch upon a few related-but-maladaptive strategies: delusion, deception, and denial. To varying degrees, anyone can hold a false belief about reality despite evidence to the contrary. That's a delusion. We can deceive ourselves into believing something that isn't so. That's a deception. People can also deny what is in front of them. Denial is a well-known strategy for dealing with uncertainty, as in response to hearing your cancer diagnosis or the unexpected death of a loved one. The point is that many of us use these maladaptive strategies to reduce uncertainty.

THE UNORTHODOX MINDSET ABOUT UNCERTAINTY:
Some Uncertainty Must Be Absorbed

The unorthodox mindset toward uncertainty distinguishes between distinct kinds of uncertainty. Leaders expressing this mindset aim to reduce the uncertainty that is reducible and absorb the uncertainty that is irreducible.

EXPRESSIONS OF THE UNORTHODOX MINDSET

You can identify the unorthodox mindset in yourself or others by noticing the common expressions of this mindset: accepting ambiguity, reaching for humility, and trusting in experimentation.

Accepting Ambiguity

A leader with an unorthodox mindset toward irreducible uncertainty accepts that rightness is absent and unattainable. He or she understands that ambiguity—the presence of multiple, unclear, or conflicting interpretations or outcomes—is inherent in irreducible uncertainty. Accepting inherent ambiguity is the beginning of absorption.

Having experience with ambiguity makes it easier to accept. Familiarity allows us to welcome the ambiguity of irreducible uncertainty as an unexpected guest, staying curious about what it may bring.

For example, a senior nursing executive's organization recently announced the dissolution of a long-standing joint venture and the acquisition of a new set of hospitals in another region. Before this, the organization had undergone rounds of restructuring. Her role had changed several times. I noticed her holding uncertainty with levity. Curious, I asked how she was able to sit with uncertainty in this way. She shrugged and chuckled. "There's nothing I can do about it. And it has been this way since I came here. Things have worked out." Familiarity with ambiguity helped her absorb what was irreducible uncertainty.

Therefore, a practical strategy for increasing our ability to welcome ambiguity is putting ourselves in situations where ambiguity and the attendant irreducible uncertainty is high. When doing that, it's important to have good support to help you navigate the challenges that will come. Learning to be successful in those ambiguous, irreducibly uncertain environments grows familiarity and helps us out in the future. We can follow the same strategy to develop other leaders.

Faith is another way I see leaders absorb irreducible uncertainty. What I mean by *faith* is the confidence that things will turn out the way we hope or the conviction that something we can't see yet will come to pass. It's faith in people, purpose, and process working together, resulting in a way forward. This faith helps leaders relax their hold on orthodoxy, resisting the pressure to reach for control, rightness, and simple stories. It helps them accept the ambiguity of irreducible uncertainty, convinced that things will work out in the end, even when things are brutal, and they can't yet see a path forward.

Whether we tap into faith or take advantage of familiarity, the beginning expression of absorption is recognizing and accepting ambiguity.

Reaching for Humility

Humility absorbs irreducible uncertainty.[37] In action, the humble leader recognizes the insufficiency of knowledge and prediction in complexity. So humble leaders relax their hold on expertise and expand their curiosity about what is possible. Humility positions the leader to need more perspectives from more people. These leaders know that their perspective is an insufficient resource. It's not because these leaders think others are necessarily better at knowing, though they may be. These leaders understand that others are different, and difference adds to what is possible.

Humble leaders cultivate environments where many possibilities emerge from many voices and subsequent experiments abound. In complexity, you never know what may work or not. The organization is in trouble if solutions are derived from experts (leaders), because they can't know enough in complex environments to find the most valuable answers. When looking for the "many possibles," leaders with an unorthodox mindset about uncertainty cast a vast net, dramatically increasing the number of people working to move things forward. That approach places trust in distributed leadership, the conviction that solutions will emerge from a plurality of voices.[38]

Trusting in Experimentation

Irreducible uncertainty is absorbed by experimenting. Rather than wait while hunting for the right answers, leaders act. They form quick hypotheses, identify several reasonable solutions (experiments), and place their bets, simultaneously putting all or most of their experiments in play. Afterward, they watch for what happens, adjusting based on the results. Some bets will pay off, and others will not. Unorthodox leaders take this approach, because many possibly valuable ideas and solutions exist in complexity. We don't know what they are until we try them out. The intention is to nudge the system's inclinations closer to its purpose, mission, or goals.

Interestingly, some bets may seem small but have an enormous impact. Some will have favorable outcomes, and some will not. Leaders must observe the system as their experiments unfold because we cannot anticipate how things will work out in complex environments until they do. If something works well, leaders amplify it, encouraging its spread. If it doesn't, the leader ends the experiment decisively.

Experimentation is the adaptive, absorptive response to irreducible uncertainty. It is how leaders avoid being paralyzed by complexity, waiting for the right solution. Experimentation is the action arm of absorption and how organizations find adaptability in the face of irreducible uncertainty.

MAKING THE SHIFT
Before the Shift

Be Prepared for "Triggered" Responses

Before you can make a shift, you must avoid being triggered by uncertainty. Our brains don't like uncertainty, because the brain's primary function is to predict. If the brain can't predict, it perceives uncertainty as a threat, compelling us to adopt protective actions and behaviors.

When a threat happens—being "triggered"—our limbic system shuts down access to our creativity, curiosity, and ability to see future possibilities. This is not helpful when things are uncertain. Triggering moves us to take flight or fight, drawing upon self-protection strategies intended to keep us safe. When triggered, we no longer have access to our best selves. Instead, we become task focused in our actions and closed in our thinking, reaching for certitude about rightness, greater control, and simple stories.

We can avoid that pitfall by making different choices after we're triggered. The most useful choice is to notice when you're triggered and then pause. Every one of us manifests limbic-system triggering in distinct ways. Pay attention to what happens in your body when you're triggered, and you'll notice a pattern. That patterned physical response is your clue that something is amiss for you, and once you recognize it, you can choose what to do. Pausing—whatever that looks like for you—is the superior choice. It allows your limbic system to settle down, which helps you be curious about how you might respond.

Be Prepared for How Uncertainty Spreads

Another thing to be prepared for is how uncertainty can act like an organizational infection. To avoid making your organization sick, thoughtful leaders modulate their actions to minimize triggering events in others. If uncertainty is shared in an ill-informed way, it can trigger entire organizations. This can be especially detrimental—like a sickness—when an organization needs to increase adaptation. If an uncertainty infection spreads unabated, entire organizations lose the ability to adapt.

Sharing uncertainty is necessary. Avoiding, withholding, or trivializing uncertainty is just as detrimental as sharing it in ways that trigger people. The effective approach is acknowledging the difficulties uncertainty brings, while noticing the opportunities it harbors.

Along this line, it's tempting for some leaders to take advantage of uncertainty as a powerful action driver and use its infectious nature to gain organizational movement. The concept of a "burning platform" gets close to this notion. A leader should consider burning platforms as mass triggering events—creating an "uncertainty pandemic" on purpose.

Once infected with that kind of pandemic, organizations lose the capacity to be creative, curious, and open to future opportunities. While a leader may gain movement or energy from a burning platform, most individuals in the organization will focus that energy on survival, not increasing organizational adaptability. This is the opposite of what leaders need most from their organizations in challenging times, so a burning platform is not helpful.

WHY SHIFT

Because Irreducible Uncertainty Is Exhausting

Irreducible uncertainty is why leaders need to shift. It has a nettlesome way of resisting our efforts to rid ourselves of it, even though we want to. We typically (orthodox mindset) double down, reaching for more control and rightness, and get locked into our simple stories. When we fight with irreducible uncertainty, it is exhausting. The more complex things are, the more effort is required to deal with it in this way.

My clients describe leading complex systems as if the uncertainty inherent in them is reducible as "hard" or "heavy." For them, leading healthcare is like being Sisyphus from Greek mythology, forced to roll an immense boulder up a hill, only for it to roll back down every time it neared the top, repeating his actions for eternity. Wrestling with irreducible uncertainty as if it's reducible is like pushing a giant rock up a hill daily and starting all over tomorrow. Instead, leaders need to absorb the irreducible uncertainty, liberating themselves from rock pushing. Shifting toward the unorthodox mindset about uncertainty begins that liberation.

Because Trying to Reduce Irreducible Uncertainty Causes Harm

Attempting to reduce irreducible uncertainty is hard on leaders, but it's brutal on followers. Followers are on the receiving end of efforts to gain more control, rightness, and actions born out of simple stories. When leaders try to reduce irreducible uncertainty, they reach for things that give them a better sense of control. As they reach for more control, leaders reduce the autonomy of their followers. Loss of autonomy (increased compliance and subjugation) is a primary contributor to workforce burnout. A poor leadership relationship with irreducible uncertainty harms organizations, contributing to healthcare's significant workforce challenges.

HOW TO SHIFT

Recognize All Kinds of Uncertainty

Shifting is about doing something with uncertainty when it shows up. Each kind of uncertainty has unique qualities and consequences, so it's important to recognize which of the four you are dealing with. Each kind is amenable to certain approaches, actions, and behaviors. If you recognize the four kinds of uncertainty, you can make better choices about how you relate to it.

Discern the Irreducible from the Reducible

The most important thing is accurately discerning which uncertainties are reducible, and which are not. Avoid the trap of thinking that all uncertainty is reducible—that all uncertainty is either stochastic or epistemic.

You may be getting trapped if you find yourself thinking that your uncertainty about what may happen will dissipate if you have enough data and predictive analytics. That might reflect a belief that all uncertainty is stochastic.

You may be getting trapped if you find yourself thinking that your uncertainty will go away if you find the right experts, people with the right experience, or gather enough stakeholder feedback. That may reflect a belief that all uncertainty is epistemic.

To avoid being trapped in complexity, you must account for the variability that is inherent in systems (aleatoric uncertainty) and the result of various interpretations of reality (ontological uncertainty). Neither of these are reducible, and they run rampant in complexity. The critical concept is that the more complex the system, the more irreducible the uncertainty. Don't try to reduce what is irreducible; absorb it instead.

Gain Comfort with Discomfort

It's OK to be uncomfortable. It's OK to be uncertain. Embrace the discomfort of irreducible uncertainty. The more familiar you are with it, the easier it is to meet uncertainty at your doorstep with a smile. Getting comfortable with discomfort is not reducing. It's absorbing uncertainty. Remember, absorption is not a reduction strategy.

A critical thing to notice is how the expressions of the unorthodox mindset about uncertainty both absorb irreducible uncertainty *and* reduce reducible uncertainty. This unique attribute shows how the unorthodox mindset adds to the orthodox mindset but doesn't replace it. The unorthodox mindset expands your behavioral options, which may increase your comfort with irreducible uncertainty while reducing what's reducible. Expressions of the unorthodox mindset are helpful with all forms of uncertainty, while the usefulness of the orthodox expressions is limited to stochastic and epistemic uncertainty.

Ultimately, there's no right or wrong way to relate to uncertainty. The crucial thing is finding the most helpful ways to relate to all forms of uncertainty and knowing why you choose to do what you do.

MINDSET SIX—CHANGE

AN UNORTHODOX MINDSET ABOUT LEADING CHANGE

Change Is Emergent, Not Just Planned and Managed

ILLUSTRATION 6. *Complexity Makes Linear Change Models Less Useful.*

UNDERSTANDING CHANGE

Our beliefs about change are closely related to how we understand the workings of the universe and how our lives unfold. These beliefs influence our views on leadership. Change and leadership are so closely related that, for many, change *is* leadership.

We hold beliefs about change tightly, because they are foundational to understanding our personal and professional existence. Questioning foundational beliefs can be so unsettling that many shy away from doing it. However, the healthcare industry's efforts to transform itself cannot be successful without carefully examining change and how it unfolds in systems.

Examining our beliefs about change is being curious about change. Curiosity relaxes our hold on what we believe the most, a necessary precondition for shifting. Loosening the grip of an orthodox mindset requires closely examining widely held beliefs about change. It requires curiosity about the true nature of change, the language we use to describe change, and how we know what change is. Understanding change in these abstract ways is an essential first step for shifting toward unorthodoxy.

OUR UNDERSTANDING OF CHANGE IS INCOMPLETE

Change Is Difficult to Define

The phenomenon we call "change" has long been debated among philosophers, theologians, and scientists.[39] After centuries of trying to define change precisely, a universally accepted definition is elusive. It is a phenomenon, but we understand it incompletely. Change lacks a definitive definition.

Definitions serve as attempts to unveil the true nature, essence, and reality of something. Lacking a complete definition means no one knows for sure what change is or how it works. Any mindset we may have about change, therefore, is also incomplete. In essence, we aren't certain what change is. But if we remain curious, the uncertainty opens us to consider different mindsets about change.

Varied Descriptions of Change

Description is the language of subjective experience, inherently personal, contextual, and varied. While descriptions of change vary, change itself is a singular phenomenon. There aren't different kinds of change, only different descriptions.

Suppose a family moves to a new city. Afterward, the parents describe the change as a fresh start leading to career advancement and a better life. Their teenage daughter describes it as a forced dislocation, imperiling her athletic development and worsening their lives.

Despite their varied descriptions, they experienced the same change: they moved to a new city. Their various descriptions express their unique experiences with change, highlighting how change is a phenomenon with different descriptions.

Descriptions vary because mindsets vary. Mindsets are powerful determinants of how we experience and then describe our world. Our brains use mindsets to filter what information to keep and what to discard. That limits what we notice, creating an incompleteness in our understanding of what we experience. Mindsets construct an incomplete "story" about whatever we experience. Therefore, whatever story we create about a change we experience matches our mindset about change and is always incomplete.

Mindsets also determine the language we use to describe our change experiences. Descriptions are our attempt to tell ourselves and others what was "real" about our change experience. In other words, our mindsets, through language, construct a reality for us about change.

The absence of a definitive definition and the propensity for incomplete descriptions leaves us open to considering other mindsets about change. Being curious about change and how we experience it helps relax a tight grip on change mindsets.

A DESCRIPTIVE EXAMPLE:
The Notion of Linear Motion in Change

Describing Change with Linear Motion

To illustrate these points further, let's consider the notion of motion as it relates to change.

The orthodox mindset suggests that change follows a straightforward path, guiding individuals or organizations from one fixed point to another. The best change efforts progress smoothly and as expected, without deviation, ultimately improving results.

The belief that change is progressive and linear stems from 17th- and 18th-century definitions of change. Key influences include Enlightenment Age philosophy, which championed reason and progress, defining change as a steady march toward a better future. In the same era, Newton's laws of motion defined change as a predictable, linear, and controllable process, resisted in direct and equal opposition to that motion. Additionally, the dominant Judeo-Christian theology of that era, with its linear view of time from Creation to Judgment Day, defined change as a straight path with a clear end, a story unfolding in a predictable way over time.

Even though those Enlightenment Age definitions incompletely represent the phenomenon of change, they infuse current change management theory. You may not have consciously thought about them, but they have seeped into your education and experiences. They shape your mindset about change by creating beliefs about what is real about change.

Regarding the notion of linear motion, 17th-century definitions create beliefs that shape the mindsets that determine the words we use to describe change. For instance, consider how the Enlightenment's linear perspective on change still lingers in our language today. When we discuss change, we often use terms and phrases that imply a steady, step-by-step progression, as if organizations move forward predictably, much like the Enlightenment philosophers envisioned the march of reason and progress.

Our descriptions matter a great deal. Language about change reinforces our definition of change. Definitions frame our beliefs. Beliefs craft our mindsets. Mindsets determine the language of description. Therefore, descriptions are important, because they create a self-reinforcing cognitive loop regarding change. The only way to escape it is by being curious about change and careful with our words.

Another reason descriptions matter is that they become the cornerstone concepts in our change models. An example is the concept of linear motion inherent in the most popular change models used in healthcare today.

Change Models Include Descriptions of Change with Linear Motion

The most common change models in healthcare assume a progressive linearity to change. For example, John Kotter's famous change model envisioned transformational change moving linearly through eight sequential steps (Figure 12).[40]

Each step is a conditional prerequisite for the next. First, you create a sense of urgency (Step 1). Once completed, you form a powerful guiding coalition (Step 2), and so on.

Kotter posits that most transformational efforts fail because leaders don't accomplish a step or don't follow them sequentially. Proponents of Kotter's process often acknowledge that change sometimes feels like it stops, regresses, and then restarts. But those caveats still presuppose linearity. Going backward is just as linear as going forward. Pausing is merely a stop somewhere along the linear progression.

1	Establishing a Sense of Urgency
2	Forming a Powerful Guiding Coalition
3	Creating a Vision
4	Communicating the Vision
5	Empowering Others to Act on the Vision
6	Planning for and Creating Short-term Wins
7	Consolidating Improvements and Producing Still More Change
8	Institutionalizing New Approaches

FIGURE 12. *The Eight Steps of Kotter's 8-Step Change Model.* (Source: Kotter International. Used with Permission. Modified from John P. Kotter, "Leading Change: Why Transformation Efforts Fail," *Harvard Business Review,* January 1, 2007, pg 4. https://hbr.org/2007/01 /leading-change-why-transformation-efforts-fail.)

While change models like Kotter's have and continue to serve as valuable guides of successful organizational change, they also shape our reality about change by describing how change efforts ought to unfold.

Reconsidering Descriptions of Change with Linear Motion

The prevailing view about change is increasingly at odds with what science tells us: change isn't linear. Change doesn't unfold like a well-working machine in predictable and plannable steps. Change is like a leaf in a swirling storm, tossed about by unexpected gusty twists and turns.

Advances in scientific fields such as complexity, chaos theory, and nonlinear dynamics show that change doesn't follow a straight line.[41] These fields of science contribute to different models, where the notion of motion in change is more like a leaf blowing in a storm than a train on a track. Modern science suggests a fundamentally different relationship between us and change, supporting a mindset shift about what change is.

A pandemic is like a swirling storm. During COVID-19, dramatic change occurred, but it had nothing to do with conforming to a predefined plan or sequential stages. There was no end state. Nothing was predetermined. It was continually evolving.

Providers needed to adapt rapidly: switching to telemedicine, perfecting patient flows, managing equipment shortages, and incorporating ever-changing guidelines. The pandemic tested adaptive capabilities when new variants appeared, demanding fundamentally different approaches. Success was measured by adaptability and staying true to purpose, mission, and financial sustainability, not by achieving a predetermined and quantifiable endpoint.

It often takes events like a pandemic for us to notice mindsets that no longer work well. For some, the COVID-19 pandemic fundamentally reshaped their mindsets about many things, including the nature of organizational change. It was an industry-wide wake-up call, shifting, for some, their most familiar mindset about change.

Changing the Description to Include Nonlinear Motion

Change models like Kotter's are comforting, because of their predictability, and valuable, because they've been helpful; however, they describe change in ways that rarely exist today. In nonlinearity, progressive steps don't happen, even if we try to make them happen.

People, processes, and the strategic environment change so fast that the results achieved during a step (in models like Kotter's) erode before you can finish it. Or, by the time you reach the end, the results you've worked so hard to achieve are no longer helpful. In complexity, the context changes so quickly that leaders don't have the luxury of the time or predictability that models like Kotter's presume.

When navigating a world that resembles less a machine and more a swirling storm, models that presume linearity don't apply. For his part, Kotter acknowledged this by moving away from his earlier, linear model.[42] Rather than steps to traverse sequentially, he now depicts change as eight accelerators (Figure 13).

FIGURE 13. *Kotter's Eight Accelerators of Change.* (Source: Kotter International. Used with Permission. From: Bedard, Alex. "The 8-Step Process for Leading Change." Kotter International Inc. Kotter International, April 7, 2022. https://www.kotterinc.com/methodology/8-steps/. Accessed 13 Sep 2023, and Kotter, Change (2021)).

By renaming steps as accelerators and redefining them, Kotter dropped the idea of a sequence of steps toward a predetermined end. Instead, Kotter represents his model as a circle of disconnected spheres surrounding the Big Opportunity.

In the graphical depiction of his new change model, Kotter intentionally removes connecting lines between accelerators. Also, the circles around the named accelerators are incomplete. The gaps and absence of connecting lines emphasize that accelerators are not discrete stages, steps, or functions. Instead, they reflect areas of activity that are in continuous interdependent interaction with each other, often in unpredictable and unplanned ways.

The accelerators orbit around the Big Opportunity, which acts as an organizational gravitational force pulling people, ideas, and resources together. The Big Opportunity attracts the accelerators, generating change. Notice that the type of change accelerators generate is an emergent change, not sweeping centrally planned change initiatives following a sequence of carefully orchestrated steps. That's why they are "accelerators" and not "steps."

Kotter renamed the accelerators, using language acknowledging that leaders don't initiate change. Instead, he describes how leaders cultivate and enable emergence, leveraging the change inclination of complex systems. Therefore, "accelerators" better describes the nature of change in complexity. Because language shapes reality, Kotter's close attention to descriptive words and graphics is powerful and essential.

Understanding that change models reflect a constructed reality about change, generated from mindsets about change, helps leaders realize that different mindsets are available. Kotter discovered this and adjusted his model. If Kotter can do that, so can we.

HOW SYSTEMS CHANGE

We have explored two descriptions of change: one that is familiarly linear, predictable, and progressive, like the workings of a machine, and another that is nonlinear and unpredictable, like a leaf in a swirling storm. Let's consider these two descriptions of change while contemplating how systems change.

All Systems Are Inclined to Change

Change is inherent in all systems. Every system is inclined to change and does so in ways that match its design. As several have said, "Every system is perfectly designed to get the result that it gets,"[43] which means that every system is perfectly designed to change how it does. Leaders don't determine how systems change: systems do that.

The change inclination of complicated systems is stability. Complicated systems change incrementally and predictably, through a forward-moving, linear progression. When orthodox-minded leaders encounter this inclination for stability, they often describe it as resistance or inertia, something to overcome.

The change inclination of complex systems is emergence. Complex systems change unpredictably through novel and transformative adaptations that occur quickly without central or controlled planning. When orthodox-minded leaders encounter this inclination for emergence, they often describe it as chaotic, something to control.

Leaders don't determine how systems change, but they can, and often do, accelerate or hinder whatever change inclination a system may have. How leaders affect change depends on the system and how leaders interact with it.

To Affect System Change, Match Its Inclinations

Suppose an enterprising leader, Joyce, deployed Lean management and manufacturing practices to improve patient throughput in a stand-alone community-based ambulatory surgical center—a mostly complicated system.

Joyce worked with her team to create a value-stream map of the process from admission through discharge. Using cross-functional teams, including frontline staff, her team worked intensively for a few days to redesign workflows and implement immediate changes, (i.e., a Kaizen event).

When things improved, the team set up standard operating procedures, called Standard Work, to ensure consistency and keep the gains achieved. Standard Work became part of the training for inexperienced staff, promoting a uniform level of care. The behavioral approaches associated with Lean effectively identified interventions and solutions that improved patient cycle time. In this case, Lean worked well for Joyce.

Joyce moved on, bringing her reputation and change-management experience to a large metropolitan academic medical center—a mostly complex system. Tasked to improve operating start times, she again deployed Lean, but it did not result in improvements, and, in some instances, performance deteriorated. She was not successful. She was convinced the problem lay in the system and others, not in her approaches, and so she eventually left the organization.

Another enterprising leader, Sharon, who had experience and knowledge about Lean, stepped in. However, Sharon had extensive experience in another management methodology called Agile, which emphasizes adaptive planning, prompt delivery, and continuous improvement.[44] After noting the complexity of the system she was working with, Sharon elected to deploy Agile instead of Lean methodologies. She encouraged establishing a cross-functional team of key stakeholders, each holding essential roles in the operating room function. This "scrum team" self-organized and set up daily stand-up meetings—called "daily scrums"—to retrospectively review what went well and what they could improve. They quickly adapted new plans focused on targeted areas of improvement.

The work to improve was ongoing, with an on-the-fly feel, focused on patient and staff needs as the basis for defining their work. They heightened their focus during slower periods, dividing change efforts into short, manageable phases—called "sprints"—with specific goals. The system responded with remarkably improved overall start-time performance.

Attributing success to the new leader, Sharon, or to the Agile approach is tempting. But it wasn't that Agile worked and Lean didn't, or that the innate leadership qualities of Joyce were inferior. Success came from matching approaches to the systems' change inclinations.

The scientific roots of Lean management and manufacturing date to the late 19th and early 20th century and work well in the systems that dominated that era—simple and complicated. As complexity increases, approaches like Lean lose effectiveness because they presume linearity, among other things. On the other hand, Agile works well in complex systems because Agile draws upon the sciences of chaos theory, nonlinearity, and complexity.

The key takeaway is that systems have inherent change inclinations. Leadership approaches successfully used in one system may be ineffective or detrimental to another. This is because the change inclinations of the system, not the leader, determine how change happens. To be the most effective at affecting system change, leaders must match their and others' approaches to the change inclinations of the system.

Recognizing that systems have inherent tendencies toward change is an important insight. Leaders can improve their effectiveness by aligning their approaches, actions, and behaviors with these inclinations. Of course, that requires the ability to shift mindsets about change. Understanding different change inclinations offers yet another way to loosen a firm grasp on a particular mindset about change.

THE ORTHODOX MINDSET ABOUT CHANGE:
Change Is Planned and Managed for Resistance

The orthodox mindset about change is that change is progressively linear, something to plan and manage, especially for resistance. Leaders with this mindset approach change by crafting a vision, finding strategic opportunities, and reducing those into actionable initiatives. They set milestones and metrics to gauge success. These leaders presume resistance and deploy various change management models to gain buy-in and ensure alignment.

EXPRESSIONS OF THE ORTHODOX MINDSET

You can identify the orthodox mindset in yourself or others by noticing the common expressions of this mindset: creating a vision, managing resistance, and following a plan.

Creating a Vision

Within organizational change, the leader's vision is central to strategic direction. They and their vision become the prime movers of transformative shifts, the orchestrators of new organizational realities. Their vision is a rallying cry that mobilizes collective effort and sustains momentum. In this way, the leader's vision serves as a change catalyst, converting abstract ideals into tangible actions and long-term strategies. Therefore, in the context of leading change, vision elevates the leader with the unique ability to start, direct, and inspire transformational change.

Vision defines direction, instills linear motion, and lays the groundwork for deciding success or failure. It determines what metaphorical "buses" we must "get on" or "off." It is often the first question the board asks of senior executives: "What is your vision for the company?" Vision, our belief in its vital importance to leadership, and our conviction that great leaders have it, is a core expression of the orthodox mindset.

Managing Resistance

The orthodox mindset holds that people always resist change. Indeed, change is often difficult, and it generates behavioral shifts. The orthodox mindset about change interprets those behavioral responses to change as resistance.

To better understand resistance, notice that the root word is *resist*, which means exerting a force in opposition to something, be it literal or metaphorical. Opposition is a force applied directly against another, in this case, change. In other words, resistance presumes linearity to change. It implies that change pushes us in one direction, and we oppose it in an equal and opposite direction, alluding to Newton's lingering influence and his definitions of change and motion.

The critical point is that we make sense of the behaviors we see in others as resistance because our mindset tells us that's what change entails. If resistance is a given, overcoming it becomes a leadership imperative. Subsequently, various change management models offer insights and strategies for persuading people to align with a change plan and how to overcome resistance.

Following a Plan

Change is an initiative with a plan. The plan is carried out in clearly defined steps that transpire predictably over time. Project managers map and check progress using Gantt charts or similar tools.

Those overseeing the plan carefully check progress, looking for achieved milestones—completed steps within the planned time and resource use. Adhering to the predicted plan serves to define success or failure. If the change initiative deviates from the plan, it's considered "at risk." If the initiative doesn't achieve the intended outcome, it's a failure.

Planning presumes the system is complicated and places trust in the system's change inclination for stability. The first presumption is that the conditions initiating the change remain stable throughout the change process and persist afterward. The second presumption is that the system will settle into a new, improved, steady state after the change. These presumptions of stability are prerequisites of planned change initiatives.

Planning becomes a quintessential management function. Plans serve as a road map with multiple purposes. They specify the direction, pace, means, and ends of change.

THE UNORTHODOX MINDSET ABOUT CHANGE:
Change Is Emergent and Led for "Adaptance"

The unorthodox mindset about change is that it emerges naturally due to the innumerable interactions between people, processes, and organizational resources. Emergent change is enabled by leaders, unleashing its potential in complex systems while suppressing the things that get in the way. Few words are available to accurately describe how individuals interact with nonlinear change. Therefore, I propose a new word, "adaptance," to describe how individuals respond to nonlinear change.

EXPRESSIONS OF THE UNORTHODOX MINDSET

You can identify the unorthodox mindset in yourself or others by noticing the common expressions of this mindset: co-creating a co-evolving vision, reframing resistance, and following emergence.

Co-Creating a Co-Evolving Vision

Leaders do not have a unique ability to see the future. It is as obscure to them as it is to anyone else. Vision is still essential, but it isn't embodied in a leader. A leader can help craft a vision by working with others, creating it together, or "co-creating."

Co-creation eschews the idea of change as planned, managed, and implemented by a central guiding hand or hands following a singularly crafted vision of the future. Instead, leaders use collective dialogue with various stakeholders to formulate vision, solutions, and strategies iteratively. Co-creation is a "crafting together."

Therefore, leaders are not the architects of vision or envisioning change, merely the enablers. They nurture an organizational ecosystem where discussions and ideas about vision, direction, and change happen organically. Multiple internal and external influences shape the interactions and dialogue, all working together to create a vision.

Additionally, context, systems, and people constantly adapt in response to and with each other over time—they evolve together. In other words, they co-evolve. In this dynamic environment, vision continuously changes as the environment, system, and the individuals in the system interact and evolve together. So vision also co-evolves. Leaders with an unorthodox mindset work to co-create a co-evolving vision with others.

Reframing Resistance

Our language about change constructs reality about change. We must be careful about the words we use. The word *resistance* is a prime example.

With an unorthodox mindset, people don't resist change. They do experience change and respond to it. Leaders see and make sense of those responses through their mindset about change. If their mindset is orthodox, they interpret those behaviors as resistance. If their mindset is unorthodox, they make sense of them differently.

I propose that leaders with an unorthodox mindset describe people's response to change as *adaptance*, not resistance. To better understand adaptance, we must have a basic understanding of self-protection strategies and their origins.

Our brains are exquisitely sensitive to environmental shifts, especially the unexpected, like change. Deep in a more primitive part of the brain, far removed from our reasoning centers, our limbic system interprets change as a threat to our survival. The limbic system responds to change by releasing a cascade of neurochemicals. The neurochemicals can quickly trigger sweeping physiological and cognitive changes that result in behavioral responses—self-protection strategies. Humans don't entirely control these survival responses, because they often occur quickly, without our rational awareness.

Self-protection strategies are learned behavioral responses we use to keep ourselves safe. Over time, these strategies became subconscious, and we deploy them automatically whenever our brains perceive a threat. Each of us has favored strategies that have worked for us previously, which is why we continue to use them. However, these strategies are usually unhelpful in organizational settings and with organizational change.

The critical point is that self-protection strategies are not resistance. They are the behavioral responses used to engage and wrestle with change. Self-protection strategies are a means of processing change while trying to stay safe and survive. The distinction between self-protection and resistance matters, because the leadership strategies for addressing resistance are entirely different from those addressing people in survival mode. Resistance is something to overcome and defeat. Survival calls for a helping hand, extended in empathy and compassion.

Furthermore, resistance presumes linearity—a force directly opposed to another, pushing against it. Because change in complex systems is nonlinear, using a word like *resistance* to describe our interactions with change is unhelpful and misleading.

Dealing with nonlinear change is like surfing. Surfers can't and don't resist or oppose the forces at play in the wave. They either go with the wave or opt out. The surfer may not like what's happening. Maybe the wave is too big or too fast. Perhaps she's not as skilled as she needs to be to stay with the wave. Nevertheless, she doesn't resist the wave; she has to go along with it, even though it's uncomfortable.

This metaphor highlights that we need a word that better describes how the surfer is with the wave—without an underlying assumption of linearity. Adaptability or adaptation comes to mind, being an effective response to change. However, both words imply an action-reaction relationship with change. Change *A* leads to adaptive response *B*, a linear, equal-opposite reaction. While *adaptability* and *adaptation* may be more suitable than *resistance*, they also presume linearity and don't meet our needs.

To construct a better word, we can begin with "resistance" and build on it. Resistance is the action or state of resisting—or opposing change.[45] Using that as a starting point, a suitable definition for *adaptance* could mirror *resistance* as the action or state of adapting.

Furthermore, breaking adaptance into the root and suffix helps make better sense of this novel word. *Adapt* means to make suitable to requirements or conditions.[46] The suffix *-ance* is derived from Latin and forms nouns that describe a state, quality, or action. In this case, it nominalizes action into a descriptive noun, imparting a sense of ongoing, interactive, nondirectional behavior. In other words, adaptance describes a complexity-fit relationship with change, like a surfer in a relationship with the wave—a nonlinear, constantly active interaction with change.

Resistance and adaptance stand in juxtaposition. One term reflects a linear opposition to change, and the other reflects a nonlinear, ongoing, and often-uneasy interaction with change. Adaptance suits an unorthodox mindset about change because it better describes how people experience and interact with nonlinear change. And it isn't resistance.

Following Emergence

Change emerges spontaneously, arising from the myriad, nonlinear interactions among elements that are simpler than the whole but not necessarily simple. For example, some novel ideas to improve patient throughput emerge among the innumerable, nonlinear daily interactions between physicians, nurses, and administrators across multiple hospitals, clinics, and other services. Someone notices something that could be better, takes it upon themselves to pull together a group to work on some change project, and then deploys it. Notably, a central authority does not approve, direct, or control these interactions or whatever arises from them. Emergence might result in a new way of dealing with patients, a creative use of the electronic health record, a novel policy adjustment, or a unique strategic opportunity not noticed centrally.

Emergence is typically a locally derived response to situations experienced at the interface between the organization and the stakeholders—patient, payer, or employer. In this way, emergence transcends the constituent parts of a healthcare organization. It gives rise to new and unforeseeable patterns or behaviors that are unknowable by the reduction and isolated study of individuals or specific system elements.

The nature of emergence makes planned change counterproductive in complex systems. Nonlinear interactions are uncontrollable, and emergence depends upon them. Planned change acts as a mechanism of control, dampening nonlinearity, thus starving the system of the emergent properties inherent in it. Planned change ultimately undermines adaptability.

Conventional change models are, therefore, unsuitable in complex systems. Instead, leaders must adopt approaches, actions, and behaviors that align with the change inclinations inherent in complex systems, as reflected in the recent adaptations to Kotter's model.

Leaders expressing an unorthodox mindset acknowledge, enable, and defend emergence. They intentionally eschew centrally planned and deployed change initiatives, preferring and promoting locally mediated efforts (experiments). Leaders carefully watch how those locally derived change experiments affect the inclinations of the entire system. If the impact is favorable, they work to promote and expand the uptake of those experiments system wide. If they are unfavorable, they work with the originators of the experiment to stop it quickly. Leaders with an unorthodox mindset about change follow emergence.

MAKING THE SHIFT
Before the Shift

Be Prepared to Face Cognitive Barriers

The cognitive and systemic barriers to shifting from an orthodox to an unorthodox mindset about change are substantial, more than for any other mindset. The main reason it is demanding work is that change is a concept born out of deeply rooted beliefs about the universe, time, human nature, and the purpose or nature of leadership itself.

To make a shift requires leaders to visit, question, and adjust those deeply rooted beliefs. That is never an easy task for adults. It usually requires a thought partner, like an executive coach, to work with the leader as they explore their thinking about these topics.

Many leaders are disinclined to explore the necessary cognitive territory, because it's risky, discomforting, and may seem like a waste of valuable time. Yet the challenges that make it difficult also make it worthwhile.

Be Prepared to Face Organizational Barriers

Another reason shifting is difficult is because the orthodox mindset is an industry norm. Leaders widely accept, reinforce, and hold the orthodox mindset as unquestionable truth. One small example of this is the belief that people always resist change.

The deep entrenchment of the orthodox mindset has profound implications. It creates significant organizational and cultural inertia, as it is often normative and ingrained in an organization's culture, if not the entire industry.

Expressing an unorthodox mindset in orthodox-infused contexts invites substantive professional and organizational challenges for a leader. People question leadership approaches that don't fit the culture or norms.

Be Prepared to Be an Outlier

Most healthcare executives are aware that the approaches of the past are increasingly ineffective. There's a genuine and widespread hunger for alternative methods that will lead to the long-desired transformation of U.S. healthcare—one that sets the industry on a sustainable path, advances the common good, and doesn't imperil the entire economy. That will never happen unless there is a leadership transformation, which cannot occur without a mindset transformation first.

If you shift toward the unorthodox mindset, you will position yourself as an industry outlier and transformative trailblazer, precisely what the industry requires. I want to encourage you to take the risk and do it. The transformation healthcare needs will not happen any other way.

WHY SHIFT

Because Function No Longer Follows Form

Larger systems are the trend in U.S. healthcare. These large organizations are corporate bureaucracies structured or formed to function as complicated systems. Most organizations are led and run as such, consistent with their design and intended function.

Because corporate bureaucracies are, by design, complicated systems, their change inclination is stability. When functioning as designed, change in these systems happens incrementally, resulting in predictable adaptations that steadily move the organization forward. These are marvelous entities that have transformed the world, but they are slow adapters. And that's why their time has passed.

One reason they are far less viable today is that the context in which these corporate bureaucracies exist is increasingly complex, requiring quick adaptations to survive. Furthermore, as these corporate bureaucracies grow larger, with more hospitals, clinics, and geographic reach, they become increasingly complex. Even though they are designed and led as complicated systems, increased complexity shifts the change inclinations of the system away from stability toward emergence. Consequently, these large organizations begin to function like complex systems even though they are designed, structured, and run as complicated systems.

If form (structure) is to follow function, then an organization that functionally works as a complex system while structured as a complicated system is a difficult challenge. In these cases, function has decoupled from form, creating mindset choices for leaders of healthcare's corporate bureaucracies. The decoupling of function from form leaves leaders with three possible approaches for dealing with the challenge. All three approaches serve as a basis for shifting toward unorthodoxy.

First Approach: Force Function to Follow Form

One approach, which is the most common, is to force the organization to function in ways that match the intended design. Leaders with an orthodox mindset will work to create greater centralization and tighter operational controls to end their organization's creeping complexity tendencies. This approach reflects the conventional meaning of systemness, which we now know is not genuine systemness. In pursuit of this kind of systemness, considerable attention and effort are applied to drive a high degree of standardization across the enterprise. Those actions serve as a doubling down, forcing function to follow form.

The consequences of this approach, however, are unpleasant. Two significant issues arise. The first is that the only way to force function to follow form in these large systems is by increasingly drawing upon power sources that convert to control. As leaders use power to increase control, they decrease autonomy and push the workforce closer to subjugation. This approach increases burnout, reduces morale, and leads to high workforce turnover. It doesn't go well.

The second major issue is the increasingly complex competitive landscape. Successfully forcing function to follow form places corporate bureaucracies in a noncompetitive position. If the context is complex and competitors function as complex systems, competitors will adapt quickly and seize strategic opportunities faster. Clearly, it is not a viable long-term strategy. It violates the Law of Requisite Complexity. Avoiding the unpleasant results of this approach is one reason why shifting to unorthodoxy makes sense.

Second Approach: Adapt Form to Follow Function

Another choice is to transform the organization so that form follows function. That would mean restructuring and redesigning healthcare organizations for complexity, a wholesale dismantling of corporate bureaucracies. The sweeping changes needed to do that in healthcare would be challenging. And that's an understatement.

Dismantling would require a radical transformation of industry norms, leadership mindsets, governance, and policy reforms. Systems would need to be redesigned with the goal of becoming ambidextrous organizations rather than corporate bureaucracies.[47]

If "form follows function" is a useful truism, changing how the healthcare industry structures its organizations to match complexity better is a superior approach. The reality and associated risk of what would be needed to make it happen quickly is daunting, but the potential reward could be remarkable if leaders and their teams can navigate the organizational risk of transformation.

If leaders and their organizations wish to take on the challenge of this approach, they must begin by shifting their mindset about change toward the unorthodox.

Third Approach: Leave Function Decoupled from Form

The remaining possibility is to accept the challenge without trying to resolve it. In this case, leaders match their leadership and management approaches to fit complexity, aligning how they work with how the system functions, not how it is structured.

They accept the challenges of leading in an organization where form doesn't always follow function, where a complicated system structure constantly works against complexity-fit leadership. You may notice that this approach feels a lot like seeking harmony with polarity: you are correct. The form-and-function challenge results from the inherent polarity of complex systems.

And that's why this third approach is a difficult one. Relating to polarity is challenging for all of us, one complexity-fit healthcare executives face daily. This third option also requires access to the orthodox and unorthodox mindsets about change. It's another reason why shifting toward unorthodoxy makes sense.

HOW TO SHIFT

The goal of shifting is to beneficially leverage the inherent change inclination of complex systems: emergence. Emergence amplifies organizational adaptability, positioning the organization to thrive in complexity. Cultivating organizational emergence begins by adopting an unorthodox mindset about change.

See Emergence

Shifting requires seeing emergence for what it is—inherent adaptive change inclinations in complex systems. Emergence is change that happens without planning. A leader can begin their shift toward an unorthodox mindset by paying attention to and being curious about unplanned change. The shift starts by noticing emergence.

Rather than considering spontaneous change to be an undesirable deviation, be curious about how that emergent change came about. Carefully notice how the change influences the system. Notice if it nudges system outcomes closer to achieving the organization's purpose.

Resist the temptation to compare the emergent change to the standard process. That's the orthodox mindset at work. Be more interested in the results the emergent change generates and whether they are superior. That's the unorthodox mindset at work.

If the emergent change does result in improvement, consider how you might encourage its spread, amplifying its influence on the entire system.

Be mindful of how your response to the change cultivates or squelches more emergent behaviors. Reprimanding leaders while terminating the emergent change because it doesn't fit a centrally planned initiative, process, policy, or procedure stifles emergent tendencies. Encouragement and appreciation for the creativity, adaptability, and courage it took to develop something novel and new tends to cultivate more emergent behaviors.

Let Go of Planning

The nature of complex systems is their unpredictability, which leads to high degrees of uncertainty. Much of that uncertainty is irreducible. In the face of that uncertainty, planned change offers false comfort. By careful planning, leaders think they can diminish the irreducible uncertainty inherent in change in complex systems. Planned change cannot reduce what is irreducible. Instead, leaders must rely on emergence and adaptability for change.

Planned change is better suited for complicated systems because it presumes that a linear cause-and-effect relationship exists and is knowable. Those kinds of relationships are absent in complex environments.

Planned change counters emergent change, controlling the system to change in designed ways. Because the inclination of complex systems is emergence, planned change deteriorates how complex systems function as more control is applied.

Leaders who fit with complexity relax their dependence upon planning. Instead, they apply methodologies—like Agile—designed to unleash emergence, allowing the organization to adapt in real time to the needs and challenges of the system.

By relaxing their hold on planned change, leaders with an unorthodox mindset cultivate and encourage emergent change, fostering an environment of self-organized initiatives.

Acknowledge Adaptance

Change is threatening to people. Therefore, self-protection strategies are inevitable and create friction with change. It's not that people are resisting change. They are surfing it, working to understand what it means for them. It isn't resistance you're observing. It's adaptance.

Leaders with an unorthodox mindset deploy approaches, actions, and behaviors intentionally designed to work with adaptance, empathizing with the survival strategies in others while enabling emergence. These leaders work with others to help make sense of change while addressing the threats others are experiencing.

The goal is not to eliminate survival behaviors. We need them, and they are at the core of our humanity. The goal is to diminish the heightened sense of threat while elevating and noticing those things that help people thrive.

When unorthodox-minded leaders see adaptance, they connect with others, supporting them as they learn to adapt. At the same time, these leaders work authentically to expand awareness of the opportunities that change brings, co-creatively finding ways to thrive with, not just survive change.

PART THREE

MINDSETS ABOUT LEADING COMPLEX SYSTEMS

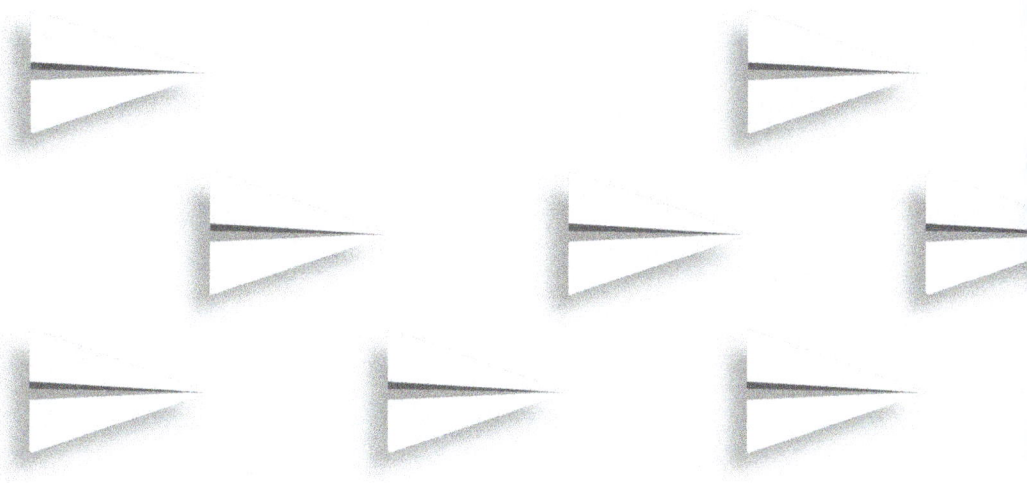

MINDSET SEVEN—FIRST WORK

AN UNORTHODOX MINDSET ABOUT LEADING WELL

The First Work of Leadership Comes First

ILLUSTRATION 7. *The First Work.* The First Work is the foundational and nonnegotiable work required to lead well in complexity. It is on the "work" side of a work-life balance, not the life side.

UNDERSTANDING THE FIRST WORK

Leading well is demanding, and complexity makes it even more difficult. A handful of essential strategies helps leaders do better in complex environments. I call one of those strategies the First Work.

Leaders are like elite athletes who depend on their entire being to meet challenges and pursue peak performance. To attain peak performance, people require periods of stress followed by recovery. That holds for leaders as much as athletes. Absent a balance between stress and recovery, human performance deteriorates.

Paying attention to stressors, recovery, and performance begins by prioritizing the fundamentals of high performance. For elite athletes and leaders, sometimes the fundamentals are easily overlooked. Being so basic, it takes intentional effort to pay attention to them, and if they are neglected, performance suffers. Leaders must pay attention to the fundamentals to perform at their best. The basics come first before other leadership tasks unfold.

The First Work is a critical competency for leaders who want to be skilled at navigating complexity. The First Work includes a spectrum of strategies, actions, and behaviors that foster and maintain holistic well-being. The First Work is vital for high-performance leadership. Putting it succinctly, to lead well, one must be well.

LEADING IS WHOLE-BEING WORK

Acknowledging Our Wholeness

Leadership emanates from the holistic self, which includes our physical, emotional, intellectual, and spiritual dimensions. These dimensions comprise our whole being. That means that leading—all the approaches, actions, and behaviors we deploy to generate leadership—results from the entirety of our being, encapsulated in a human body. Leaders sometimes overlook this. They forget about their bodies. Moreover, leaders do not merely *have* a body; they *are* a body. Leaders are embodied, holistic beings that "work" within and with a system.

The Multifaceted Demands of Healthcare Leadership

Leaders challenge, and are challenged by, the systems they lead. Those challenges stress the leader's holistic self. By "stress," I don't just mean emotional tension. I refer to more-global adaptive challenges or external pressures. In this sense, stress is a stimulus that provokes an adaptive response in all the domains of our being. A leader cannot escape this adaptive response. It is part of what it means to be alive, inherent in our nature.

Leading healthcare is a multifaceted, adaptive challenge to this embodied holistic self. The challenges press and test leaders on all fronts: physically, emotionally, intellectually, and spiritually. The varied and comprehensive stressors that leaders experience are similar to what athletes encounter when training.

Parallels With Elite Athletes

Athletes take full advantage of adaptive challenges. A training regimen is the intentional application of stressors to solicit an adaptive response. For example, athletes practice repetitive movements, stressing the body to ingrain physical skills, like spending hours on the driving range practicing a golf swing. The involved domains of their being adapt to the athlete's practice regimen. That's how athletes improve their performance.

Practice for elite athletes is multisystem. In addition to conditioning and strength exercises stressing the physical body, athletes practice repetitive visualization and meditative practices, stressors on the mind. They learn to be on a team and compete against others, challenging and growing meaningful relationships. Some draw upon their faith to bring a sense of purpose and meaning to their sport.

A successful training program is a harmonious, intentional, and comprehensive challenge to the athlete's holistic self. It engages and tests the athletes on all fronts, soliciting an adaptive response in multiple domains. We recognize a successful adaptive response to these intentional stressors as improved performance on the field of play.

Like elite athletes training for peak performance, healthcare leaders face challenges that stress their whole being. Unlike athletes, who can control the stressors they encounter with the help of a skilled coach, the stressors a leader encounters are primarily unstructured and unrelenting. The unplanned nature of the challenges poses significant hazards for a leader. While leaders always adapt to stressors, in some cases, the adaptations lead to success; in others, they do not. That's why leaders must carefully consider their stressors and how they maximize an adaptive response.

The Fundamentals of Elite Performance

Leaders and athletes must pay close attention to fundamentals to achieve peak performance. For example, the fundamentals of basketball include the mechanics of taking a shot. For swimming, it's head position and breathing. For golf, it's the grip on the club.

Every endeavor has a set of fundamentals required to perform well. If people neglect the fundamentals, they will not perform at an elite level. While fundamentals vary, they are always nonnegotiable necessities. You cannot achieve peak performance in any discipline without attending to the fundamentals of that discipline.

Fundamental to leadership are the approaches, actions, and behaviors necessary to maximize the natural adaptive response to stressors. One fundamental is *recovery*.

Human beings do not adapt during periods of stress. They adapt after periods of stress, during recovery. If recovery is inadequate, improvement doesn't occur, and peak performance is impossible. Importantly, this fact applies to all domains of our being, not just the physical. Adapting, growing, and reaching full performance potential depends on adequately recovering from stressors.

For athletes, this means taking time between training sessions and incorporating active and passive recovery work such as rest, stretching, and massage. For leaders, the nonnegotiable fundamental of recovery is the First Work.

THE FIRST WORK

The First Work Described

The First Work refers to a suite of leadership approaches, actions, and behaviors that foster and sustain holistic well-being. It is the leadership work that creates recovery. The First Work enables an adaptive response to the stressors inherent in leading. The First Work is:

▸ The First Work of Physical Health: This domain involves a nutritious diet and regular exercise that builds strength, balance, and stamina. It includes sufficient sleep, preventive care, and avoiding risky behaviors such as not wearing seatbelts or other activities that risk disability or death.

▸ The First Work of Mental Health: While physical well-being strongly and favorably influences mental health, distinct cognitive strategies, such as self-reflection and reframing negative thoughts, are essential. Lifelong learning and creative endeavors cultivate a resilient, adaptive mindset that sustains mental well-being.

▸ The First Work of Emotional Health: Growing and attending to emotional expression and awareness fosters a leader's ability to forge authentic, trust-based relationships characterized by empathy, compassion, and humility. This intentional practice enhances emotional resilience.

▸ The First Work of Spiritual Health: Meditative practices, mindfulness, and faith-based activities help ground leaders in a profound sense of meaning. Exercised with discernment, it can enhance a leader's ethical decision-making, emotional resilience, and ability to foster community. It can also encourage empathy, long-term thinking, and adaptability in irreducible uncertainty.

▸ The First Work of Relational Health: Humans need nurturing, meaningful, positive relationships to be healthy. Devoting time and attention to partners, family, and community helps leaders as individuals find purpose and meaning in their lives and work.

Why Is It First?

The First Work is first because everything else leaders do suffers if it is absent. It is a bedrock body of work that leads to and sustains health, upon which leading well is established. The First Work is recovery. Without it, adaptability fails, and leadership suffers. That's why recovery is fundamental—the inescapable first contributor to peak performance. Therefore, the First Work comes before any other leadership work.

Why Is It Work?

The tight connection between leadership success and the First Work moves it away from the *life* side of a work-life balance equation to the *work* side. The First Work is critical work for leading well. This means the First Work is not play, not a nice-to-have, or some add-on to a day, trying to squeeze it in if you can. The First Work is fundamental, critical, bedrock leadership *work*.

The First Work isn't easy to do. It takes planning, preparation, an investment of resources, daily effort, commitment, grit, and trade-offs. Most importantly, it takes time. It sounds a lot like work because it *is* work.

IF THE FIRST WORK IS INADEQUATE

Maladaptation in Leaders

Our holistic self is in a constant tussle with leadership environments and their attendant challenges. The tussle generates tension and pressure, which are stressors. Those stressors unavoidably cause an adaptive response.

In leadership, sustained stress, pressure, tension, fatigue, or anxiety—being under duress—coupled with inadequate recovery overwhelms the adaptive capacity and capability of the leader. That results in an unsuitable response or maladaptation. (See Mindset 3—Adaptability)

An Example of Maladaptation in Leaders

Blair is a new CEO who prefers to be direct and make quick, reasoned decisions. She is more willing to take risks than most. While relationships matter to her, she is most concerned about results. She prefers to stick to business in her communication, being clear, specific, brief, and concise. If others bring innovative ideas or suggestions, Blair prefers that they bring compelling data and information to support them. The board of directors hired Blair in part because her behavioral preferences matched the organization's needs.

As time went on, inevitably, her stressors increased. When her stressors reached moderate levels, Blair's behaviors shifted. Others began to experience her as demanding, egotistical, and aggressive. Blair became abrasive, controlling, and opinionated when the stressors became extreme.

Blair's set of behavioral preferences are unique to her. Every leader has their own, and like Blair, everyone changes their behaviors under duress. A leader's change in behavior under duress is almost always detrimental to their success.

Even though her behavior changes were significant, Blair didn't fully appreciate how others were experiencing her. Few leaders do when they are under duress. She believed her behavior changes were mild and necessary. If others told her about what they noticed, she thought their complaints reflected resistance to her ideas and the changes she was enacting.

Blair responded to her increasing stressors in a typical way: she worked more. Consequently, Blair set aside her yoga, meditation, and gardening routines. It was hard to find the time for those things. Additionally, she was new to the community, having moved from out of state to take the job. She was also alone after a recent divorce.

Months after moving, she had yet to unpack fully. Finding time to eat during the day was hard, so she lost weight. Long days at work led to late nights, living on take-out. Dinners were alone, sitting on the floor, food atop unpacked boxes. She wasn't sleeping well.

Blair's adaptive response—becoming an abrasive, controlling, and opinionated leader—didn't work well. The changes in her behavior reflected a genuine neurophysiological and psychological adaptation to her stressors. They resulted from her holistic self trying to adapt suitably to the stressors she faced.

Her adaptive responses, however, were unsuitable, because her adaptive capacity and capabilities were overwhelmed. Instead, she experienced a maladaptive leadership response, and the behaviors that came with it got in her way.

To be clear, the cause of her maladaptive behavior shift was not the stressors. It was her lack of attention to recovery. She wasn't doing the First Work. For Blair, that would have included her yoga, unpacking her home and making it a sanctuary, working to build meaningful relationships, and getting connected with her new community. Instead, she didn't have enough periods of recovery to adapt in suitable ways to the stressors she faced.

The Consequences of Prolonged Maladaptation

The usual approach in healthcare leadership is to skip the First Work. Like Blair, many leaders find their roles all-consuming, leaving little time for other things. Consequently, the stressors are prolonged and unrelenting, and recovery is absent. Neglecting First Work is a surefire way to undermine performance, sometimes ending a career. It's a surefire way to damage health, sometimes destroying it. Unaddressed, the resulting maladaptation is usually destructive.

For elite endurance athletes, persistently inadequate recovery causes a clinical condition called overtraining syndrome (OTS), a potentially career-ending maladaptive response to unremitting stress. It results in multisystem changes reflected in hormonal, immunological, neurological, and psychological disturbances. The only treatment for OTS is rest. Most athletes who succumb to OTS never perform at the same level, even after adequate rest and recovery.[48]

For leaders, inadequate recovery can precipitate burnout, a potentially career-derailing condition akin to OTS. Burnout manifests as a maladaptive response to persistent stress, characterized by a constellation of symptoms that include alterations in hormonal and immunological functions, cognitive impairments, and psychological disturbances. Just as athletes experience diminished performance, fatigue, mood changes, and increased susceptibility to illness due to overtraining, leaders facing burnout exhibit decreased effectiveness, exhaustion, emotional instability, and compromised health (table 4).

The parallels are not happenstance. Both conditions represent the maladaptive response in human beings when they experience unrelenting stress in the absence of recovery—a warping of the inherent adaptability of the holistic self.

This means that "what doesn't kill you makes you stronger" is a lie. What makes you stronger is *recovery* after stress. Working 24/7 is not a good thing, and it will never be. This is why the First Work is

PARAMETERS	OVERTRAINING IN ATHLETES	BURNOUT IN LEADERS
Physical Symptoms		
• Fatigue	●	●
• Insomnia or Disturbed Sleep	●	●
• Decreased Performance	●	●
• Frequent Illness or Infection	●	●
• Muscle and Joint Pain	●	○
• Headache	●	●
Emotional Symptoms		
• Irritability/Cynicism	●	●
• Anxiety	●	●
• Depressive Mood/ Depression	●	●
• Lack of Motivation	●	●
• Emotional Exhaustion	●	●
Cognitive Symptoms		
• Decreased Concentration	●	●
• Impaired Judgment	●	●
Social Impact		
• Social Withdrawal	●	●
• Interpersonal Conflict	○	●
Performance		
• Decreased Efficacy	●	●
• Disengagement	●	●
• Career Derailment	●	●

TABLE 4. *Comparison of Overtraining Syndrome and Burnout Signs and Symptoms.* ● = commonly observed, ○ = generally not observed. (Source: Table 4 is an aggregation of multiple sources, including the personal experiences of the author, Michael Hein, as an athlete, coach of elite athletes and physician, in collaboration with ChatGPT, Open AI, November 8, 2023.)

imperative. The First Work is a body of leadership recovery work that the best-performing leaders focus on first.

THE ORTHODOX MINDSET ABOUT THE FIRST WORK:
First Work Is Optional

The orthodox mindset about the First Work is that it is not work. It may be considered important, but it is neglected routinely by leaders because it's on the *life* side of the work-life equation. Therefore, it is not part of leadership work. When leadership's "real" work increases, the First Work becomes another item that gets considered and then, too often, deprioritized. The First Work, therefore, is optional.

EXPRESSIONS OF THE ORTHODOX MINDSET

You can identify an orthodox mindset by noticing how you and others relate to the First Work. Expressions of the orthodox mindset are ignoring and marginalizing the First Work and exhibiting maladaptation.

Ignoring the First Work

Ignoring the First Work manifests when it's absent in routine dialogue. It isn't a topic of discussion among peers during casual conversations. No one shares or asks about restoration during your last vacation. They may ask where you went, whether you had a lovely time, or if your kids behaved well. But there's no curiosity about how your vacation helped you recover, restore, or rejuvenate as a leader. For example, you don't share, nor does anyone ask, about the long weekend you spent participating in a silent retreat at the local Benedictine monastery. The First Work is just not part of the discourse in the workplace.

Its absence may indicate that others don't practice the First Work, so there's nothing to discuss. Or they may practice the First Work and not discuss it, because they don't think it's leadership work. Regardless, its absence as a topic of interest at an organizational level is an indicator.

Other indicators are that well-being, self-care, or reflective practice are not present on formal agendas. There are no professional development opportunities focusing on personal growth and restoration. Conferences, developmental work, and retreat schedules go from 7 a.m. to 5:00 p.m., with a 30-minute lunch. The social hour and dinner follow, starting at 6:00 p.m. There's no reasonable time in the day for people to pay attention to the First Work unless they're willing to shorten their sleep, skip part of the day, and risk absence.

A typical workday calendar mirrors another indicator: the "always on" leader, who doesn't appear to take time for restoration. The approach of the "always on" leader implies an absence of the First Work. They may be doing it, but their observable behaviors and actions convey that they are not. A packed calendar and constant connection are an unspoken message that the First Work is something to ignore.

Marginalizing the First Work

Another way leaders express an orthodox mindset is by pushing the First Work into the margins, squeezing it in somewhere in the day. The notion of a work-life balance fuels marginalization. *Balance* is a time equation problem to solve, pitting work and life against each other to reach a détente. It is a zero-sum competition, with the First Work on the equation's life side.

Given that the demands of work and life fluctuate wildly, for most, any notion of balance remains elusive. Moreover, the needs of leadership are pervasive and relentless, creating significant pressure to work more and live less. Consequently, the First Work gets pushed to the margins of life.

A contributing factor is the idea of managing time. The Industrial Era brought us the notion that time is a finite resource to be divided, allocated, and optimized for maximum productivity. We now use time to manage work, aiming for maximal efficiency. Packed calendars and long days are a result. If calendars are full of work, there's little time left for the First Work. It gets pushed to the margins.

Achieving maximal productivity by managing time has an aim—an outcome, a product, or a result. This outcome-focused approach tends to value the results more than the process. In this case, achieving results from leadership work matters most. The way to achieve those results quickly is by maximizing work through the efficient use of time. The amount of time contributed depends on how much is necessary to attain the desired outcome. In other words, the end tends to justify the means.

A consequence is enormous pressure to take as much work time as necessary to achieve results promptly. To accomplish that, leaders allocate more time to work, leaving less time for other endeavors, including the First Work. So First Work gets marginalized.

Exhibiting Maladaptation

When leaders behave in ways that harm their leadership or the organization, it most likely represents a maladaptive response. As we noticed with Blair, the key is that absent sufficient recovery, leaders maladapt, and their behaviors are the indicator.

It may seem odd that we choose self-defeating behaviors when maladapting. But what's occurring is the brain is perceiving the stressors and subsequent maladaptation as a social threat, perhaps risking a leader's status. A leader may make sense of the threat in several ways, but all leaders reach for familiar self-protection strategies that have previously kept them safe. These strategies are almost always unhelpful.

It's relatively easy to see maladaptive self-protective behaviors in others. It's much more difficult to notice them in ourselves. As we are entering a maladaptive state, we may have some sense that things are askew. We feel unsettled. Our lives seem narrower, smaller, or closed.

A sense of hope and opportunity escapes us. It feels like everything in our lives revolves around work.

Further along into a maladaptive state, we may have some sense that we're not at our best with others. Whatever our behavioral inclinations, they become amplified, a warping of what are usually our strengths.

Unhelpful behavioral shifts are an early indicator of a maladaptive state, the inevitable consequence of prolonged periods of ignoring and marginalizing the First Work.

THE UNORTHODOX MINDSET ABOUT THE FIRST WORK:
First Work Is Mandatory

The unorthodox mindset about the First Work begins with the understanding that sustained high performance, including leadership, depends upon a holistic self that is well. If there is a rigorous focus on operational outcomes, there is an equally rigorous focus on the holistic well-being of leaders and their teams. The First Work is the mandatory, nonnegotiable, foundational leadership work that enables a sustained focus on results.

EXPRESSIONS OF THE UNORTHODOX MINDSET

You can identify an unorthodox mindset by noticing how you and others relate to the First Work. Expressions of the unorthodox mindset are attending to and promoting the First Work, while exhibiting adaptability.

Attending to the First Work

When the unorthodox mindset about the First Work is present, it's not just a topic of conversation. It is that. But the First Work is also getting done. Because it's getting done, it's a natural part of the banter and discussion among colleagues.

The entire team knows some details about a colleague's recent cycling trip in the wilds of Utah. There's a discussion about the chief operating officer's experience and learnings at a yoga retreat in Arizona.

Considerable curiosity exists about what people do to build resilience, recover, and rejuvenate. Because the First Work is considered a critical component of successful leadership, it finds its way into meeting agendas, events, calendars, and friendly banter.

Not only do people cultivate interest in the First Work through curiosity and discussion, but they also serve as guardians and protectors of the First Work. There's a vigilance for the deterioration of energy states or aberrant behaviors in themselves and others. When noticed, it solicits a check-in. These brief moments, often in private, are inquiries about how things are going with the First Work.

What underlies these discussions is that the leaders have informally, and sometimes formally, committed themselves and others to the First Work. A compact arises between them—we do the First Work around here. What follows is accountability among the team, keeping the First Work at the forefront of what they are trying to accomplish together. Consequently, there is active, ongoing, deliberate attention to the First Work.

Promoting the First Work

We can see the unorthodox mindset when leaders promote the First Work, pulling it away from the margins of life and making it central to work—an essential, bedrock leadership discipline.

Paying attention to the First Work in routine discourse promotes its stature. Beyond that, there's active promotion, when an organization offers a monthly day off for rejuvenation. Another team routinely discourages email exchanges after hours and on the weekends. A CEO insists that her leader stay home when ill. She checks in later, encouraging her colleague to rest, recover, and avoid work.

One organization I worked with actively promoted First Work by including well-being in its strategic plan, establishing metrics and measures to monitor and increase its stature and persistence in its corporate culture. In another organization, the executive team has an annual three-month-long fitness and diet challenge, logging time spent exercising and counting days where they followed some elements of a dietary regimen. They celebrate the winners with a small cash award and considerable bragging rights for the rest of the year.

Leaders actively promote the First Work in multiple ways. They express their expectations that it gets done and make their own practice of it obvious. These leaders promote the First Work, because it's central and essential to leading well. It isn't optional. It's mandatory.

Exhibiting Adaptability

When leadership is challenging, as it is in complex healthcare organizations, and leaders are at ease amid complexity, I say they are "holding their role well." Holding a role well describes a global behavioral portfolio that reflects adaptability.

When we have the capacity and capability to adapt, and those adaptations are suitable for our context, that's adaptability. When leaders adapt suitably to the stressors they face, their approaches are well-matched to their context. In that case, we observe leaders who seem to be with their role in ways that suit them well. They are more at ease in their work and seem to have the energy and wit to navigate all the challenges that come their way.

These leaders can stay curious, open to multiple perspectives, retain optimism, and see opportunities in their challenges. They are more inclusive, trust their teams to complete the work, and are more facilitators than commanders.

These observable behaviors are unlikely to be entirely innate. More likely, among the many mindsets they hold, they believe that the First

Work is mandatory. They think the First Work is essential to leading well. So they do the First Work and promote it, while paying attention to it in others.

MAKING THE SHIFT
Before the Shift

Understand the First Work Imperative

The issue I encounter most when discussing this aspect of leadership with executives is convincing them that the First Work is leadership work. My dialogue with them reminds me of similar discussions with my patients. Trying to persuade patients to eat healthily, exercise, and keep their weight down to avoid high blood pressure, diabetes, or heart disease was notoriously tricky. But that didn't diminish the fundamental necessity to do so or the validity behind my recommendations. The same applies as I implore leaders to pay attention to the First Work.

You are a *corporate athlete*.[49] You cannot lead well unless you are well.[50] Your recovery must match your stress. It is not optional if you want to succeed in complex healthcare organizations. You are not an exception to nature. You have a body. That body of yours is your leadership platform. Everything you are or will be as a leader depends on your body's health and fitness. If it is unfit, so is your leadership. It is that simple.

Before you shift, you must understand and accept that caring for your whole being is inescapably *leadership work.* Please, please do it. You will be a much better leader in complexity if you do.

Draw Upon Your Experience

You likely have experience with the First Work. You've tried things you liked and others you didn't. Some First Work stuck with you, and some quickly slipped away. Likely, you learned valuable things about yourself as you experimented with and practiced the First Work. Maybe you found that you had to exercise in the morning or you wouldn't get to it, being too tired and uninterested after a long day. Perhaps you found yoga surprisingly helpful physically, emotionally, and spiritually. Those insights into your nature are clues that can help you find and sustain a First Work routine.

Before you shift, reflect on what has hindered your ability to stick with the First Work. Identify what things got in your way before and consider strategies to avoid or address those barriers. In essence, look for patterns that didn't work, learn from them, and avoid them this time. Build upon those insights. Do this before you attempt to make the First Work central to your leadership work.

WHY SHIFT

It Mitigates the Strain of Complexity

Attempting to lead complex healthcare organizations takes a toll. Complexity is tough to deal with. Burnout, the maladaptive response to unrelenting stress, is high in healthcare senior executives. That is worrisome, because burnout correlates to increased depression, suicide, and inferior performance. Not to mention increased departures from executive positions, whether voluntary or involuntary.

In 2022, Witt-Kiefer reported that 74 percent of executive healthcare leaders had felt burnout in the previous six months.[51] Of those who reported burnout, 43 percent often or always thought about leaving their position. Many were looking to leave the industry. Indeed, the median tenure of hospital CEOs in the U.S. is about 3.5 years, representing a 16 percent annual turnover rate.[52]

The First Work is a means of mitigating these consequences of complexity. It's a potent antidote, one particularly effective if it's part of the corporate culture.

It Contributes to the Bottom Line

The First Work isn't merely a well-being issue. It's a bottom-line concern. High turnover from burnout disrupts continuity, incurs recruitment costs, and can destabilize long-term strategic initiatives. Burnout and turnover consequences cascade down the organizational hierarchy, affecting the entire workforce. Burnout negatively affects clinical outcomes, clinical productivity, and patient satisfaction.

Shifting your leadership focus to integrate the First Work fundamentally reorients this dynamic. It prioritizes the process of being well in order to lead well, placing equal importance on how things get done rather than just focusing on results. Promoting the First Work with others and doing it yourself doesn't just mitigate burnout and attrition. You create an organizational culture that is more agile, humane, and capable of navigating the inherent complexities of healthcare. Paying attention to the First Work is not a distraction. It increases the likelihood of bottom-line success.

It Nurtures the Adaptive Arena

Complex systems must have a robust Adaptive Arena to excel. The Adaptive Arena in a complex organization is a challenging and demanding domain. Success within the Adaptive Arena is dependent upon a leader's adaptability.

When an outcome-focused approach dominates, it deemphasizes the means of achieving those outcomes. Consequently, well-being garners little attention, even though it is essential to the workforce and to a leader's adaptability. An excessively results-focused approach can starve the Adaptive Arena of adaptive capacity by disregarding The First Work. However, the First Work is the source of the vital energy necessary in the Adaptive Arena for emergence, the adaptation engine of complex organizations. If the First Work is absent, the Adaptive Arena is in peril.

Organizational stagnation often follows, as the workforce staggers under the weight of the many and varied stressors inherent in complex organizations. Without robust attention to, promotion of, capacity for, and ability to do the First Work, those in the Adaptive Arena cannot adapt suitably.

If leaders desire a workforce that moves swiftly, with resilience and creativity, in the face of innumerable challenges and dynamic change, they must attend to and promote the First Work. It can't be limited to a handful of enlightened executives. An organizational culture that cares for the whole person is only achievable if leaders live out the First Work while encouraging and expecting everyone else to do the same.

HOW TO SHIFT

Seek Harmony, Not Balance

Work and life are not problems to be solved. They are a polarity awaiting harmony. To shift, you must jettison the notion of finding a balance between them, because it forces an unnecessary choice between two opposites. It is also unachievable and marginalizes the First Work. Rather than seek balance, seek harmony among the many domains of your being, including your work.

Leaders who successfully make a shift move away from strictly compartmentalizing their lives into work and life, meticulously trying to allocate equivalent time to each. Instead, they move toward harmony by setting clear priorities *for their life* and establishing boundaries that allow for flexibility. They stay mindful about where they focus their energy, ensuring work and life each receive their due.

It's not about carving out a perfect equilibrium between the two. It's about fostering an interplay where each aspect informs and enhances the other, leading to a dynamic, holistic integration, tailored to one's authentic way of being in the world. Harmonizing still requires choices about where to spend energy. Sometimes, those choices are tough. The path to harmony is not always an easy one.

Manage Your Energy, Not Your Time

Leaders making the shift move away from managing time to managing energy.[53] They cultivate a high-energy state to which they align their most demanding work.

High-energy periods are part of your circadian rhythms, naturally waxing and waning. So these high-energy periods are limited in duration but occur in a patterned way.

You already have a sense of what time of the day your energy is at its peak. For example, early-rising morning people are likely at their peak energy state in the mornings. Night owls typically experience their peak energy state in the evenings.

Leaders shift by learning to take advantage of their rhythms, ordering work around energy, not a calendar. The calendar becomes a tool for matching work with high-energy states rather than a tool to match work with available time.

When managing energy and not time, activities that rejuvenate and renew become critical to performance. These leaders appreciate the high-energy costs associated with complexity and work to mitigate the risk to their performance by putting the First Work front and center in their leadership. The First Work becomes the fountain of energy necessary for leadership, mitigating maladaptation. Absent, the energy wells from which the leader draws dry up, leaving them unable to adapt suitably.

Find a Nonnegotiable Routine

Finding a nonnegotiable routine begins with a decision that declares where the First Work belongs in your preferred way of being in the world. One of my clients said, "I switched the First Work from my *wish* list to my *will* list." He began his shift by declaring his intentions. His statement encapsulates the beginning place for most of us when contemplating a change in our approaches, actions, or behaviors.

The routine you seek is nonnegotiable, because the First Work is both fundamental and foundational to your leadership; it belongs among the things in your life that you pay attention to before anything else. Once established, it becomes an immutable aspect of your schedule. Other commitments rarely override your commitment to the First Work. Over time, it becomes a habit you consistently adhere to and even need. It is indispensable for being the leader you need and want to be in complexity.

What makes it a routine is that it happens regularly, in a patterned cadence. There are three levels of your First Work routine to pay attention to: the micro-, meso-, and macro-routines.

- **Micro-First Work** happens multiple times daily and lasts just a few minutes. A notable example is taking a few minutes to meditate at lunch and during breaks. It may be taking a cleansing breath or a reflection before every meeting. It's "micro" because it's brief, frequent, and impactful.

- **Meso-First Work** occurs no more than once a day but at least weekly. The typical meso-First Work is an early-morning routine that includes exercise, meditative practice, spending time with family, and visualizing significant interactions forthcoming in your day. It doesn't have to be in the morning. For many, it is daily. If not, leaders do the work on specific days of the week. The critical thing is that it happens at least once a week.

- **Macro-First Work** occurs just a few times a year. For example, taking a holiday every quarter, or a two-week vacation twice a year. Ideally, work doesn't come with you on your holiday or vacation. However, some leaders find reading about leadership, thinking about high-level strategy, noodling ideas, and reflecting on their overall performance rejuvenating. That works for them, and it may work for you too. The essential thing is to make sure you are working on recovery. From a First Work perspective, recovery must be the primary focus and outcome of your vacations and holidays.

Everyone is different, and no routines are the same. But the most adept leaders follow this pattern: micro-, meso-, and macro-routines of the First Work.

MINDSET EIGHT—PURPOSE

AN UNORTHODOX MINDSET ABOUT WHY

Purpose Is Trustworthy

ILLUSTRATION 8. *Purpose Is Trustworthy*. People make better autonomous decisions if they know the purpose.

UNDERSTANDING PURPOSE

Leaders do better in complexity when they know their personal purpose and act on it. That's because purpose grounds leaders amid uncertainty, offering resilience in the face of change. When so much is unknowable, purpose guides leaders like a compass. Not only is purpose a trustworthy compass, but it also moves people and organizations forward in a coordinated way.

DEFINING PURPOSE

Purpose is a fundamental reason for being. It is like bedrock, anchoring our lives, while providing direction and meaning. It answers the profound question, "Why do I exist?"

Living out our purpose is not just about pursuing personal fulfillment. Purpose moves us toward something larger than ourselves, working in us and through others to create a legacy that lasts. In this way, purpose acts as a powerful force. Harnessing the power of purpose can lead to extraordinary outcomes, both personally and professionally.

Our purpose derives from the core values we hold, our lived experiences, and the insights we have about life and the world around us. Our values, experiences, and insights contribute to our beliefs, philosophies, and mental models. All these elements coalesce and shape our sense of purpose.

Our purpose can change, but it generally remains stable, a consistent force at work in us over long periods. If it does change, it usually deepens or widens to accommodate new experiences or insights. Our purpose is like a river that flows through our lives, following a well-worn channel; yet its path may alter after floods or other disruptive events.

Every person and organization have purpose, whether known or not. Finding our purpose takes work, but it is knowable. Knowing our purpose matters, because it motivates our approaches, actions, and behaviors. In other words, purpose *moves* us.

Purpose and Motivation

Leading is about moving organizations and people forward, which requires motivation. One approach to understanding different motivators is to classify them as either *extrinsic* or *intrinsic*.

Extrinsic motivators exist outside of us. Common extrinsic motivators are money, promotions, or praise—anything external that moves us to meet expectations or follow demands and requests.

Intrinsic motivators, on the other hand, are internal to us. They draw upon personal desires and core values, moving us to pursue things that satisfy us, are in our self-interest, or are worthy of our lives. Purpose connects us with all these qualities. So purpose is an intrinsic motivator, and it is a powerful one.

Leaders use purpose by knowing and combining it with the personal purposes of others. This approach generates a sense of shared purpose. Leaders can also work to align shared purpose with organizational purpose. In this way, leaders use purpose as a powerful intrinsic motivator, moving people and entire organizations forward in a coordinated way.

Purpose and Effectiveness

A leader can use purpose to advance their effectiveness. The leader may be intrinsically motivated by their purpose and choose to rely on extrinsic motivators when leading others. Or a leader may choose to connect their purpose with others, relying on intrinsic motivation through shared purpose. Either way, purpose is often a pivotal motivator.

If the leader taps into purpose, it will shape the approaches, actions, and behaviors they choose—the "how." Those choices determine the attained outcomes and results—the "what." Effectiveness for leaders is achieving the "what." But effectiveness is more than that—otherwise, the end would always justify the means. That's why effectiveness includes *how* leaders achieve results. For instance, a leader's ability to nurture individual growth and collaboration while adhering to ethical standards is also effective leadership.

An effective leader does not merely reach a goal. They pay attention to *how* they reach the goal. With purpose in mind, effective leadership begins with purpose—the "why." That leads to an effective, purpose-driven "how," which generates certain results, the "what."

THE PURPOSE-PASSIVE LEADER

Sometimes, leaders aren't well connected to purpose. Perhaps leaders aren't aware of their purpose, or how they lead doesn't align with it. Very few leaders are entirely detached from a sense of purpose, but it happens. Regardless of the reasons, I broadly categorize leaders not well connected to purpose as "purpose-passive" leaders. Purpose-passive leaders may not have a sense of purpose, or they don't engage with it for assorted reasons.

Suppose purpose is entirely absent from a leader. In that case, it may be that the leader questions or denies purpose. Perhaps that results from an existential crisis, or the leader believes life inherently lacks purpose.

More likely, purpose is present in the leader but *unrealized*. The leader may not yet know or understand what their purpose is. Or maybe the leader knows their purpose but has yet to consistently align their approaches, actions, and behaviors with it. In that case, the leader hasn't integrated purpose into their life choices or careers. Their purpose is present but *unaligned*.

Then again, perhaps a leader knows their purpose but has disengaged from it due to burnout or disillusionment. In that case, their purpose is present but *unattached*.

An Example of Purpose-Passive Leadership

Consider John, known throughout his organization as a no-nonsense operator. He is an exacting, detail-focused, and metric-driven fellow. People experience him as intense and demanding, constantly focused on achieving measurable results quickly. Throughout his thirty-year career, John's approach has yielded increased productivity and efficiency whenever he took on a new role. His new teams typically respond to his approaches, delivering tangible results quickly.

For many, those kinds of results exemplify leadership effectiveness. John had a long history of that kind of effectiveness, fueling his career path for decades.

John knew his purpose but rarely integrated it into his leadership. He chose not to expose that part of himself to others, thinking it was too personal. John's leadership was *unaligned* with his purpose.

That was one reason John focused on tangible, short-term gains. He believed that effective leaders consistently achieve results, something he called "wins." Achieving results motivated John, because he liked to win. For him, that was the purpose of leadership.

Where John saw "wins," his team saw an endless stream of meaningless metrics. So John's team lacked purpose in their work. They felt the transactional nature of John's leadership and struggled with sustained engagement and resilience.

John's approach relied on extrinsic motivators, and that fostered flagging motivation among his team, reflecting poorly on John's effectiveness. Consequently, John typically remained in positions for about three years, choosing to leave whenever he sensed decreased performance in response to his leadership. At other times, John was let go because his teams or peers grew weary of his approach.

Like John, purpose-passive leaders tend to focus on short-term, measurable results. They are motivated by those results and expect others to be as well. These leaders tend to rely on extrinsic motivators, which lose potency over time. Many find the transactional work this approach fosters intolerable. In response, they seek other opportunities that offer a more purpose-driven environment or actively work to remove the leader.

THE PURPOSE-DRIVEN LEADER

On the other hand, if leaders know their purpose and integrate it into their approaches, actions, and behaviors, they are purpose-driven. For these leaders, purpose is a dependable and powerful motivational force.

These leaders share their purpose, which inspires and motivates others intrinsically. That draws others to the leader, creating close connections united by purpose. Like ripples in a pond, shared purpose tends to spread from one person to another. Over time, a shared purpose can ripple through the entire organization. If that happens, purpose becomes a powerful way to unite and coordinate organizational movement. Shared purpose can become part of what others have called "shared consciousness."[54]

Purpose also fosters tenacity and adaptability as the leader and team face challenges. Intrinsic motivation has more staying power than extrinsic motivation, so those motivated in this way persevere. That's how purpose reliably keeps people moving forward together in ever-changing conditions. Purpose-driven people can excel amid change, staying focused on long-term impact while effectively addressing immediate demands.

An Example of Purpose-Driven Leadership

Stefani was the purpose-driven CEO of 65 primary care clinics. She routinely shared her purpose: to bring healing through loving relationships. Her team trusted her, because her approaches, actions, and behaviors consistently reflected her stated purpose. Kindness, civility, and compassion dominated her leadership style, whether with patients, providers, or team members.

In an ongoing dialogue about what living out "healing through loving relationships" looked like in primary care, Stefani found many who shared her purpose. Over time, the leadership team adopted patient-centered care principles aligned with their shared purpose. They incorporated those principles into the core values of the clinics, which then served as guideposts and accountability standards for everyone.

Stefani continuously worked to foster a team culture deeply committed to "healing through loving relationships." She consistently connected the work anyone did with this co-created, shared purpose. By doing this, Stefani cultivated a shared consciousness throughout the organization.

Shared consciousness offered directional clarity about why they did what they did, as well as how they went about doing it. Their shared consciousness informed the strategic choices they made. It informed their hiring decisions and how they defined success.

Stefani's approach led the organization to outperform others clinically and financially. Workforce turnover was low. Physician engagement was high, as was team-member satisfaction. Stefani and her organization were highly regarded and sought out for advice.

Purpose-driven leaders like Stefani tend to focus on long-term results. The ongoing realization of purpose motivates these leaders and those around them. The dependence on intrinsic motivation cultivates an environment where everyone sees the connection between their co-created "why" and their daily "how" and "what." Many find this kind of workplace transformational. People stick around, love their work, and give more than what's called for.

THE ORTHODOX MINDSET ABOUT PURPOSE:
A Trustworthy Road Map in Known Territory

Both purpose-passive and purpose-driven leaders can hold an orthodox mindset about purpose. A purpose-passive leader with an orthodox mindset will craft a trustworthy road map to achieve the leader's vision. A purpose-driven leader will do the same, but the vision will align with their purpose. Moreover, these leaders will rely heavily on their past experiences and expertise—known territory—to make decisions and to tell others how to realize the vision they created.

EXPRESSIONS OF THE ORTHODOX MINDSET

Expressions of the orthodox mindset are approaches, actions, and behaviors intended to create coordinated organizational movement. You can find an orthodox mindset in yourself or others by noticing the common expressions of this mindset: leading with "what," relying on extrinsic motivation, and exhibiting rigidity.

Leading with "What"

Leaders with an orthodox mindset tend to lead with the "what"—their vision for the organization. That vision may be unrelated or loosely connected to an organizational purpose. If purpose serves at all, it is secondary to vision. In essence, orthodox-minded leaders aim to create a *shared vision*.

Creating a shared vision of the future is paramount to these leaders' success. To be effective, they must gain buy-in to the vision they created. So these leaders strive to inspire and persuade others to pursue the vision, and pursuing the vision is accomplished by following a plan.

Leading with "what" is characterized by detailed planning and a focus on metrics. Leaders usually approach this from the top and then work to spread the work through initiatives and directives. That creates a centrally planned path toward the vision, primarily relying on extrinsic motivators. In this case, realizing the vision *is* the organizational purpose.

Consider Daniel, the CEO of a regional multihospital organization. His vision was an organization that operated at a 15 percent EBIDTA so that they would have the capital resources necessary to invest in regional growth. Daniel aggressively pressured all the hospital presidents to achieve the budget targets assigned to them. The plan focused on productivity targets and workforce reductions necessary to achieve the vision.

Laura was one of those presidents. She led several rural hospitals where payer mix, demographics, and provider constraints challenged her organization. Concerned about the impact of Daniel's unrelenting pressure and plan, Laura worked with her team to reinvent ways of delivering care in their region, using fewer resources. When Laura advanced some of those solutions to Daniel, he was unimpressed. Daniel told Laura that it wasn't her job to derive innovative solutions. Instead, she was to follow the plan and execute it quickly. In Daniel's view, pursuing creative ideas hindered Laura's ability to focus on her assigned tasks—innovation was a distraction.

To sustain motivation, Daniel repeatedly and publicly threatened the termination of hospital presidents, including Laura, if they could not achieve his monthly and quarterly targets.

There are benefits to Daniel's top-down, extrinsically motivated, directive-driven approach. It ensures unity, everyone strives to achieve the vision. It simplifies decision-making and gives clear directions and specific priorities. That can, indeed, be motivating for teams, helping them feel like everyone is working toward some well-defined goals. Expectations are clear, as are the consequences. Some leaders appreciate that kind of clarity.

Trusting Extrinsic Motivation

A leader's mindset about purpose uniquely influences where they place their trust. Like Daniel, leaders with an orthodox mindset about purpose trust their ability to see the future and motivate others to pursue it.

They also trust their road maps, the scripted sequence of steps to achieve the vision. Because a road map defines the path forward, it reduces uncertainty. It explains where the organization is going and how to get there. This approach rewards the team with clear success metrics, which tend to work as extrinsic motivators. As the team achieves the metrics, it affirms their capabilities, a form of external reward.

The road map often draws upon a leader's current and operational experiences, reflecting the assumption that their past experiences and strategies will be just as effective today as it was previously. Operating in this kind of known territory simplifies measures of success—the leader knows what must happen to achieve the vision. Working on the plan bolsters confidence—We are getting it done! Hitting the plan's predefined targets acts as extrinsic motivation, rewarding timeliness and defining success.

The road map also identifies individual performance that deviates from the path. It defines what is going right and what isn't. That distinction helps leaders hold others accountable. Noncompliance with the plan has consequences, including possible termination, another powerful extrinsic motivator.

There are consequences to depending on extrinsic motivation. Extrinsic motivators decrease a sense of autonomy, because they are transactional in nature. Extrinsic motivators involve a coercive exchange: the leader exerts control to generate efforts from others to realize a reward, follow a directive, or avoid punishment.

Leaders that exert control diminish autonomy (see Mindset 4—Power). Leaders can only take that so far before others rebel or resist. That's one of the reasons why extrinsic motivators have limits. Another is that their impact diminishes when the external factors are absent or removed, like achieving a short-term goal or removing punishment. Transactional exchanges do, indeed, motivate, working well for routine or straightforward tasks in the short-term. But they lack the depth and staying power necessary for creative, complex problem-solving.

An overreliance on extrinsic motivators often leads to decreased job satisfaction. Extrinsic motivators also reduce intrinsic motivation, a perilous loss for organizations requiring adaptability.

Leaders focused on extrinsic motivation may achieve quick wins. But those wins often come at the cost of long-term organizational health and team-member engagement.

Exhibiting Rigidity

A leader with an orthodox mindset about purpose focuses on achieving a vision measured by tangible results and tends to be intolerant of variations or deviations from the plan. Furthermore, operational metrics determine success and take precedence over deeper, purpose-driven goals, which are absent or considered less important.

These leaders lean toward directives, prioritizing control and compliance. They focus on and pressure others to execute assigned tasks, driving efficiency. Deviating from expected performance, or straying from the established road map, usually results in a vigorous rebuke and refocus. Their leadership focuses on strategic priorities and associated plans and initiatives. This unyielding focus creates rigidity, shaping an organizational culture that favors predictability and consistency over creativity. That kind of culture is suitable for stable environments but hinders adaptability and innovation, which is problematic in dynamic settings.

Furthermore, people who prefer a creative, adaptive, and innovative workplace leave the organization. The people who stay are those who prefer the clarity of predictability, prescribed work, and efficiency. Over time, this self-selection process creates a workplace that struggles with change and is uncomfortable with autonomy. That's how an orthodox mindset about purpose tends to foster a compliant workforce, reducing adaptive capacity and capability. In the long-term, an orthodox mindset about purpose creates organizational rigidity, making the organization resistant to change and unable to adapt.

THE UNORTHODOX MINDSET ABOUT PURPOSE:
A Trustworthy Compass in Unknown Territory

Leaders with an unorthodox mindset about purpose trust and rely on purpose to guide and motivate others to make good decisions that move the organization forward. In other words, purpose is a compass, not a road map.

The territory to traverse is unknown, because the current state is unlike anything encountered before. Past experiences and expertise contribute little toward accurately discerning a future.

Recall that it's always uncertain where the organization may end up in complex environments. So complex systems are constantly traversing unknown territory. That's why leaders with an unorthodox mindset about purpose trust and rely on purpose as an organizational compass. It's more trustworthy than vision.

EXPRESSIONS OF THE UNORTHODOX MINDSET

Expressions of the unorthodox mindset are approaches, actions, and behaviors intended to *co-create* coordinated organizational movement. You can see the unorthodox mindset at work in you or others by noticing the common expressions of this mindset: leading with "why," trusting intrinsic motivation, and exhibiting resilience.

Leading with "Why"

Leaders with an unorthodox mindset lead with "why"—approaches, actions, and behaviors aligned with purpose. They also connect and work with others to link their purpose with the organization's. Essentially, the unorthodox leader actively cultivates a *shared consciousness* rather than a shared vision. By shared consciousness, I mean that the unorthodox leader actively cultivates a shared understanding of and commitment to the "why" (purpose), rather than just the "what" (vision).

That doesn't render vision obsolete. Unlike the orthodox-minded leader, for whom vision defines purpose, for the unorthodox leader, purpose defines vision. In this way, purpose anchors the organization in the "why," while vision offers a dynamically changing "what." This purpose-driven approach fosters a coherent direction for the organization, albeit with a changeable destination. Shared consciousness is a compass, not a road map.

It's important to note that shared consciousness enables and is essential for adaptability. That's because shared consciousness draws upon diverse perspectives and is naturally inclusive. Furthermore, shared consciousness promotes and relies upon distributed leadership, tapping into and harnessing collective intelligence. Once unorthodox leaders cultivate shared consciousness, they trust and rely on it to inform the decisions made through distributed leadership. Others have called this kind of trust in shared consciousness "empowered execution."[55] Empowered execution characteristically results in a nimble, active, and resilient workforce.

The unorthodox leader cultivates shared consciousness by advancing and cultivating shared purpose. In this way, they not only lead with the "why," but they trust in and rely upon purpose to move the organization forward in a coordinated way.

Trusting Intrinsic Motivation

Purpose is a powerful intrinsic motivator, innate to people. Viktor Frankl, in his theory of logotherapy, suggested that the will to find meaning in life is a primary motivational force.[56] Research in cross-cultural psychology has shown that purpose and meaning are valued across diverse cultures.[57] From an evolutionary standpoint, having a sense of purpose may have provided social cohesion and cooperation benefits, contributing to survival and well-being. This suggests that purpose is a deep-rooted aspect of human nature, serving as a universal source of human motivation.[58]

There are individual differences, of course. So leaders must consider cultural variations and historical contexts when using purpose to motivate others. However, purpose as an intrinsic motivator is a universal human trait. That renders it trustworthy.

With that knowledge, leaders can cultivate shared consciousness, depending on it to guide the decisions of distributed leaders. That's how leaders with an unorthodox mindset about purpose motivate others and trust them to make good purpose-driven choices. Instead of relying on their abilities to craft a compelling vision, unorthodox leaders trust others to pursue purpose.

Building shared consciousness is not easy work. It requires leaders to know and be known by those who work with them. Leaders must recognize the diversity of purpose within their team and actively work to help align that diversity with the organizational purpose. They align that diversity by fostering an environment that welcomes and celebrates individual contributions. They also amplify connectivity through inter-action and robust information exchange.

In short, these leaders cultivate high-trust environments, where constructive conflict is the norm. Team members genuinely commit to the group's purpose-driven decisions and hold each other accountable for those commitments. Together, they are in hot pursuit of a co-created vision realized through shared consciousness.

Satya Nadella, CEO of Microsoft, did all of that.[59] He famously shifted Microsoft's culture by advancing a "growth mindset."[60] Nadella said the leadership team began their journey by "sharing their personal passions and philosophies," including their purpose.[61] The leadership team encouraged the workforce to be curious and try new things, finding solutions aligned with customer needs and organizational purpose. Leaders, including Nadella, explicitly encouraged the workforce to do things not found in the strategic plan, what they called "off-strategy" solutions.

Nadella also focused on promoting empathy as a critical cultural characteristic. He described empathy as knowing and understanding customers', employees', and partners' needs, perspectives, and purposes. Nadella believed empathy was essential for innovation and growth.

Nadella's emphasis on empathy and a growth mindset cultivated a cultural shift that reinvigorated Microsoft's purpose. That approach aligned the intrinsic motivations of its employees and customers, leading to innovations and strategies that resonated more effectively with customers. Nadella's unorthodox-minded, purpose-driven leadership drove Microsoft's resurgence and success.

Nadella became CEO of Microsoft in 2014. At the time, many thought Microsoft was irrelevant; it was losing out to innovative competitors.[62] Due the complex nature of how leadership behaviors impact organizational performance, it's difficult to measure the direct impact of Nadella's purpose-driven leadership. However, a favorable correlation between high employee engagement and operational results is well-known, and higher employee engagement is invariably correlated with purpose-driven environments.[63] Therefore, it's not unreasonable to consider routine business metrics as corollary measures of Nadella's leadership effectiveness.

In the business world, stock performance is often used as a surrogate measure of leadership effectiveness. Following that convention, we might "measure" the results of Nadella's purpose-driven leadership by looking at stock performance over Nadella's tenure. In 2014, Microsoft stock sold for $34 per share. Today's stock price is over $400, outperforming the NASDAQ Composite threefold over the past ten years. Nadella's transformation of Microsoft has led many to consider him the most successful CEO in the tech industry.

Microsoft's transformation under Nadella's leadership is an excellent example of how an established organization, mired in bureaucracy (much like nearly all large healthcare organizations) can successfully make the shift to unorthodoxy.

Exhibiting Resilience

Purpose is stable. When leaders anchor themselves to purpose, they are less likely to be overwhelmed by change. They can better absorb complexity's inherent ambiguity, placing their trust in a purpose-driven present rather than an unpredictable future. That approach imparts confidence and hope, helping leaders see opportunities even when the future is highly uncertain.

The unexpected doesn't knock them off some predetermined course. That's because leaders with an unorthodox mindset about purpose don't carry a road map; they have a compass. Their trust is placed in the purpose-driven adaptability of themselves and others, not in the clarity of their vision. That keeps these leaders grounded and resilient, making them more effective in complexity.

Jens and Anita are hospital presidents working within the same healthcare organization in the same urban market. The hospitals they lead are similar in size and function. The regional organization struggles financially, so both leaders are under considerable pressure to perform. Neither has been with the organization for more than a few years. Each plays a critical role in the organization's overall success.

Jens criticizes senior executives for lacking a clear organizational vision and strategic plan. Instead, senior executives discuss fulfilling the organizational mission. Jens finds that guidance vague and unhelpful. He wants the leaders to tell him explicitly where the organization is heading and what the plan is to get there. Jens feels accountable for results but lacks clarity about which matters most. Jens has voiced these concerns consistently and is frustrated, as the desired clarity has not been forthcoming. In private, Jens thinks he was misled during his recruitment and is resentful. He is actively looking to leave the organization.

Anita notices how much change has happened during her short tenure. She marvels at how senior executives have navigated these changes, staying true to their repeatedly voiced organizational values. Anita feels invigorated by the invitation of senior leaders to align herself and her hospital with the organizational purpose, thinking they trust her to make good decisions advancing the organization.

While the performance of her hospital isn't as good as Jens' hospital's, Anita sees hope and opportunity. She points to the purpose-driven cultural transformation she oversees. Indeed, her hospital's improved performance was initially slow, but recent performance metrics are improving rapidly. She attributes escalating success to her team and their creative ideas and solutions.

Like Jens, Anita feels the pressure to perform. Unlike Jens, she finds herself energized by the work and excited about the future. Anita admits that she doesn't know what the future looks like, but she likes how her team is figuring it out.

The contrasting experiences of Jens and Anita illustrate the transformative power of anchoring leadership in purpose. Jens, who sought clarity and direction from a traditional organizational vision and strategy, was frustrated and disillusioned. His reliance on external directives, which weren't forthcoming, left him feeling disconnected and disempowered, eroding his resilience and commitment to the organization.

In contrast, Anita's focus on the organization's core purpose gave her a compass for navigating uncertainty. Her story underscores how a deep connection to purpose is a wellspring of resilience. Purpose enables adaptability, keeps hope alive, and energizes leaders even in the most challenging circumstances.

MAKING THE SHIFT
Before the Shift

Be Prepared by Knowing Your Purpose

You can't shift if you don't know what your purpose is. First, you must believe that personal purpose exists and then work to figure it out. That's foundational work for leaders and those who coach them.

Finding your purpose requires reflection, a historical survey of your life, and noticing the things that sustain and invigorate you. Purpose also connects with your core values. If you know what those are, your values can lead you to your purpose. A helpful thing about core values and purpose is that they are consistently present throughout your life. So a historical review of the patterns in your life can sometimes be a window to finding your purpose.

Leaders can usually find their purpose and distill it into a brief personal purpose or mission statement. In one organization I worked with, all their leaders introduced themselves by saying, "I'm on a mission to . . ." followed by their mission/purpose statement. That's a powerfully positive practice.

Be Prepared to Align with Purpose

Shifting requires living out your purpose. That means consistently aligning your approaches, actions, and behaviors with your stated purpose.

Consistency and alignment are critical. If a leader's stated purpose misaligns with how they show up, it breeds cynicism. Cynicism about purpose is a cultural cancer, quickly eroding trust and organizational performance.

Leaders who succeed in complexity have clarity about their purpose. They make daily choices that consistently align their approaches, actions, and behaviors with their purpose.

WHY SHIFT

Because Purpose Grounds and Sustains You

Healthcare leadership is demanding and challenging. The intellectual, physical, and emotional requirements are extreme, sometimes brutal. Satisfactory results are hard-won and often elusive. The solutions leaders relied on in the past offer diminishing returns or no benefit today. Moreover, pressed on all sides, healthcare requires rapid adaptation.

Most leaders I coach are skilled healthcare executives with decades of experience. Faced with these challenges, they often tell me they have done everything they know, but their organizations are still not performing well. That these experienced leaders are at a loss for how to find success is a testimony to how difficult things are. For many leaders, the challenges, rapid change, and struggle to succeed lead to fatigue and burnout. Some are utterly demoralized.

What's remarkable is that not every leader feels that way, even when facing similar challenges. Some are enthusiastic about the future, invigorated by the changeable world, seeing hope and opportunity, whereas others only see trouble. I'm fascinated by this difference. Two leaders, like Jens and Anita, can be in the same organization, running comparable facilities, in the same community, under the same leadership. Yet they make sense of their worlds in two completely different ways.

One key differentiator is how the leader connects with purpose. Purpose-driven leaders tend to do better amid profound uncertainty. Even though their context may be brutal, they believe they and their organization will prevail and improve. Shifting toward an unorthodox mindset about purpose will ground and sustain you amid profound uncertainty and change.

Because Purpose Is a Strategic Asset

Being grounded and sustained, believing that you and your team will prevail, is a powerfully beneficial attribute. It helps people avoid feeling trapped, stuck, or powerless. It tends to generate tenacity and perseverance. The combined effect is an ability to see what is possible amid the mess of complexity. Purpose, in short, infuses adaptance, which is a powerful strategic asset, especially in complex contexts.

One cannot overstate the value of purpose as a strategic asset. It influences every aspect of an organization—from its strategic planning to day-to-day operations. It affects team-member engagement and customer satisfaction. Purpose drives coherence between what an organization says and what it does. It ensures that its strategies and actions align with organizational core values. This coherence is critical for building trust and credibility among stakeholders. All these things favorably differentiate the organization from most others.

Purpose must be deeply embedded and authentically practiced to be a strategic asset. For purpose to realize its full potential, it requires more than just a well-articulated statement; it needs leaders who consistently and repeatedly prove their commitment to purpose. That commitment manifests through organizational processes and decisions that integrate purpose in an observable way.

Purpose only has strategic power if leaders are all-in and trust in purpose as a dependable compass. If that happens, purpose becomes the cornerstone of a sustainable competitive advantage generated from an environment conducive to growth, innovation, and resilience.

HOW TO SHIFT

Understand Your Need for Control

Because our brains are prediction machines, we reach for things that increase our ability to predict what comes next. Many reach for greater control to decrease the discomfort that comes with unpredictability. But when things are complex, leaders must relax control and trust in something else. That something is purpose. A complexity-fit leader shifts their trust away from control toward purpose, which is trustworthy.

Making a shift away from control unsettles most leaders. It stirs skepticism, doubt, or fear. Trusting and relying on others to make good, purpose-driven decisions in times of change, uncertainty, and ambiguity is no easy feat. One client responded to this idea by asking me, "What am I supposed to do, then? I'm the leader!"

Our notions of leadership are so wrapped up in control and decision-making that shifting our trust away from that familiar way seems unthinkable. Most leaders envision subsequent chaos, profligate spending, and unrestrained inefficiency. Leaders also fear that others may make decisions that determine the leader's success, maybe even cost them their jobs! That's part of why it's hard to make this shift.

If shifting makes you feel like you're no longer in charge, reconsider what being in charge means. Reframe your work in ways that affirm your critical role in advancing cultural norms that derive from a purpose-driven mindset. Instead of being in charge by making good decisions, you're now being in charge by helping others make good decisions.

Embrace the Fear of Failure That Comes from Others

Many are afraid of failing, whatever failing means. A reticence to relax our need for control often derives from the fear of failure. Trusting others to do things that decide our success can be unsettling, especially if we need autonomy. Shifting means embracing the possibility that our failure might result from the approaches, actions, or behaviors of others. That is extremely hard for many, including me.

Who doesn't remember working as a group on some class project, only to find your classmates less concerned about the final grade than you? In those situations, we faced a choice. Either we went with the group, accepting the lesser grade, or we reached for greater control, taking charge of the group, telling people what to do. Or we did all the work ourselves, accepting whatever grade we could achieve.

Some of us went to the teacher and pleaded for individual grades rather than group ones. In essence, we asked the teacher to assess our leadership based on what *we* did, not what the *team* did. Many leaders want to be graded on their performance, not on the performance of others. Those leaders are fine if others contribute to their *success*, especially after doing what the leader told them to do. However, many leaders are uncomfortable trusting others to do whatever aligns with their purpose, having subsequent successes *and* failures attributed to their leadership.

The stakes involved are much higher than those for a school project, of course. Our careers, livelihoods, and sometimes the lives of others are on the line. Trusting others to do the right thing, following purpose, is not trivial. Most of us would rather reach for greater control, because we trust ourselves more than others. Unfortunately, that rather natural response is the opposite of what works well in complex contexts.

A successful shift toward unorthodoxy requires leaders to embrace a fear of failure resulting from the choices of others. It means maximizing the likelihood of others making good, purpose-driven choices that result in organizational success.

Find A Story Worth Your Life, or Create One

To shift, find a "story" that's worth the one life you must live. Living out your purpose is your story. That's one reason personal purpose is a profound gift to a leader. If you know your purpose and live it out, your life will be richer and more rewarding. If you are passive about purpose, I invite you to create a story worth your life. Find your purpose and pursue it with enthusiasm! It may be that health-care leadership is that pursuit. It may be that it is not. No matter. Whatever story is worth your life, it will be better if you have found your purpose.

MINDSET NINE—STORIES

AN UNORTHODOX MINDSET ABOUT REALITY

Our Stories Are Always Incomplete

ILLUSTRATION 9. *Sensemaking Stories.* We create "stories" about reality. Those stories help us make sense of what is happening. They are true, but they are not THE Truth. Our stories are always incomplete.

UNDERSTANDING STORIES

A leader's mindset about "stories" strongly affects how others experience the leader. This mindset may be more impactful than any of the other mindsets in shaping how others feel and respond to a leader's approach.

The way leaders make sense of what happens around them deeply shapes their approaches, actions, and behaviors. Put another way, what the leader believes about their sensemaking stories guides everything the leader does. The impact on an organization is profound.

My coaching clients consistently return to focus on this specific mindset more than any other. They see its importance and find themselves consistently challenged by it. Let's look at some ideas about this mindset and see if the same may be true for you.

What Stories Are

By *story*, I mean a sensemaking narrative, the descriptive explanations we create about what happens around us or what we experience. We create stories about everything.

These stories are more than the mere recounting of events. They are the way our brain interprets and assigns meaning to our experiences. Because our brains craft these stories based on our mindsets, perspectives, and emotions, our stories are always unique and subjective. While our stories may be similar to the stories of others, they are never the same.

Our brains are story-making machines. They adeptly and rapidly craft narratives about what's happening. This remarkable ability is a necessary part of existing in the world as healthy adults. We must craft our sensemaking stories in order to stay safe and function normally.

Even though we readily and automatically create these stories, we often don't notice them. Furthermore, we tend to believe our stories to be true, convincing ourselves that we know how or why things happened the way they did. Because we're so good and well-practiced at creating stories, we have confidence in our ability to be right about reality.

This matters a great deal. Our stories determine the approaches, actions, and behaviors we take, influencing our decision-making, solution-finding, and relationships. They shape how we make sense of our organization and what we do about it. In short, stories describe and shape how we interact with the world, and that's why they matter.

What Stories Are Not

Stories are not fiction. Our sensemaking stories are not fiction. They describe what we believe to be true about our world. Our stories are genuine and truthful to us. If our brains are healthy, we don't intentionally make things up about reality. We don't falsely imagine things, events, or experiences.

Of course, we can intentionally mislead or be false. But that's not what these sensemaking stories are. Stories reflect our honest efforts to make sense of what we experience. They are our truthful descriptions of reality.

It's important to note that we also craft stories about our organizations and how they function. That means our stories determine what things we consider important. They determine whether we think something is a strategic opportunity or a threat. They shape our relationships, who we affiliate with, and who we stay away from. We craft stories that explain the approaches, actions, and behaviors of others. In short, our stories are our reality, shaping all our interactions.

Stories are not perspectives. Our sensemaking stories are not our perspectives, either. Perspectives are the *specific lenses* through which we view situations or topics. We create our stories from the viewpoints that our perspectives provide. Keep in mind that the broader framework of our mindsets is what shapes our perspectives. Think of it this way: our mindsets shape our perspectives, and our perspectives shape our stories.

Therefore, our perspectives act like cognitive lenses, regulating our understanding of our experiences. They are the vantage points through which we create the stories we do.

For example, an orthodox mindset about systems (Mindset One—Systems) holds that organizations are complicated, rather than complex, systems. One perspective from that mindset is that results are always knowable and predictable. A familiar story about a leader can result: suppose the leader admits they don't know why something unexpected happened. In that case, the story about their leadership becomes, "The unexpected happened because the leader wasn't on top of things. Good leaders know how things happen."

The relationship between mindsets, perspectives, and stories is not linear. While mindsets shape perspectives, and perspectives shape stories, they also loop back and influence each other. Our stories reshape our perspectives, and our perspectives change our mindsets. Perspectives are dynamic, evolving with new experiences or information, and they can actively shape, not just filter, our perception and engagement with the world. So mindsets, perspectives, and stories coexist in an interdependent, three-way relationship. Each continuously informs and reshapes the other.

For example, if the story is that good leaders are always on top of things, that informs our perspectives about unexpected results—the unexpected shouldn't happen. Our perspective that the unexpected shouldn't happen reinforces or informs our mindset about organizations and how they function—good organizations function in predictable ways, just as complicated systems do. Therefore, organizations that function like complicated systems are good.

This relationship is both helpful and problematic. It is helpful, because the elements all work together to create a cohesive and quickly accessible way of making sense of reality. It's problematic, because the relationship favors a self-reinforcing view of reality. It's self-reinforcing because we don't see reasons for changing our views. Our brains discard inputs that don't fit what we already believe. We are naturally disinclined to reexamine our views of reality. The self-reinforcing nature of our stories can trap us in one story, leaving us closed to others. That's a problem for leaders.

Stories are not optional. Lastly, stories are not optional. We must create them. We wouldn't understand what is happening around us if we didn't. Without our stories, we couldn't respond to threats and opportunities in helpful and healthy ways.

Let's illuminate how our brains must create a story and how readily a normal brain does it. Read the three brief statements below, slowly. As you read each sentence, see if you notice what your brain is doing with it.

▸ A man cuts into your lane and makes you slow down.

▸ A woman yells at a child in the check-out line.

▸ A politician disparages a colleague on a live mic, saying something not intended to be heard by others.

Notice your stories. Why did the man cut you off? Was it because he was rude or because he had just learned that his wife was in the emergency room after an accident? Were you driving a car, riding a motorcycle, or a bike, or were you a competitive swimmer in a race? Were you on a six-lane freeway or a two-lane road?

What about the women yelling at the child? Were you in a store or a hotel? Was she a sister, a mother, or a stranger? Was the woman poor or rich? Was she yelling because she was an unfit mother or a rude customer? Or was she yelling because the two were siblings and it was a case of sibling rivalry?

What story about the politician did you craft? What did the politician say? Was the politician male, female, gay, or straight? Was the politician a person of color, or were they White? Were swear words involved? What political party were they from?

I didn't give you much to go on. But your brain didn't hesitate to fill in the blanks. You might wonder where the stuff you added came from.

The answer is that the statement I provided likely triggered a memory or an image for you, something from your past experience or something you've heard about. Your brain drew upon your mindsets, perspectives, and previous sensemaking stories and influenced what you added, filling in the blanks. Everyone does this. I'd get ten different stories if I asked ten people about each sentence.

Our brain *always* fills in the gaps, based on our mindsets. Remember this about our brains: in the absence of information, people *must* make up a story. It's an inescapable consequence of the way our brains work. All of us create stories, and we do it all the time. Stories are not optional.

Complete and Incomplete Stories

We craft our stories intending to approximate reality. Some of our stories are closer to reality than others. And some think their stories *are* reality, which makes their stories complete.

Complete stories are those that match reality. And stories that don't match reality are incomplete. In other words, some stories can be more or less complete than others. That's an unusual way to use the word *complete*, which typically doesn't include degrees of completeness. But I will use it in this unusual way: *complete* can have degrees of completeness.

Imagine you baked two pies and sliced each into eight pieces. In this case, a complete pie includes all eight slices. Then imagine you invited four guests to dinner, and each, including you, enjoyed a piece of pie. Cleaning up, you noticed that one pie had a single piece missing. The other pie had four pieces missing. Both pies were now incomplete. But the pie with one slice missing was "more complete" than the one missing four. That's what I mean by degrees of completeness.

If a story is complete, it is the full representation of reality—the whole pie. If it's incomplete, it has various degrees of completeness—part of the whole pie. Our stories about reality are more (one slice missing) or less (four slices missing) complete than others. Let's look at stories and how they can be more or less complete.

How Complete and Incomplete Stories Work

Justin was the new chief medical officer (CMO) for a small, rural regional multihospital organization. He was a native of Sweden, and English was not his first language. Justin preferred direct, brief communication, and that's how he communicated, especially when stressed.

After several months, the human resources director informed Justin that several employees had filed complaints against him. They claimed Justin was verbally aggressive and demeaning, creating a psychologically unsafe work environment. This unexpected feedback surprised Justin, because had had never received complaints like that before. He was appalled by the accusation that he had created an unsafe workplace.

Moreover, Justin learned that two of his peers had encouraged others to lodge complaints against him via the incident reporting system. This news, along with his insecurities about his English language skills, led Justin to think that his peers and the staff were conspiring against him. Justin thought they were doing that because they were biased against "foreigners." His conviction that many rural Americans harbored prejudiced views toward individuals from other nations reinforced his belief.

Justin's story went like this: Complaints were filed against me, because I'm a foreigner who doesn't speak English well. These people don't like foreigners, so they are trying to get rid of me. Notice how Justin created his story based on some prior beliefs and personal insecurities as he tried to make sense of the unexpected feedback he had received.

Months later, in the context of coaching, we found Justin's story to be incomplete. Justin's use of English was so good that no one knew it wasn't his first language. Few were aware he was from Sweden. But his peers had, indeed, encouraged people to file their complaints. There were good reasons for why Justin's peers did that.

Before Justin's arrival, the institution had spent years building a high-reliability organization (HRO), a workplace safe from harm. All staff underwent training during their HRO journey, encouraging everyone to speak up if they noticed something that could lead to harm. In this organization, speaking up meant filing an incident report, which Justin's peers encouraged.

Based on prior training about how harm happens in healthcare, some staff thought Justin's directness shut down dialogue, which they knew increased the likelihood of patient harm. Some had expressed their concerns about Justin's approach to their supervisors, who were Justin's peers. Justin's peers then reminded the staff to use the incident reporting system if they noticed things that could lead to harm.

Thankfully, all involved decided to dialogue about these things. A new understanding dawned after people learned that English was not Justin's first language, and that Northern Europeans, like Swedes, typically tend to prefer direct and clear communication. This recognition helped demystify Justin's approach, previously perceived as overly aggressive. It was an explanation, not a justification, for Justin's behavioral preferences. Justin learned he needed to modulate his preferred approach.

Furthermore, Justin realized that the people around him did not harbor prejudice against him. On the contrary, many were unaware of his native language and cultural background. They welcomed that news with genuine curiosity and regard.

Justin did what we all do. He created a sensemaking story about what he experienced and believed it to be complete. Absent complete information, his brain worked to fill in the blanks, drawing upon his mindsets.

Because Justin and others remained open to different stories, with time and discourse, everyone could create a more complete and helpful story in the end.

THE ORTHODOX MINDSET ABOUT STORIES: Our Stories Are Complete

The orthodox mindset about stories is that they are complete. If they are not, they can be or ought to be. Leaders with this mindset seek out complete stories and hold them with certitude, confidence, and conviction. In other words, the story they have is the right story.

EXPRESSIONS OF THE ORTHODOX MINDSET

You can identify the orthodox mindset in leaders by noticing the typical expressions of this mindset: believing their story is complete, holding tightly to one "right" story, and diversifying stories for compliance.

Believing Their Story Is Complete

Leaders with this mindset demonstrate considerable confidence and certitude about their sensemaking abilities. They know or can know all that needs to be known. These leaders believe they should, can, and do create complete stories.

Their confidence in crafting complete stories comes from our historical understanding of the universe and its workings. That understanding includes believing that every interaction leads to a knowable result and that we can always know what happens if we reduce things to small enough elements. Therefore, good leaders can understand what is happening with enough time, data, and expertise. They can and should be able to craft a complete story.

The leader's certitude about the completeness of their story extends to the subsequent approaches, actions, and behaviors they take, which, of course, affects their decision-making, solution-finding, and interactions. These leaders tend to be decisive, directive, stubborn, methodical, and tenacious.

Holding Tightly to One "Right" Story

Complete stories are right stories, and they harbor the "right" answers. All other stories are, to varying degrees, wrong. That means there's always a right or wrong way to proceed, one best way to do things. Additionally, there are ways that things should be or ought to be. In short, complete stories evoke *rightness*, a collective belief that there is one best way to think and act.

When leaders believe their story is complete, they are justifiably reluctant to consider others. Any other story must be wrong to some degree. That is why these leaders tend to hold tightly to the one right story they have.

In this context, accepting other stories is an admission of being wrong or ill-informed. Consequently, their approaches, actions, and behaviors would be less than best. Those are uncomfortable considerations for leaders with this mindset. That makes it harder for these leaders to take on multiple perspectives or consider alternatives. They hold tightly to their one right and complete story, which profoundly shapes their actions and how others experience them.

Holding tightly to one right story often cultivates organizational rigidity. It narrows access to other stories, solutions, ideas, or processes that may be equally right or even superior. One "right" story is a slippery slope toward arrogance and overconfidence. A leader may insist on their story as the only correct one, creating an inflexible, my-way-or-the-highway leadership culture.

Diversifying Stories for Compliance

Fostering an inclusive environment that values and respects individual differences and provides equitable opportunities is a moral, ethical, and legal imperative for everyone. However, the motivation for diversity differs between those leaders with orthodox and unorthodox mindsets about stories.

Leaders with an orthodox mindset often view diversity primarily as a means to fulfill moral, ethical, and legal obligations, rather than as an opportunity to derive a more complete sensemaking story. Leaders with this mindset don't need a more complete story because they already have one.

What leaders with an orthodox mindset about stories need is for others to believe in the complete story they crafted. Therefore, these leaders' primary motivation for diversity is to invite and inspire diverse *followers*, not to include or listen to diverse stories. Diversity becomes primarily about including other followers, not finding and including other stories. If they have diverse followers, they have complied with diversity and inclusion.

THE UNORTHODOX MINDSET ABOUT STORIES:
Our Stories Are Always Incomplete

The unorthodox mindset about stories is that they are *always* incomplete. By incomplete, I mean inherently limited. The limits come from various aspects of human cognition, the insufficient nature of the tools and processes we use to discern reality, and the inscrutable nature of reality itself. These limitations also apply to understanding the organizations we lead and how they derive the outcomes and results they do.

Consequently, certitude always comes with caveats. Confidence derives from the ability of many to co-create the most complete story possible. The leader's confidence in what is known or knowable resides with others, not just themselves. These leaders know they can always have a more complete story, even though their stories will always be incomplete.

EXPRESSIONS OF THE UNORTHODOX MINDSET

You can identify the unorthodox mindset in yourself or others by noticing the typical expressions of this mindset: believing their story is always incomplete, holding all stories with an open hand, and diversifying stories for completeness.

Believing Their Story Is Always Incomplete

Leaders with an unorthodox mindset know that their stories are always an incomplete representation of reality. That includes stories about their organization and how it functions.

Even if the leader pulls everyone together to better understand the organization and its function, their expanded knowledge will remain incomplete. That is the nature of organizations that are predominantly complex systems. They are not fully knowable. Incompleteness, therefore, stems from the nature of complex systems, not just the limits of human cognition.

Human cognition does, indeed, impair our ability to know reality fully. Our mindsets, perspectives, and stories work together to filter out things that don't fit with what we *already believe*. Our stories help us by acting like a cognitive shield, protecting us from an onslaught of information that would otherwise overload our senses. We cannot escape this fact about how our brains work, nor should we want to. It keeps us safe and functioning as healthy people. Still, it impairs our ability to acquire a complete story.

What we're learning about autism helps us understand this better. Autism spectrum disorder (ASD) is characterized by differences in sensory processing. Individuals with ASD often experience sensory input more intensely or differently than neurotypical individuals. This heightened sensitivity can lead to what some describe as sensory overload, where the individual finds it challenging to filter extraneous stimuli. That inability is overwhelming or distressing, resulting in characteristic behavioral responses.[64]

Predictive processing theory suggests that the brain constantly makes predictions about incoming sensory information based on past experiences and adjusts these predictions based on new information.[65] Some theorize that individuals with ASD have impaired predictive processing capability. It's a model that provides insights into how individuals with ASD might experience the world differently. It also illustrates the extreme challenges arising from an inability of the brain to filter out what it considers extraneous noise, using preconstructed narratives to anticipate what is useful and what is not. Autism helps us appreciate how essential these cognitive filters are for all of us.[66]

Our stories help us impose order and coherence on our experiences, acting as a vital filter. Even though our stories are normal and necessary, they are inherently incomplete because our brain filters out what it considers nonessential information. What our brains consider nonessential is anything that doesn't fit our mindsets, perspectives, and stories.

If we ignore this about ourselves, then we will be perpetually prone to miss new or unexpected vital information. That's because our brain doesn't naturally notice what we filter out. Leaders with an unorthodox mindset about stories understand this. So these leaders earnestly seek *many* other stories, listening to learn from the stories of others. As a result, they often adopt parts of the sensemaking stories of others, changing their own.

Consequently, one hallmark of these leaders is their curiosity. They hunt for the most complete story they can find, driven by necessity. They are authentically humble, because they embrace the inherent incompleteness of their stories, freely admitting that they don't and can't know completely. They listen deeply, with a reverence for other individuals, genuinely curious about their sensemaking stories and how they were derived. They actively delve into the mindsets of others, if allowed, because mindsets are the fountainhead of stories.

Pursuing a more complete story moves these leaders to connect and collaborate with others, working together to co-create the most complete story they can. That approach includes embracing and cultivating constructive conflict, because they know conflict is the exchange of incomplete stories, adding to everyone's understanding.

Holding All Stories with an Open Hand

Once the leader realizes that their stories will always be incomplete, it's much easier for these leaders to let go of the notion of "rightness." This is what I mean by an *open hand*. There are no right stories to hold tightly to. They hold every story, including their own, with an openness to other possibilities.

That liberates these leaders to hold many potentially useful stories, rather than being concerned about finding the best or right one. They stay curious about the merits of many other stories. That openness tends to generate many different solutions, answers, and ideas.

Let's revisit my coaching client, Justin. He held tightly to one story that he believed to be complete: "These people want to get rid of me, because I'm a foreigner." We both paused to notice his story when he brought it into our coaching session. Staying curious, we wondered why and how he derived the story he did.

We both accepted his first story without judgment, acknowledging its truthfulness without elevating it to the Truth. Then I asked Justin, "How else might you make sense of the same information you have access to?" That is a crucial question to answer when trying to create and consider other stories.

It was tough for Justin to answer that question, not unlike trying to pry open a tight grip. He held onto his first story tightly, because he felt threatened and falsely accused.

Justin relaxed the cognitive grip on his first story by finding more than one story. One story Justin considered included the role of the HRO in what happened. Another story acknowledged Justin's tendency for directness when under stress. Again, we set aside any notion of rightness about any one story, holding all three with an open hand.

Just thinking together about two other possible stories was helpful for Justin. It opened his mind to potentially more-useful, if not more-complete stories. It lowered his sense of threat, and he didn't feel trapped anymore.

Holding multiple stories helps leaders avoid getting stuck in one story, which limits their options and constrains their choices. Multiple stories keep the leader curious, humble, and open to understanding their organizations better.

Diversifying Stories for Completeness

Leaders with an unorthodox mindset about stories value diversity and inclusion for reasons beyond ethical, moral, and legal considerations. These considerations are critical, but not central, to their thinking.

These leaders need and want diversity because of the different stories and insights diversity brings. They know lived experiences and insights shape mindsets, generating different perspectives, which shape sense-making stories. Including different sensemaking stories leads to more complete stories, leading to better decisions, plans, and strategies. Leaders with this mindset *need* diversity to create a more complete story, which is their primary motivation for diversity.

One behavioral hallmark of this mindset is its strong tendency to include diverse stakeholders in decision-making processes. These leaders want and need as many diverse participants as possible. These leaders call upon the many and advocate for extreme transparency and radical inclusion, creating a free flow of information and dialogue. They work to develop extensive feedback mechanisms, opening direct and robust communication lines to the leader. It's not unusual for others to criticize their approach as reckless or naïve. Indeed, leaders with an unorthodox mindset about stories recklessly hunger for diversity, because diversity is what creates the most complete stories possible. That's what helps organizations comprised of predominantly complex systems thrive.

MAKING THE SHIFT
Before the Shift

Be Prepared for Genuine Humility

Humility begins with knowing and accepting your limitations. That is, not thinking higher of yourself than you ought. No matter how intelligent, wise, or experienced, all people have inherent cognitive limitations that are never entirely escapable. Those limitations impede everyone's ability to completely understand what is happening around them. The foundation of leadership humility is knowing that your stories are and always will be incomplete.

Your experience doesn't help you much, either. In complex systems, everything is new to some degree. Your past can't fully inform the present, even less the future. So your confidence and certainty in any story derived from your past experiences or expertise is equally incomplete. In fact, stories highly dependent on our experiences and expertise may be more of a trap than an aid, because they are likely to be too simple.

That means the source of truth about your organization and how it functions does not exist in you but in many others. Effective leadership of complex systems is less about what you know and more about what "we" can know together. Leaders must rely upon others to co-create the most complete, yet still incomplete, story about how things are. The leader's primary responsibility is to foster an environment that amplifies and elevates opportunities for co-creative, co-evolving sensemaking stories about the organization and how it functions.

Therein lies the beginning of genuine leadership humility: limited confidence in what we can know, greater confidence in what others know, and a reliance on others more than ourselves to see the organization in the most complete way possible.

Be Prepared for Reverent Curiosity

Humility positions leaders to be genuinely curious. If you're humble, you depend and rely upon curiosity, driven by the conviction and certainty that you don't and can't hold a complete story. It is a form of curiosity driven by genuine need, rather than by an abstract or external leadership principle.

Furthermore, you're not curious because you want to figure out how to persuade others to believe your story. You're curious because you value the story the other person has. You *want and need* their story. Their diverse stories will help you and the organization gain the most complete story possible.

A genuine hunger for learning the other person's sensemaking story demonstrates reverence for the other person. Reverence is an uncommon word today, but it means deep respect for someone or something.

As you express your genuine curiosity in pursuit of a more complete story, you show respect and attribute dignity to others in a very tangible way. You're showing them that they matter to you and the organization. In short, you show reverence for the other by being genuinely curious about their story and how it is derived. That's what I mean by being reverently curious. Remember that you can't be reverently curious unless you are genuinely humble first.

Be Prepared to Learn

Humility and curiosity position you to learn as you inquire about other stories. In this case, you're not curious about how their story is wrong, (i.e., different from your right story). Neither are you curious about what you may think are the flaws in their stories. You're not advancing something you know that they don't. Instead, you want to listen to learn.[67]

Listening to learn is not just about understanding something or someone else. Understanding is discovering someone else's sensemaking story and intellectually acknowledging how the other person came up with it. That's not learning. It's merely mental assent. Learning demands more.

Listening to learn means you are the student, and the other is teaching you. You willfully submit to their instruction. You trust and depend on them to educate you, expanding your understanding. When listening to learn, you *take into yourself* what they share and make it your own, even if just for a moment. It's not that you must agree, but you must listen. Listening to *learn* demands genuine humility and reverent curiosity; listening to *understand* does not.

People who consistently listen to learn are rare. It's not easy to do. If you've been fortunate enough to work with someone who does listen to learn, you remember what it feels like. It feels like you matter greatly. These leaders listen to you, not because of your title, role, or experience, but because you are different, a valuable source of learning. Leaders who listen to learn genuinely care about you and what you think. They exude an openness and eagerness toward others and are viewed as approachable and down-to-earth. These leaders are memorable and highly impactful people in our professional lives.

People respond to leaders who listen to learn. They are willing to go beyond what the leader asks and exceed expectations. Though rare, leaders who listen to learn are profoundly influential.

WHY SHIFT

Because Complete Stories Trap You

You make decisions based on what you believe to be true. If you believe your story to be complete, that one right-and-true story will shape how you lead. And it can trap you. Here are two ways complete stories trap us.

You Get Trapped in Your First Story. We usually think our first story—the one that first springs to our mind as we see or experience something—is complete. Recall how difficult it was for Justin to move beyond his first story. It took work on his part and mine to consider alternatives. Just like the rest of us, Justin thought his first story was complete or right. And, as is almost always the case, he held tightly to his first story because he thought it was complete.

Moving beyond your first story is hard for everyone because we tend to believe it's the truth. If we think our first story is the truth, there's no need for another. That's why we hold our first story so tightly. Any other story would not be the truth.

Unfortunately, your first story is almost always the least complete, rendering it faulty. Our first story is a true story, but it's rarely, if ever, the truth. That's why our first story is often the least helpful story to act on, resulting in less-than-ideal outcomes. And that's the trap. The trap for leaders is responding to your first story, believing it is complete when it is not.

You Get Trapped in Complexity. Given the nature of organizations that are predominantly complex systems, we can never know everything about them. That affects our sensemaking stories. It means that whatever story you have about your organization and how it functions is inherently incomplete. It's incomplete because you cannot know or understand everything that matters.

Holding incomplete stories about organizations that are mostly comprised of complex systems is not the main problem. The main problem arises when we don't realize our stories are incomplete and make decisions based on them. Actions bolstered by confidence and certitude in what we think is a complete story—when it is not—almost always makes things worse. Unforeseen and unintended consequences run amok, deteriorating organizational performance, especially over the long-term. That's how complete stories in the context of complexity trap leaders.

HOW TO SHIFT

Notice Your Stories

The first step is to notice your stories. That seems straightforward, but most of us pay little or no attention to the narratives we construct about what is happening around us. Seeing those stories takes considerable curiosity and self-reflection, especially at first. It's even more difficult if your emotions are involved. A skilled executive leadership coach is beneficial here, noticing your stories with you. Working with another person, like a coach, can help you grow the "muscle" necessary for readily noticing the many stories you create.

Practice Storytelling

Your brain is already a storytelling machine. So go with it. Once you notice your first story, create some more. What other ways might you make sense of the same observations and experiences that led you to your first story?

Practice creating and carrying more than one story around with you. Sometimes, I put it this way to leaders, "Carry three stories with you." It's a catchy phrase from Jennifer Garvey-Berger that many leaders I've coached find helpful. It forces them to notice their stories and pause to craft a few more. If leaders practice sensemaking storytelling, carrying three or more stories around, they are much less likely to get trapped.

Holding onto at least three stories brings liberty. It frees the leader from getting trapped by their first story. It positions them to consider multiple possibilities in complex contexts.

Diversify Your Stories

Diversity and inclusion are crucial on multiple levels. For our discussion, I focus on one part of diversity and inclusion: the necessity of diversity for crafting more complete stories about the organization you lead.

To shift, leaders must grasp how diversity is essential for successfully leading healthcare organizations comprised of complex systems. Diversity is not just a matter of compliance, which is vital in and of itself. Diversity is the *only* means for accessing the most complete sensemaking stories possible, essential for effectively leading complex systems.

The best decisions in complex systems are born out of the most complete stories possible. The results and outcomes generated in response to the most complete stories about complex systems will be superior.

Diverse sensemaking stories come from a diversity of lived experiences. To shift, leaders must include people who have lived experiences that are very different from one another and very different from themselves. Absent that diversity, leaders will not be able to develop a more complete understanding of how their organizations generate the results that they do. They will only find the most valuable solutions or decisions if they seek diversity. That's what makes diversity and inclusion a *strategic advantage* in complex systems. Diversity fosters a more nuanced and comprehensive understanding of reality. For you to make this shift, I encourage you to thirst and hunger for genuine diversity and inclusion. Successful leadership of complex healthcare organizations depends on it.

MINDSET TEN—CURIOSITY

AN UNORTHODOX MINDSET ABOUT KNOWING

Curiosity Is Preventive Medicine

ILLUSTRATION 10. *Curiosity as a Mindset.* Curiosity that transforms organizations manifests as listening to learn, not to win and not to fix.

UNDERSTANDING CURIOSITY

Successful leaders are curious. They always want to know more about themselves, the world, and their organizations. Curiosity is an essential leadership characteristic of several mindsets. But it can also be a mindset itself. When curiosity is a mindset, it powerfully shapes the leader. It changes how a leader experiences and interacts with their organization and life in general. Not only that, but curiosity has a unique way of mitigating the substantial challenges of leading complex organizations.

DEFINING CURIOSITY

What Curiosity Is

Curiosity is a natural part of being human that compels us to explore and seek information. It is the powerful desire to learn, an intellectual and experiential hunger. Curiosity is the primal need to know. As we satisfy that hunger, we gain knowledge and experience. We discover new things about ourselves and the world around us. Absent curiosity, progress and personal growth are impossible.

Likewise, curiosity is pivotal to leadership. It's essential for growing self-awareness, adapting to change, understanding organizations, and making good decisions. Many consider experience, rather than curiosity, the crucial ingredient of leadership growth and development. But experience is merely the accumulated effect of curiosity, underscoring the fundamental nature of curiosity itself.

While curiosity is powerful and innate, the degree or intensity of it varies. We are less curious when we are confident or certain and more curious when we are humble. We are less curious when we perceive a social or physical threat and more curious when we feel safe. We can also be selective about our curiosity, focusing on some things while ignoring others. What we are selectively curious about can be categorized into *dimensions of curiosity.*

Four Dimensions of Curiosity

Curiosity has multiple dimensions, and each dimension determines what we are curious about, depending on what's happening and which mindsets we are using. Four dimensions of curiosity are:

Specific Curiosity: This dimension seeks information to address immediate, practical goals. For example, a hospital leader might review nurse-to-patient ratios to improve staff schedules and patient care. Specific curiosity is targeted inquiry, seeking specific answers to a particular concern. When leaders believe that the right or best answers exist, that the world works through direct, cause-and-effect relationships, or that the past informs the future, they primarily engage with specific curiosity. Specific curiosity seeks the answers they want and need.

Social Curiosity: This dimension seeks different perspectives, motivations, and emotions of others, like gathering team input on proposed operational changes. This is the dimension of curiosity that leaders select and depend on when they co-create coordinated movement. It's the principal means of building trust and creating inclusive, collaborative environments. Social curiosity builds the connections leaders need to drive distributed leadership and build interdependent, high-performing teams.

Experiential Curiosity: This dimension seeks to learn through direct involvement and observation. It involves experimenting and exploring, underpinning what I and others call "sensing" the system. It is the dimension of curiosity that helps build experience and expertise.

For example, a leader might join a departmental team to experience their workflows. These leaders aim to detect system patterns and dynamics that lead to organizational outcomes. In essence, they are noticing the inclinations of the system.

This dimension differs from specific curiosity, because it's not seeking answers. It isn't about deciding and telling or finding and fixing. It's about seeking to understand through exploration and experimentation; leaders *experience* the system themselves or through the sensemaking of others. Experiential curiosity allows leaders to make good sense of the complex systems they lead.

Reflective Curiosity: This dimension encourages leaders to reflect on their behaviors, learning how and why they take the approaches and actions they do. They look inwardly to understand how their mindsets shaped the results and outcomes they realized. It is through reflective curiosity that leaders grow and develop.

For example, Sandra, the CEO of a regional healthcare organization, engages a leadership coach. Sandra learns new things about herself through assessments, feedback, and coaching. As a result, she changes her leadership approaches, actions, and behaviors. With those changes, she is more effective, contributing to improved organizational performance. Reflective curiosity moves us to explore our inner landscape, a necessary journey for becoming a better leader.

A leader must be aware of the different dimensions of curiosity, because they determine what the leader notices or doesn't. More importantly, the dimensions determine how others experience the leader—how the leader cultivates trust and collaboration or how the leader instigates personal and organizational change. Whatever dimensions of curiosity a leader engages in will impact their leadership profoundly.

Curiosity as a Mindset

A leader's relationship with curiosity can be more than merely using one dimension or another. Curiosity can be a mindset if the leader embraces all four dimensions simultaneously. As a mindset, curiosity becomes the foundation for understanding ourselves, relating to others, and interacting with the world. When curiosity is a mindset, it becomes a cognitive stance taken in relationship to the universe.

In his seminal book, *Curious? Discover the Missing Ingredient to a Fulfilling Life*, Todd Kashdan describes curiosity as more than a psychological trait. He promotes curiosity as a profound existential stance that can define a leader's engagement with the world—a mindset.[68] A curiosity mindset invites a continual openness to new experiences and a willingness to explore the unknown, especially in the face of challenges and uncertainty. Kashdan states that the enduring inquisitiveness fostered by a curiosity mindset results in a richer interaction with life. A curiosity mindset enhances personal meaning and satisfaction.

By positioning curiosity as a "central life force," Kashdan underscores its foundational role in knowledge acquisition and leadership development. He affirms that the most influential leaders approach their roles with a curiosity mindset, embracing the unknown rather than clinging to certainty.

Embracing curiosity as a mindset equips leaders to navigate complex challenges with adaptability and insight. It also transforms the very nature of leadership, making it an adventurous journey of continuous discovery and growth. Curiosity also acts like preventive medicine, keeping leaders grounded amid the dynamic, uncertain, and ambiguous world of complexity.

Curiosity and Listening

Even though a curiosity mindset is transformational, curiosity itself is not directly observable. We can only see curiosity through the behaviors it inspires in others: most notably, how they listen.

If we listen well, we use all our senses—sight, sound, touch, hearing, and even smell—paying close attention to everything our senses pick up. While that seems straightforward, few of us are exceptionally good at listening.

There are several reasons why. One is that all of us are selective listeners. It's challenging for our brains to process all the sensory input we can access, especially if we are unpracticed at listening with all our senses. In addition, as we've already discussed, our brains tend to filter out things that we aren't expecting, leading us to miss things. Not because we are neglectful or lazy, but because we're human.

Our brain focuses on what it perceives as most pertinent. This process is protective, helping us avoid overload and focus our attention on what is important to us. That's part of why it's good to know about dimensions of curiosity. Our brains will ignore information from the dimensions that don't interest us, impairing our listening ability.

Becoming an effective listener in complexity requires expanding what we consider relevant. We do that by deliberately engaging all dimensions of curiosity: listening with our whole being. As we do, we train our brains to welcome more information, including more of the unexpected.

When leaders listen with their whole being, they affect others profoundly. Such leaders are perceived as approachable, open, and authentic, leaving others feeling heard, understood, and valued. That is how a leader's engagement with all four dimensions of curiosity transforms an organization's culture.

Various Ways Leaders Listen

Nearly all leaders work hard to improve their listening skills. But there are many ways to listen, and we don't always practice the most useful ones. Knowing many ways of listening helps a leader access the more helpful ways, shying away from those that may get in their way. One of my favorite descriptions of ways to listen comes from Jennifer Garvey Berger.[69] I favor her list because it is easy to remember and useful. She describes three ways to listen.

Listening to Win. Listening to win is grasping for certainty and striving for rightness. We look to discover what is wrong and strive to make things right. We engage almost exclusively with specific curiosity, seeking facts or details, relying on experiences and expertise. We tune into what we think are weaknesses, flaws, or gaps, and fight to fill in what's missing. Listening to win is a competitive form of listing. It closes us down to other points of view, as we're only interested in getting our way or being right. It leads to a "decide and tell" approach, something like "I'm right. You're wrong. So do what I tell you to do."

Listening to win is fast, allowing us to deal quickly with an issue and move on. Because it's expedient, listening to win is tempting and familiar, especially in a crisis. In a crisis, there's a limited need for dialogue and a heavy reliance on the leader's experience, perspective, and expertise. Listening to win might be an appropriate way of listening during a crisis, but outside of that setting, using it comes at a cost.

Being on the receiving end of listening to win rarely feels good. Not only does it leave us feeling unheard, but it's clear that the leader who is questioning us isn't interested in anything we have to say. They are indifferent to our ideas, perspectives, and motivations.

Listening to win shuts down communication, connection, and collaboration. It erodes trust (unless in a crisis) and eliminates opportunities for constructive disagreement. As such, it leads to compliance, not commitment. It positions the leader to hold others accountable, destroying ownership and distributed leadership. Ultimately, a heavy reliance on listening to win imperils team and organizational performance.

The useful opportunities for this way of listening are rare. Leaders who routinely rely on it create damage out of proportion to the benefits gained from its expediency. Yet it's a common way of listening.

Listening to Fix. Listening to fix is mainly about offering advice. We listen for the best way to move forward or how to do things right. We focus on understanding things just enough to provide a solution or plan, preventing a deeper understanding of the issues. Like listening to win, it is an expeditious way of listening. It allows us to spend just enough energy and time to discern a path forward, fix the problem, and move on.

Often, the motivation behind listening to fix is the desire to be helpful. While this may differ from listening to win, listening to fix also relies on specific curiosity. Sometimes, it draws upon social curiosity, too, but in a limited way. We only want to know enough to help us figure out how to fix the issue.

Listening to fix can feel paternalistic, hierarchical, and tutorial. The leader presupposes they know or understand something better. Consequently, the leader-receiver relationship tends to be transactional and devoid of empathy. Listening to fix leaves the receiver feeling incapable and dependent, as it presumes a need for help and advice. By routinely offering "help" and "advice," a leader may inadvertently hinder growth and prevent the development of collaborative interdependence within teams.

Listening to fix undermines trust, because the receiver believes the leader doesn't trust them to know how to do things. If we sense that someone doesn't trust us, it diminishes the trust we reciprocate.

There's a place for listening to fix. After all, much of our work in healthcare is providing medical advice and treatment. Listening to fix is essential to some degree. However, if listening to fix dominates leadership, it promotes a culture of dependency. That's not much of an issue in complicated systems, where hierarchical structures and control work well. However, it is a big problem in complex systems, because they depend on distributed leadership and increased adaptability. Listening to fix undermines those things.

Listening to Learn. Listening to learn is the least common way to listen, partly because it demands so much from us. And because so few leaders do it well, the rest of us don't have many to emulate.

Listening to learn requires humility. It requires a genuine reverence for whomever we're listening to. It requires that we be students of one another—a form of submission to the experience and expertise of someone else. Those are not easy things for most leaders.

Listening to learn also requires the leader to simultaneously engage with all four dimensions of curiosity. That takes considerable intention and effort. It's more taxing than listening to win or listening to fix and not as expeditious. It's not as expeditious because listening to learn depends less on specific curiosity. It's taxing because it relies heavily on social, experiential, and reflective curiosity, which take more effort and time.

The impact of listening to learn on others is dramatic. Leaders who listen to learn leave others feeling included, valued, and heard—because they are! The receiver feels influential and important to the leader and the organization. That cultivates deep, trust-based connections, motivating people to work together toward a shared purpose. Listening to learn garners enthusiasm, influencing others to bring their best efforts. It also cultivates distributed leadership, an essential component of complex systems.

While listening to learn may demand much more from the leader, it is transformational. It is also essential in complex environments, where leaders must be able to sense the system as completely as possible. That's impossible unless the leader routinely and simultaneously engages with all four dimensions of curiosity: listening to learn.

THE ORTHODOX MINDSET ABOUT CURIOSITY:
The Path to Certainty

Like other orthodox mindsets, the orthodox mindset about curiosity focuses on control, predictability, and efficiency. Curiosity for the orthodox-minded leader is a means for gaining greater certainty.

Orthodox-minded leaders value curiosity but use it to achieve specific tactical and strategic outcomes. Leaders with this mindset may sometimes access all four dimensions of curiosity, but specific curiosity dominates their cognitive landscape. Therefore, leaders with an orthodox mindset about curiosity prefer listening to win and listening to fix.

EXPRESSIONS OF THE ORTHODOX MINDSET

You can identify the orthodox mindset about curiosity in leaders by noticing its typical expressions: relying on specific curiosity, pursuing certainty, and using curiosity for control.

Relying on Specific Curiosity

Leaders with an orthodox mindset employ curiosity as a deliberate tool for specific, often short-term organizational gains—it's merely a tactic. This kind of curiosity seeks concrete facts or data that directly inform a decision or problem. It is a pragmatic, if not mechanistic, use of curiosity. That makes specific curiosity expedient. The leader is not necessarily interested in the "why" or "how" unless it directly affects the leader's immediate goals.

Others may experience these leaders as decisive, directive, and confident. The leader's interest in other perspectives is limited. For example, a leader I coached once said, "If I listen to other perspectives, I might give the impression that I think they are right." He did not offer that comment in jest. Feedback from his 360-degree evaluations affirmed that nearly everyone who worked with him found him bullheaded and dictatorial. Leaders pursuing specific curiosity acknowledge different perspectives, but their primary aim when doing so is to reinforce their views or find flaws in the views of others. Like my client, these leaders are not interested in taking on other perspectives.

Expedience makes this approach attractive, especially in fast-paced, demanding environments with limited time. Given the pressures of leading healthcare, it's a standard approach.

Relying on specific curiosity draws heavily from individual experience, expertise, and patterned leadership behaviors. That makes it reasonably successful when dealing with simple or complicated problems, situations, or systems.

The problem is that most fast-paced and demanding environments today result from complexity. Relying on specific curiosity in a complex context is the least helpful approach for leaders. It leads to oversimplified solutions that invariably result in poor organizational performance.

Pursuing Certainty

Leaders with an orthodox mindset about curiosity are in pursuit of certainty. Certainty means realizing the predicted results by finding the right solution, idea, or direction. This is complementary to, yet different from, relying on specific curiosity. Pursuing certainty addresses the organizational need for stability and predictability to control processes and systems. It focuses on finding predictable outcomes and minimizing organizational surprises.

Pursuing certainty uses curiosity to confirm existing assumptions rather than challenging or expanding them. It relies on specific curiosity but seeks a particular explanation for why things went awry. These leaders also draw upon social curiosity but in a limited way. They focus on discovering what happened, who contributed to the unexpected result, and assigning blame. Or they may rely on social curiosity to determine how best to gain buy-in to the leader's perspective or plans.

These leaders are good at noticing opportunities for improvement and are proficient at driving organizational efficiency. Others may experience these leaders as engaged, helpful achievers who drive operational success. They tend to be intelligent and insightful, due to years of experience. The teams they lead tend to be task focused and purposeful, preferring established practices over novelty and innovation. These leaders vigilantly find deviations and deploy corrective actions, aiming for compliance with standard practice.

Pursuing certainty is a utilitarian approach to perspective taking. Leaders use knowledge gained from the perspectives of others to secure greater efficiency and standardization. There is limited interest in expanding understanding through other perspectives to find novel, innovative, or potentially valuable variations.

The pursuit of certainty sets up an interesting dichotomy. The more knowledge a leader gains through specific and (maybe) social curiosity, the more their degree of uncertainty decreases. As their perceived degree of uncertainty decreases, so does the leader's need for curiosity. This creates a self-reinforcing disinclination toward curiosity and a growing reliance on experience and expertise, leading to intellectual and organizational stagnation. That traps the leader in established ways of thinking and doing things. The result is individual and organizational rigidity and hubris.

Leveraging Curiosity for Control

Leveraging curiosity for control is strategically using curiosity to align others with the leader's aims. It's about understanding and controlling others to achieve the leader's needs.

The difference between the previous expressions of the orthodox mindset about curiosity and this one is the interpersonal focus. Instead of using social curiosity to take on multiple perspectives or co-create a shared purpose, leaders use it to garner buy-in.

These leaders want to know the perspectives of others, what motivates them, and what moves them emotionally. But they use that knowledge as leverage, using coercive and positional power to get others to do what they want. In other words, as Dwight D. Eisenhower famously stated, "By leadership we mean the art of getting someone else to do something that you want done because he wants to do it, not because your position of power can compel him to do it, or your position of authority."[70]

The leadership "art" Eisenhower refers to walks a fine line between manipulation and influence. When the leader combines social curiosity with coercion, compelling others to follow their vision, it's about control—"getting someone else to do something that you want done." It's a subtle form of manipulation that leaders frequently use to create, but not *co-create*, coordinated movement. Leaders who leverage curiosity for control often think that they're being influential. Instead, these leaders are using social curiosity, in combination with their power, to gain greater control over others.

Meet John, a senior executive who is leading a team through organizational change. He sets up individual meetings with team members to enhance communication. During those meetings, John uses social curiosity to better understand his team's perspectives and motivations. Armed with this knowledge, he strategically alters conversations and employs persuasive techniques to steer the team toward his desired outcomes. While appearing collaborative, John subtly coerces his team into conforming to his agenda, eroding their autonomy. Indeed, others "want" to do what John wants. But their motivation is compliance, not commitment.

Others may experience these leaders as inquisitive and insightful. They can be persuasive. But sometimes others feel manipulated by these leaders.

There are some benefits to this approach. These leaders tend to gather like-minded people who share in the leader's vision and approaches. That generates a kind of uniformity and cohesion, minimizing conflict. In popular language, it "gets people on the bus." Leveraging curiosity for control is an approach suitable to complicated contexts, where deviation reflects something gone wrong, faulty thinking, or noncompliance.

THE UNORTHODOX MINDSET ABOUT CURIOSITY:
A Way to Absorb Uncertainty

The unorthodox mindset about curiosity focuses on influencing others and the system, eschewing the pursuit of certainty or control. It absorbs uncertainty and advances adaptability. The leader strives to remain curious and open to novelty and the unexpected. This mindset helps leaders thrive in complexity by enhancing their understanding of how their system functions.

Leaders with this mindset hold all four dimensions of curiosity simultaneously, drawing upon them to various degrees, depending on the situation. For them, curiosity is an intrinsic, exploratory way of being with the world—it defines their stance toward the universe. As such, these leaders prefer listening to learn.

EXPRESSIONS OF THE UNORTHODOX MINDSET

You can identify the unorthodox mindset about curiosity in leaders by noticing its typical expressions: relying on all dimensions of curiosity, using curiosity to absorb uncertainty, and synthesizing multiple perspectives.

Relying on All Dimensions of Curiosity

What's notably different about these leaders is that they draw upon all the dimensions of curiosity. They recognize the need for specific curiosity, though they know it has severe limitations in complex contexts. Unlike orthodox-minded leaders, these leaders fully engage with social curiosity and uniquely rely on experiential and reflective curiosity. This approach is appealing because successfully leading complex systems requires a means of knowing what the system is doing in real time. Doing that well requires full access to all four dimensions of curiosity, especially experiential curiosity. Again, this is "sensing" the system, which necessitates seeking as complete an understanding of the system as possible.

Successfully sensing complex systems also requires taking on multiple and genuinely diverse perspectives. Before a leader can take on the perspectives of others, they must first be able to suspend their own. A leader can't suspend their perspectives if they don't know what they are. Therefore, taking on multiple perspectives requires deep self-awareness, which only arises from reflective curiosity.

Leaders who rely on all dimensions of curiosity are conspicuously different. They tend to be self-reflective, self-aware, and thoughtful. They're quick to listen to learn and slow to listen to win or fix. They tend to speak last and constantly connect with others while they help others get connected. For example, these leaders value "rounding" as a means of connecting with others and experiencing the system firsthand. Others experience these leaders as approachable, humble, authentic, and vulnerable.

Using Curiosity to Absorb Uncertainty

Uncertainty is unsettling. Particularly troublesome for us is the type of uncertainty a leader cannot reduce—irreducible uncertainty (Mindset Five—Uncertainty). We successfully approach irreducible uncertainty by absorbing it. One of the best ways to absorb uncertainty is by remaining curious, which helps us resist the natural inclination to gain greater control by pursuing certainty.

Absorbing uncertainty requires the integration of all four dimensions of curiosity. Reflective curiosity allows leaders to recognize their own sensitivity to uncertainty. Experiential curiosity is essential for identifying the unexpected and emergent qualities of complex systems. Social curiosity, by taking on multiple perspectives, reduces the likelihood of surprises. Specific curiosity clarifies contributing factors, constraints, and opportunities in unexpected situations. Together, these dimensions enable leaders to distinguish between reducible and irreducible uncertainties, equipping them to absorb the irreducible.

Others experience these leaders as discerning and inquisitive, exuding steadiness in a turbulent sea of change. Their unflappable nature, especially in dynamic and volatile contexts, has a calming effect on others. These leaders also exhibit eagerness, expressing awe and wonder, with frequent exclamations of, "Isn't that interesting!"

They don't frame the unexpected as if something had gone wrong or right. Instead, they stay curious about how the system generated the results and outcomes that it did, wondering how they might nudge the system toward a more favorable performance. In their efforts to nudge, they seem uniquely talented at synthesizing creative and novel approaches, sometimes for the most vexing challenges.

Synthesizing Multiple Perspectives

Leaders with an unorthodox curiosity mindset tend to take on multiple perspectives and creatively synthesize them into uniquely practical and novel approaches. By *synthesize*, I mean they can creatively combine perspectives, even those that seem at odds with each other, deriving ideas and solutions that hadn't been available previously. This unique ability contributes substantially to organizational adaptability, a precious leadership capability, especially in complexity.

Leaders who routinely synthesize multiple perspectives are uncommon. We experience them as visionaries and genuine collaborators. They repeatedly find approaches that meet and exceed expectations. They quickly build trust and are highly approachable. They are exceptionally good at connecting with others.

Leaders who take on multiple perspectives and creatively synthesize novel approaches are perpetually curious, heavily relying on all four dimensions of curiosity. They've honed listening to learn to near perfection, and they are artfully adept at drawing out and considering the perspectives and ideas of others.

MAKING THE SHIFT
Before the Shift

Be Prepared to Let Go of Certainty

Letting go of certainty is the cornerstone of shifting. I can't emphasize the importance of this idea enough. Pursuing certainty has dominated our leadership approaches, actions, and behaviors for centuries. Gaining certainty is a powerful motivating force, deeply ingrained in our psyche. Unsurprisingly, the pursuit of certainty intertwines with historic views of leadership and management. It is difficult to dismantle the cognitive infrastructure most of us have that supports this pursuit. To unlearn the deeply ingrained need for certainty takes considerable self-awareness, intention, and persistent curiosity.

Yet it is important to make the effort to unlearn our bias toward certainty, because certainty is severely limited and often unobtainable in complexity. Correct answers or single best solutions rarely exist. In short, the pursuit of certainty in complexity is leadership folly. Since certainty is seldom obtainable in complexity, letting go of certainty is the beginning place for shifting toward the unorthodox mindset about curiosity.

As a leader lets go of certainty, they relax their reliance on specific curiosity and reach for greater dependence on all the other dimensions of curiosity. Letting go of certainty lays the groundwork for absorbing the irreducible uncertainty of complex systems. It prepares leaders to value and seek out diverse perspectives as a necessary and inescapable means for successfully navigating and being well with complexity.

Be Prepared to Embrace Genuine Diversity

By embracing genuine diversity, I mean valuing genuine diversity of thought. Before you can shift, you must advance your thinking about diversity beyond compliance concerns to the most critical strategic asset you can lay your hands on. Effective leadership of complex organizations *demands* genuine diversity, because it's the only way to craft the most complete story you can about your organization and how it functions (Mindset Nine—Stories).

Leaders must recognize that their own perspective can never be the sole arbiter of truth. All the experiences and expertise a leader brings to their leadership, and the attendant perspectives born out of that experience, do matter. But it's an insufficient and unreliable basis for deriving the most helpful leadership approaches, actions, and behaviors in complex organizations. Instead, leaders must tap into *many* others, not just a senior management team, to succeed in complexity. To take full advantage of diversity, a leader must be genuinely and vigorously curious, embracing and relying on all four curiosity dimensions—curiosity as a mindset.

In the hands of leaders who listen to learn, driven by curiosity as a mindset, genuine diversity leads to unique insights that contribute to a more holistic understanding of complex systems. Before a leader can shift, they must embrace genuine diversity with gusto.

Be Prepared to Foster a Bias for Learning

Complex organizations demand a strong bias for learning—an openness to a growing understanding of ourselves, others, and how complex organizations function. It is a bias that moves organizations away from a blame-based culture to a learning-based culture.

A bias for learning includes the notions of failing forward, being willing to take risks, and learning from failure. This is true even in healthcare, where failing may have unwanted consequences. I'm not being cavalier with this idea. Failing forward in healthcare does not have to lead to patient harm. Healthcare can innovate, take risks, and learn from nudges that shift system inclinations, sometimes undesirably, while still advancing patient safety. The status quo is not necessarily safe, and failing forward is not necessarily harmful. Resisting the bias for learning for fear of greater patient harm is a spurious defense of certainty.

Moreover, there's no place for finding blame when complex systems generate unpredictable and emergent results and outcomes. Those system results and outcomes have extraordinarily little to do with what someone did or didn't do. There will always be surprises, changes, and ambiguity in complex systems. The best response is to relax your hold on finding blame and open yourself to a bias for learning. Be persistently curious about the system. You will never be bored. In short, a learning bias supports continuous personal and organizational growth, an essential prerequisite to shifting.

WHY SHIFT

Because Curiosity Is Like Preventive Medicine

Complexity is hard to deal with and doesn't feel good when we're in the middle of it. Our brains perceive complexity as a threat, triggering a robust neurophysiological response. That response leads to self-protective behaviors and discomfort, including strong emotions.

Curiosity counteracts this response, allowing leaders to absorb the inherent uncertainty of complex systems. That helps the leader stay grounded—more adaptable and at ease, less anxious and less susceptible to rash responses. Curious leaders are better at learning and adapting as they go, sensing what's happening moment by moment. Therefore, curiosity is like preventive medicine, inoculating leaders against some of the perils that come with complexity.

Because Curiosity Fosters Adaptance

A crucial attribute for a leader in complexity is adaptance—the ability to be with change in a way that fosters growth and development. Adaptance is impossible without curiosity drawing from all four dimensions. To adapt, one must continuously learn about oneself (reflective curiosity), reconsider different perspectives on what is happening (social curiosity), stay open to novel approaches (experiential curiosity), and be in tune with particular activities and results (specific curiosity).

Curiosity enables individual adaptation and fosters a broader organizational capacity to evolve and innovate. With curiosity, leaders and their teams are better equipped to integrate diverse perspectives, embrace change, and co-create novel solutions. All are necessary for adaptance.

Because Curiosity Helps You Avoid Getting Stuck

The riskiest thing for leaders of complex organizations is getting stuck. Leaders can become fixated on finding a single right or best solution. They can get caught up in the pursuit of some ideal path forward. They can find themselves paralyzed by how fast or unpredictably things are changing and end up adapting too slowly. They can become overwhelmed by trying to control too many simultaneous interdependent interactions. Leaders of complex organizations pursuing certainty or rightness tend to make overly simplified decisions, which are often detrimental to organizational success. But if leaders stay curious, they are less susceptible to becoming trapped in responses that may work well in complicated systems but are ineffective in complex systems.

HOW TO SHIFT

Cultivate All Dimensions of Curiosity

You begin to shift by paying attention to all four dimensions of curiosity. Like most of us, you are probably quite familiar with specific curiosity.

It is the most heavily used form of curiosity, often equated with rational thought, objective decision-making, and solid business practices.

Many are also familiar with social curiosity, whether in principle or practice. However, there are varying degrees of social curiosity. Most have not yet embraced the full breadth of that dimension, which includes the need for genuine diversity and taking on multiple perspectives. You're likely to have some growth opportunities in social curiosity.

Experiential curiosity may be the least familiar to you. It's the one that relies on experimentation and exploration, serving as the foundation for experiential learning. It gets closest to sensing the system, which is essential for leading complex organizations well. The orthodox mindset about curiosity tends to disregard this dimension, preferring a find-and-fix approach. This dimension may require most of your attention.

Lastly, successfully leading complex organizations requires significant personal development beyond simply acquiring expertise and experience, (i.e., reflective curiosity). The key lies in perspective taking, the ability to notice your stories and realize they are always incomplete. That only happens with deepening self-awareness, which includes clarity about your mindsets and where they come from.

Practice Listening to Learn

Listening to learn does not come easy. It's not the most expedient approach to listening. It requires genuine humility, an authentic hunger for diversity and inclusion, and silence.

Those are just the prerequisites. Listening to learn takes practice. Notice when you are using listening to win or fix, and then question whether those were the most helpful approaches. If not, shift toward listening to learn instead.

Practice also includes noticing, learning about, and asking the most useful questions. You'll need to learn to listen with your whole being, which means learning how to be and stay fully present in the moment.

You can't listen to learn while texting on your phone during a meeting or multitasking. You can't listen to learn if you're talking. You can't listen to learn if you're in find-and-fix mode. You must be comfortable with silence, mindful of yourself, and focused on others.

The best place to practice listening to learn is during collaborative efforts, whether working through conflict, critical decisions, or creating something new. Make listening to learn your preferred mode of listening, striving to practice it everywhere. You'll be amazed at what happens.

Be Genuinely Curious About Other Perspectives

I have intentionally repeated myself about taking on multiple perspectives, because it's critical for successfully leading complex organizations. The key things to remember are that your story is always incomplete, that you must seek to create a more complete story, and that you can only accomplish that by taking on multiple perspectives.

Take on multiple diverse perspectives and creatively synthesize them. That can lead to a better understanding of the system and how it functions. Take advantage of those insights, capturing emergent opportunities as they arise, and nudge the system favorably forward.

As you do, remember that your story about the organization will always be incomplete. Even if you're really good at taking on and synthesizing multiple perspectives, you will, like all of us, still fall short of completely understanding your complex system. Humility, vulnerability, authenticity, and collaboration are the leadership qualities that position you for the greatest success in complexity. They will help you stay vigilantly curious.

The unorthodox mindset about curiosity comes with a bonus. Suppose you consistently live out this unorthodox mindset. In that case, others will think you are one of the most remarkable leaders they have ever worked with. That is a legacy worth pursuing—a story worth your life.

PART FOUR

PUTTING IT ALL TOGETHER

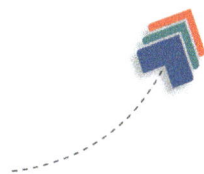

PUTTING IT ALL TOGETHER

The Orthodox and Unorthodox Leader

UNPRECEDENTED TIMES, UNORTHODOX LEADERS

Looking at each mindset individually can make it hard to see the whole leader. It is like trying to see an entire puzzle by looking at one piece. It is important to examine each mindset individually, because it can help healthcare leaders reconsider some familiar ways of thinking. However, we don't interact with the world one mindset at a time. So let's now look at the mindsets as a whole.

Suppose we found a leader who only held to the 10 orthodox mindsets. We would experience that leader quite differently from a leader with only unorthodox mindsets. When considered together, the orthodox and unorthodox mindsets create an image of two profoundly different leaders. Looking at things this way may help us better understand what it means to shift toward unorthodoxy and why it matters. Let's take a closer look at both leaders.

THE ORTHODOX LEADER

We admire orthodox leaders. They are intelligent, experienced, and decisive. They drive organizational change by creating a vision that inspires us. We examine these leaders closely, trying to learn which personal characteristics contribute to their success.

Two Defining Beliefs of Orthodoxy

Two defining beliefs stand out when we study the orthodox leader. Because these beliefs underpin all orthodox mindsets, they help us understand orthodoxy and its origins.

Organizations Are Complicated Systems. Orthodoxy views the world and organizations as comprised of mostly complicated systems, rather than complex systems. There are many reasons why.

Our educational systems instruct us in orthodox mindsets. We also gain experiences in the workforce that reinforce those mindsets, partly because orthodox mindsets prevail. Our experiences connect us with others who think similarly, creating a social network of like-minded people. That makes it seem like orthodox mindsets are the right way for all good leaders to think. These prevailing views become leadership truisms, like "people always resist change." Over time, orthodoxy is codified in policies, regulations, and the law. Together, these things create what sometimes seems to be an insurmountable wall of entrenched orthodoxy. This is how orthodoxy permeates nearly every facet of our lives, leading many to view the world as complicated.

Given the pervasiveness of orthodoxy, leaders who want to be successful adopt the associated mindsets. This has worked out historically, because orthodox leaders are well-suited for leading complicated systems. In fact, complicated systems *need* orthodoxy. Without orthodox leaders, complicated systems run amok and perform poorly.

Leaders Are Like Heroes. We admire leaders who can successfully move complicated systems forward, tending to see them as heroes. This notion of "leader as hero" is another defining belief of orthodoxy. That's because the orthodox view is that leadership comes from the leader— that is, leadership exists *within* the leader. We can see this heroic notion when we describe leaders by their leadership behaviors or other personal characteristics.

This orthodox view is why we usually attribute organizational success or failure to the leader—the athletic director may fire the head football coach because the team doesn't win, or the board may fire the CEO because the organization does not meet its financial targets. Organizational and individual success or failure results from the leader's leadership—an extension of their personal attributes.

These two defining beliefs contribute to an orthodox leader's relationship with each of the ten mindsets. By *relationship*, I mean how an orthodox leader uses the mindset to make sense of what is happening around them. If we look at those relationships as a whole, it paints a holistic picture of the orthodox leader.

A Holistic Description of the Orthodox Leader

The Orthodox Leader's Relationship with the System. An orthodox leader relates to their organization by imagining they stand apart or outside of it. They are observers acting on their complicated systems, working to ensure correct functioning. The system has no control or influence over the leader, but the leader has control and influence over the system. In short, the leader is in command of the system.

This perspective has considerable implications. Notably, an organization cannot exist or function well without an orthodox leader in command. Absent their control, we imagine utter organizational chaos. Orthodoxy positions leaders as organizational heroes, standing apart from the system, protecting and guiding it forward.

The Orthodox Leader's Relationship with Polarity. The orthodox leader doesn't see polarities; instead, they see problems. They protect and guide the organization forward by addressing these problems. Tension, friction, disruption, and conflict represent system dysfunction. When those things exist, there is a problem to find and fix.

Indeed, orthodox leaders are adept problem-solvers. That ability often leads to promotion, elevating these leaders to higher levels of organizational responsibility. The catch is that polarities—a characteristic of complex systems—are invisible to these leaders. When encountering polarity, they misinterpret the energy from a polarity's inherent tension. They diagnose a problem (instead of a polarity) and then they try to fix it.

The Orthodox Leader's Relationship with Adaptability. When these leaders misinterpret polarity as a problem, they also miss the generative energy for organizational adaptability. The energy for organizational and personal adaptability comes from the tension and conflict generated by polarities. That energy is experienced as organizational and individual pressure, which fuels change. However, in the mind of the orthodox leader, the pressure they feel comes from problems, and problems always threaten operational efficiency. If the system functions as it should, there will be no surprises and little friction. Orthodox leaders believe good systems run smoothly and predictably, like an efficient machine.

It's not that these leaders disregard adaptability. Orthodox leaders know their organizations must adapt. However, they believe adaptation must be carefully considered and controlled. Otherwise, adaptation threatens efficiency. In the orthodox leader's mind, adaptability matters, but efficiency matters more.

The Orthodox Leader's Relationship with Power. Orthodox leaders work to control complicated systems to protect and advance efficiency. Because systems include those who work in them, these leaders control how people work and their decisions. There are many ways to control people, both evident and subtle. Regardless, if power reduces autonomy, then the leader is using sources of power to achieve greater control.

That approach helps orthodox leaders take command of the system, ensuring it functions efficiently. Orthodox leaders prefer and are adept at using sources of power for control, out of necessity. It is precisely what complicated systems require.

The Orthodox Leader's Relationship with Uncertainty. The unexpected is a manifestation of uncertainty. Uncertainty is undesirable because it is uncomfortable and threatens organizational efficiency.

Orthodox leaders believe all uncertainty is reducible, given enough resources and expertise. They equate effective leadership with the ability to reduce, if not eliminate, uncertainty. Moreover, unpredictable results or outcomes threaten the leader's vision. Vision is a means of providing certainty, so orthodox leaders will work diligently to realize it.

Orthodox leaders typically create a strategic plan to accomplish this. The plan translates the leader's vision into a clear direction and actionable activities. Then, these leaders cascade the strategic plan throughout the organization, providing greater clarity and certainty about what work matters most.

The Orthodox Leader's Relationship with Change. The strategic plan also defines what must change. Orthodox leaders manage (control) that change, because if it is not managed well, change threatens organizational efficiency, predictability, and the realization of the vision. So orthodox leaders carefully craft change efforts and implement them as initiatives. Those initiatives tend to be system-wide, centrally planned, and deftly managed. These leaders expect resistance to change, preparing themselves and others to manage and overcome it.

The Orthodox Leader's Relationship with the First Work. Managing change, reducing uncertainty, and maintaining efficiency the way orthodox leaders do is demanding. As the orthodox leader takes on broader responsibilities, they encounter even more problems to fix, which increases their need for greater control. The pressure to do all those things results in a massive body of important and urgent work, packing the leader's calendar. Packed calendars, ceaseless meetings, and long days ensue, as do profound fatigue, stress, and anxiety.

In the face of increased demand for time and attention, leaders must give up something to find more time to meet the demand. While orthodox leaders consider the First Work of leadership valuable, it is not the most urgent or important work for them. So these leaders typically let the First Work fall by the wayside. It disappears from their lives, as urgent and important work dominates.

The Orthodox Leader's Relationship with Purpose. Pursuing efficiency, dealing with problems, maintaining control, and reducing uncertainty press upon these leaders. Orthodox leaders focus on getting things done in pursuit of their vision. While purpose may matter, it is not central to any of that work.

For these leaders, purpose is not a trustworthy compass. It is not something that can be relied on to guide the decisions and actions of others. Consequently, decision-making rights are centralized. That's because orthodox leaders trust themselves and a few others to decide the best ways to realize their vision. The "front line" or other stakeholders cannot be entirely trusted to make good, purpose-driven decisions that affect organizational direction.

The Orthodox Leader's Relationship with Stories. Orthodox leaders also trust their ability to make good sense of what is happening. They have confidence in the stories they create about reality. Part of that confidence derives from the belief that their past experiences inform the present and future.

Orthodox leaders tend to disregard or devalue the impact of their cognitive biases and inherent limitations. Instead, they rely on their gut. They trust their experiences. They rely on their perspectives and believe their stories are the best way to make sense of things. In other words, orthodox leaders believe their stories to be complete.

The Orthodox Leader's Relationship with Curiosity. Orthodox leaders' belief in the completeness of their own stories changes how they make use of curiosity. The primary purpose of curiosity for these leaders is to learn how to persuade others to agree with their sensemaking story, not to craft a more complete story. Therefore, curiosity for the orthodox leader is a tactical tool used to maximize the pursuit of the leader's vision for the organization. Indeed, orthodox leaders are adept persuaders, relying heavily on listening to win or fix.

The Importance of Orthodox Leaders

We need orthodox leaders. We revere them for their ability to steer organizations through challenges. They provide clear direction and decisive action, motivating us to work diligently in environments that demand efficiency and stability. Their sharp vision and defined goals help align our efforts, ensuring everyone works together toward established aims.

Orthodox leaders excel in structured organizations (complicated systems) where predictability and standardization are crucial. These kinds of organizations developed in an era of far greater stability, where contextual changes occurred slowly. That is part of the reason complicated systems function best when they are managed to maximize efficiency. When they are led in ways that match their intended function, complicated systems consistently achieve operational goals.

We changed the world by understanding, leveraging, and managing complicated systems. Orthodox leaders were pivotal in building companies into global corporations that withstood the test of time. In the 19th and 20th centuries, these giant, complicated organizations created value for billions, elevating the health and prosperity of communities and nations worldwide. Complicated bureaucratic corporations are among humankind's greatest achievements. One cannot overstate their significance and importance in advancing human civilization.

Orthodox leaders drove the industrial and corporate revolutions these companies represent. That is one of the main reasons we continue to admire and emulate these companies and their leaders.

Consider contemporary examples like Steve Jobs, whose visionary leadership at Apple transformed technology and consumer electronics, changing the world and how we interact. Likewise, Elon Musk has driven innovation and disruption in the automotive and space exploration industries with Tesla and SpaceX.[71]

Jobs and Musk embody orthodox mindsets, where control, efficiency, and predictability (at least in execution) are paramount. Their leadership is (or was) often top-down, with a strong emphasis on their unique vision and their individual abilities to shape the direction of their organizations. The consequences of Musk's leadership will continue to unfold, but it is already transformational. Though he is no longer with us, Job's vision and company continue to transform the world, with Apple being one of the most successful companies ever created. The point is that modern orthodox leaders like Musk and Jobs still lead organizations and continue to drive change through their clear vision of the future and decisive action.

Regardless of how remarkable orthodox leaders may be or how much we admire them, they are increasingly less effective today than they once were. Jobs and Musk are rare exceptions. We sometimes tolerate leaders like them if they garner dramatic results: Jobs and Musk are examples of this tolerance. Working with either is often described as difficult, their genius aside.

And how they lead is not entirely transferable to the rest of us, because most of us are not Steve Jobs or Elon Musk. We're usually mere mortals, striving to be the best leaders we know how to be. As such, success as an orthodox leader can be elusive. The diminishing effectiveness of orthodox leaders is not due to a lack of capability, intelligence, or skill. It's because the world has changed, and so have our organizations. Today's organizations are complex and, therefore, dramatically less predictable and stable. Orthodox leaders don't do well in these kinds of complex environments. Because the context has changed so dramatically, other ways of leading, born out of different mindsets, find greater success.

THE UNORTHODOX LEADER

We admire unorthodox leaders. Their holistic approaches, wisdom, and ability to stir human imagination and creativity inspire us. They drive organizational change by tapping into shared purpose, which helps us see our interconnectivity with each other. We examine these leaders closely, trying to learn how they make sense of the world. We want to emulate how they think, not just what they do.

Two Defining Beliefs of Unorthodoxy

When we study the unorthodox leader, two defining beliefs stand out. Because they underpin all the unorthodox mindsets, knowing about both beliefs helps us better understand unorthodoxy and its origins.

Organizations Are Complex Systems. Unorthodoxy views the world and organizations as comprised of mostly complex, rather than complicated, systems. This view reflects an evolved understanding of the world's workings, one anchored in complexity science, "one of the most radical new scientific paradigms of the 20th century."[72] Complexity moves us beyond the certainty that attends orthodoxy. It is an unfamiliar way of making sense of the world and its workings. Nonetheless, unorthodox leaders have embraced complexity and its implications, adding a new portfolio of mindsets to their orthodox ones. They have shifted toward unorthodoxy.

Unorthodox leaders must stimulate novel and emergent change. Accomplishing that leads to greater organizational adaptability. In fact, complex systems *need* the unorthodox leader's ability to enable an environment where adaptability thrives. Without unorthodox leaders, complex organizations wither and die, unable to adapt rapidly to an ever-changing context.

Leaders Are like Gardeners. This brings us to the second defining belief of unorthodoxy. Leaders are like "gardeners" who cultivate leadership. In unorthodoxy, leadership grows (emerges) out of an adequately prepared organizational landscape. It lives among the interactions between people, a co-created entity existing *outside* the leader. This means leadership *results* from specific approaches, actions, and behaviors. But it is not those approaches, actions, or behaviors themselves.

Because leadership exists outside the leader and results from specific ways individuals interact, anyone can be a leader. Given this understanding of leadership, we can see how leadership has little to do with title, role, or position. It does not rely on technical expertise or an individual's experience. Leadership only emerges within the relationship between at least two people. That means leadership can emerge anywhere the conditions are favorable. Leadership, therefore, is a distributed entity.

An implication of this is that organizational success or failure does not derive from any given leader. It derives from the numerous interactions of many. That means complex systems only thrive if distributed leadership thrives.

These two defining beliefs of unorthodoxy contribute to an unorthodox leader's relationship with their mindsets. If we look at those relationships, it helps paint a holistic picture of the unorthodox leader.

A Holistic Description of the Unorthodox Leader

The Unorthodox Leader's Relationship with the System. Unorthodox leaders are entangled in complex systems, unable to extract themselves to observe and act on the system objectively. The system influences the leader's understanding as much as the leader influences the system. There is no way to escape this interdependent relationship.

Because leaders are as much a part of the system as the system is part of them, leaders cannot separate themselves from the organization to "command" it. Therefore, leaders can only influence an organization through their participation in whatever is transpiring. There is no commanding or controlling a complex system.

One important implication is that to nudge or favorably move complex systems, the interdependent, influential interactions of many must be coordinated. But those coordinated efforts cannot be commanded or controlled either. They must come from a distributed leadership that is guided by a shared purpose. Absent that influence, the organization will devolve into a complicated system or slip into chaos.

While unorthodox leaders are essential, complex systems rarely respond to and don't rely on any given leader. In short, there are no heroes in complexity.

The Unorthodox Leader's Relationship with Polarity. Unorthodox leaders differentiate problems from polarities and discern the challenges of both. These leaders recognize that the tension, friction, disruption, or conflict they experience may be the creative energy of polarity, enabling an Adaptive Arena (as described in Mindset Three—Adaptability). Or it may be a problem that the leader and others must resolve. Unorthodox leaders know the difference and shift their approaches accordingly.

Recall that polarities require the leader to strike a dynamic harmony between two necessary components. These leaders seek out that dynamic harmony, aiming for an adaptive response.

The Unorthodox Leader's Relationship with Adaptability. The unorthodox leader recognizes the inherent polarity of complex systems and sees it as an opportunity to maximize organizational adaptability. They work to strike a dynamic harmony between the Entrepreneurial

Core (innovation and emergence) and the Operational Core (production and efficiency), which creates the Adaptive Arena.

From within that organizational tension, unorthodox leaders work to cultivate distributed leadership, fending off the encroachment of either pole. This allows novelty to emerge, which spurs adaptation.

Unorthodox leaders work to maximize organizational adaptability. They know adaptability is the primary source of value creation, not efficiency. For unorthodox leaders, efficiency matters, but adaptability matters more.

The Unorthodox Leader's Relationship with Power. Unorthodox leaders use power to protect and advance adaptability, drawing upon sources of power that convert to influence. They use that power to influence both poles of the inherent polarity of complex systems. They use it to protect the Adaptive Arena from encroachment while taking advantage of opportunities. And they use that power to enable widespread distributed leadership.

Unorthodox leaders use power to influence, rather than to control, because control diminishes autonomy, and autonomy is an essential precondition for distributed leadership. Since autonomy is needed for distributed leadership, foundational to emergence, and a prerequisite for adaptation, unorthodox leaders prefer power sources that convert to influence. So the unorthodox leader's preference for influence is not a stylistic choice. It is a preference for the success or survival of the complex system itself.

The Unorthodox Leader's Relationship with Uncertainty. Unorthodox leaders take advantage of uncertainty. They work with it to generate emergence, the arrival of something unexpected and not wholly intended. A surprising result or outcome means the system is functioning as designed—it is functioning adaptively. For the unorthodox leader, uncertainty must be embraced and harnessed, not eliminated.

These leaders know that there are various kinds of uncertainty. Some can be reduced, but much of the uncertainty they encounter in complex systems is irreducible, so it can only be absorbed.

These leaders don't disregard reducible uncertainty. They are as equally adept at reducing uncertainty as their orthodox colleagues. Unorthodox leaders are proficient at both ways of dealing with uncertainty.

The Unorthodox Leader's Relationship with Change. Adaptability is the healthy response to uncertainty in complex organizations. In short, adaptability is change.

Unorthodox leaders recognize this, eschewing centralized change initiatives because they are not usually helpful or successful.[73] In complex organizations, successful change efforts are mainly localized experiments that spread throughout the organization. The unorthodox leader watches for these emergent adaptations, noticing how the experiments nudge the entire system. These leaders promote those experiments if the system adjusts favorably. If the system is nudged unfavorably, the unorthodox leader works with others to shut those experiments down.

The Unorthodox Leader's Relationship with the First Work. Leading within the Adaptive Arena of complex systems is highly demanding and relentlessly uncomfortable. That's because the level of uncertainty is persistently high and the unexpected is the norm.

The inherent polarity of complex systems also causes considerable organizational and personal tension. Success as an unorthodox leader in this environment is so demanding that these individuals must be at their best daily. These leaders consider the First Work of leadership essential because it enables them to be at their absolute best. The First Work is foundational to their leadership. It's not an optional nice-to-have but a nonnegotiable on their daily calendars. Unorthodox leaders do the First Work, because they must.

The Unorthodox Leader's Relationship with Purpose: In addition to the First Work, unorthodox leaders deal with the inherent

SHIFTING TOWARD UNORTHODOXY

challenges of complexity by being purpose-driven. That's true personally, and it is how they engage with others within the complex organizations they lead.

These leaders carefully cultivate a shared purpose, trusting that others will make decisions that advance the organization toward that purpose. Because the future is primarily unknowable in complexity, any vision of some future state is, by comparison, an unreliable guide. The unorthodox leader's ability to help us stay connected with personal and organizational purpose in the face of irreducible uncertainty is one of the main reasons we admire them.

The Unorthodox Leader's Relationship with Stories. Uncertainty is the essence of complexity, and it undermines a leader's ability to know. That leaves the leader acknowledging the limits of their knowing—their stories are and always will be incomplete.

Acknowledging that their stories are incomplete keeps leaders humble, and humility keeps the leader's mind open to other possibilities. That positions unorthodox leaders to look for and take on diverse perspectives. Unorthodox leaders listen to learn and create collaborative environments, where trust-based relationships thrive.

That kind of environment is essential. It allows for enough psychological safety to share alternative stories. Leaders who understand their stories to be incomplete remain curious and open to learning from the perspectives of others.

The Unorthodox Leader's Relationship with Curiosity. Humility positions unorthodox leaders to consider curiosity the most important means of crafting a more complete story. When leaders are curious in ways that help craft more complete stories, better ideas and unique solutions emerge. Those novel ideas can sometimes strategically position the organization in remarkably successful ways. That makes curiosity a highly prized strategic asset, not a tactical approach.

The Importance of Unorthodox Leaders

We need unorthodox leaders. They foster environments of high trust, collaboration, and innovation. Those characteristics are critical in today's dynamic and unpredictable world. The unorthodox leader's ability to galvanize collective action and co-create solutions leads to adaptive, sustainable, and transformative change.

Unorthodox leaders excel in networks and ambidextrous organizations where adaptability, innovation, and swift transformation are crucial. We design these kinds of organizations to be complex, deriving rapid adaptive change in response to dynamic and volatile contexts. In short, unorthodox leaders are ideally suited for complex systems.

Historically, unorthodox leaders have played pivotal roles in advancing organizations and human civilization. Mahatma Gandhi is a notable example. Gandhi sparked independence in India through nonviolent resistance. He had a complex relationship with the concept of leadership. While he undeniably led millions with his philosophy and his actions, Gandhi himself often downplayed his role. He preferred to see himself as a servant of the people, an unorthodox leader, rather than as a hero in the conventional sense.[74]

Gandhi believed in the power of collective action and grassroots movements. He emphasized that true change comes from the bottom up, an adaptive response to local community realities. He encouraged each individual to take responsibility for their own actions and moral integrity, thereby making an appeal to autonomy and ownership. In his writings and speeches, Gandhi looked to empower others to become leaders, fostering a decentralized approach to leadership—distributed leadership.[75]

For example, Gandhi's concept of self-rule extended beyond political independence to include self-discipline and self-governance at an individual level. He encouraged people to lead themselves through self-reliance, ethical living, and community cooperation.

In addition to historical leaders like Gandhi, there are contemporary examples of successful unorthodox leaders. Jacinda Ardern, the former Prime Minister of New Zealand, is one such leader.[76] She showed unorthodox leadership by fostering unity, empathy, and effective crisis management during the COVID-19 pandemic and other challenges. Her inclusive approach and emphasis on collective well-being garnered international admiration.

Unorthodox leaders are routinely at the heart of individual and organizational transformations. That's because they enlighten us, drawing out the best we can offer. We follow these leaders, not out of compliance but from a willing subjugation of our self-interests for the benefit of many. When people work together that way, the result is invariably transformational work that tends to endure. A key thing to remember about unorthodox leaders such as Gandhi is that they co-create *movements*, not plans.

Reflecting on the defining characteristics and a leader's relationship with orthodox and unorthodox mindsets, a picture of two distinct types of leaders emerges. (See table 5 for a summary.) Yet, as awkward or difficult as it may seem, leaders today must be able to adopt both orthodox and unorthodox mindsets.

BEING AN ORTHODOX AND UNORTHODOX LEADER

Throughout this book, I've emphasized that shifting toward unorthodoxy is not about abandoning orthodoxy. It's about being adept at both and adopting the most helpful portfolio of mindsets when the situation demands it.

Which way you shift depends on your context. Being orthodox or unorthodox is not a preference or a style choice. Your goal is to adopt the mindsets that match your context—complicated systems need orthodoxy, and complex systems need unorthodoxy. Of course, that

	THE ORTHODOX LEADER	THE UNORTHODOX LEADER
Defining Beliefs		
View of Systems	Sees organizations as complicated.	Sees organizations as complex.
View of Leadership	Leadership is what leaders do: the leader is a heroic figure commanding the system.	Leadership results from what leaders do: the leader is a gardener figure cultivating distributed leadership.
Relationship with Mindsets		
Mindset One—Complexity	Observes and acts on the system from outside it, controlling how it functions.	Experiences and interacts with the system, influencing and being influenced by how it functions.
Mindset Two—Polarity	Views tension as dysfunction, reflecting problems to be solved.	Views tension as creative energy from polarity or a problem to be solved.
Mindset Three—Adaptability	Prioritizes efficiency over adaptability.	Prioritizes adaptability over efficiency.
Mindset Four—Power	Uses power to control.	Uses power to influence.
Mindset Five—Uncertainty	Reduces uncertainty.	Absorbs uncertainty.
Mindset Six—Change	Implements change initiatives.	Cultivates emergent change experiments.
Mindset Seven—First Work	Considers First Work to be on the "life" side of work-life balance.	Considers First Work to be on the "work" side of work-life balance.
Mindset Eight—Purpose	Trusts in the leader's vision.	Trusts in shared purpose.
Mindset Nine—Stories	Believes their stories are complete.	Believes their stories are *always* incomplete.
Mindset Ten—Curiosity	Views curiosity as a tactical tool.	Views curiosity as a strategic asset.

TABLE 5. *The Orthodox and Unorthodox Leader.* A holistic view with brief descriptions of the orthodox and unorthodox leader. (Source: Michael Hein, 2025.)

means you must discern between the complicated and complex. That's not always easy to do. Here are a few helpful things to keep in mind:

Learn More About Both Kinds of Systems

I introduced you to some basics of complicated and complex systems in Mindset One—Complexity. I also introduced you to Cynefin, a sense-making tool for leaders (Part One—Systemness and Why it Matters).[77] Cynefin helps leaders decide which kind of system they are dealing with. I encourage you to learn more about this tool, where it comes from, and how to use it. Regardless of which resources you use, understand that, to shift, you need to know which of the two systems you are dealing with: complicated or complex.

Avoid a False Choice

Remember that our brains prefer simplicity, so we are inclined to pick one way of thinking—right or wrong, good or bad, orthodox or unorthodox. But leading well is not an either/or choice. The choice is about being orthodox *and* unorthodox, shifting toward one or the other when it matters the most. It is about shifting your cognitive weight, leaning away from one portfolio of mindsets toward the other, like shifting your weight from your right foot to your left. Your goal is to be adaptive and to adjust to match the system you have.

Do not fall into the trap of trying to change the system to match your mindsets. That's a common error, and it can lead to considerable individual and organizational harm. To avoid that harm, carefully consider your context, the organization's purpose, and the results and outcomes you need most. Then, shift toward the mindsets that match.

Mindsets Are Not Styles

It's tempting to consider mindsets to be styles of leadership, (e.g., a "hero" leadership style or a "gardener" leadership style). However, that notion reflects an incomplete understanding of mindsets and leadership's nature, whether leadership exists inside or outside a leader.

Style suggests a preference for something, like which clothes you wear—an expression of your inclinations. In other words, style is something detached from necessity. We can wear whatever we want. If we apply that thinking to how we lead, then how we lead is merely an extension of our personality—a style.

I hope I've convinced you that that way of thinking does not serve you well. If success is about style, then success only depends on you being the right person for the right job at the right time and picking the right style—mostly luck. Successful leadership is more than luck.

Success in a complicated or complex system depends on which portfolio of mindsets a leader chooses. You shift toward whichever portfolio of mindsets is most likely to garner individual and organizational results that matter. The critical point is that the *context* determines the mindset portfolio that leads to success, not your leadership style.

BEING AN UNORTHODOX LEADER

You must be both an orthodox and unorthodox leader. However, if you're paying attention to your context, you will often shift toward unorthodoxy. It's like finding a new posture. Where you once stood mostly on orthodoxy, now you find yourself standing mostly on unorthodoxy. It's like having found a new cognitive base of operations, one that is unorthodox. The context has changed, creating the imperative to shift toward unorthodoxy.

Being an Unorthodox Leader Follows
the Law of Requisite Complexity

Underpinning this imperative to shift is the Law of Requisite Complexity.[78] This principle asserts that an organization or system must be as complex as its environment to maintain stability, adaptability, and success. The implications for healthcare leaders are that (a) you must recognize that your healthcare organization is a complex system; and (b) you must be a complexity-fit leader.

Healthcare leaders must be able to lead well to realize safe, equitable, accessible, and affordable healthcare. This has always been true. However, leading complex healthcare organizations today (and tomorrow) requires healthcare leaders suited to complexity. That is what has changed.

If leaders with orthodox mindsets lead complex organizations—which is the norm today—the leader and the organization will suffer because these leaders are violating the Law of Requisite Complexity. Leaders must fit with complexity to lead complex systems effectively. Complexity-fit leaders are leaders who have shifted toward unorthodoxy.

Because our healthcare organizations are mostly complex systems in a complex world, unorthodoxy is generally the better—more useful—portfolio of mindsets for a leader. In these unprecedentedly complex times, what's called for most is unorthodoxy.

Being an Unorthodox Leader Positions You to Achieve Genuine Systemness

That brings us back to one of this book's most important points: systemness. Systemness is an idealized vision of an organization, where all the parts work together in ways that enhance the performance of the whole. It has become a justification or explanation for the consolidation and growth of healthcare organizations. There is a widely and deeply held belief that being bigger opens the door of opportunity for being better. Once the organization is bigger and we learn how to "be like a system," we can deliver better care. Acting like a system is systemness. But what kind of system do we want to act like? As we've learned, there are many kinds of systems, and orthodox and unorthodox leaders understand systemness very differently.

For orthodox leaders, sweeping standardization leads to system-ness, which leads to efficiency and high quality. Their efforts focus on minimizing variation to optimize the function of the whole. A process or system's performance is scrutinized for deviation from a standard. If deviations exist, the leaders work to reduce that variation. This approach is suitable for complicated systems, where predictability and control are paramount.

You can reduce complicated systems to their parts to know how the whole functions. You can look at the hospital unit's productivity targets to understand the entire hospital's productivity levels. Or you can do that at a regional level, looking at each hospital to understand the organization's performance. Orthodox leaders understand system-ness as the sum of those parts equaling the whole. They believe that the whole organization will function at its best only if every part functions at its best. Another way to say that is we are only as good as the weakest link.

In contrast, unorthodox leaders view systemness as an emergent property that can only happen when the parts are free to interact in uncontrolled ways, influenced by distributed leadership. Emergence, therefore, births organizational adaptability, leading to systemness. This view is well-suited to complex systems, where emergence and adaptability are paramount.

It also means you cannot fully understand how the whole derives results or outcomes. The system is not reducible. How the parts work together creates more than can be explained by looking at how each part functions.

This inability to reduce complex systems and understand how they work is radical and profound. David Krakauer says it well: "Hence, reductionism . . . not only fails to explain complexity, but it also fails to detect it."[79] Unorthodoxy views systemness as emergent and derived from innumerable, interdependent, uncontrolled interactions among the parts of the organization. It cannot be created, understood, or even identified by looking at how the parts function. The beauty of systemness is that something magical happens when all the parts interact in this way. The whole becomes greater than the sum of the parts. That is genuine systemness.

This kind of systemness happens when a group of people works together, leading to results that cannot be explained by looking at any single individual. High-performing teams exemplify this phenomenon, whether in business, sports, or any other field. Something remarkable occurs when individuals come together with a shared purpose so deeply held that they are willing to subjugate their self-interest to it. In such an environment, genuine systemness emerges. This magic happens through the group's dynamic, interdependent interactions and collective intelligence, resulting in performance far exceeding what can be expected or explained by the sum of the individual parts. The whole becomes greater, demonstrating that genuine systemness is an emergent property that cannot be reduced merely to the contributions of each member.

Large healthcare organizations can accomplish the same thing. It requires genuine systemness, cultivating the organizational landscape in such a way that emergence grows and thrives among its many parts. For emergence to grow and thrive requires distributed leadership and an Adaptive Arena, which allow adaptability to flourish.

It's critical to understand that emergence creates genuine systemness. Without emergence, systemness doesn't exist. Since emergence is a unique quality of complex systems and is absent in complicated systems, genuine systemness is only achievable in complex systems. If you want and need systemness, you want and need complexity. That's the only system where the whole exceeds the sum of the parts.

If genuine systemness only occurs in complex systems, leaders must also be complexity-fit. To be complexity-fit, leaders must shift toward unorthodoxy. This shift is essential for realizing genuine systemness and enabling healthcare organizations to reach their full potential in these unprecedentedly complex times.

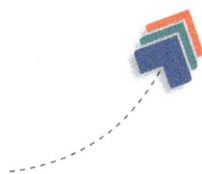

AFTERWORD

Here we are at the end and the beginning—the end of the book and perhaps the beginning of your journey with complexity. In writing this book, I aimed to offer you a complexity compass, not a road map. This is a how-to-think-it book, not a how-to-do-it book. You may have noticed that approach. I offer examples highlighting different ways to think about something but don't provide many "best practices," side-stepping the inclination to tell you what someone else did. I also downplayed detailed explanations of specific methodologies, like Agile or Lean.

I took this approach because you don't need my advice. You're intelligent and resourceful. You can sense the kind of system you are dealing with and decide which approaches, actions, and behaviors are most appropriate. You don't need me to do that for you. In short, you can create your own road map to success.

Mindsets, however, are different from examples, methodologies, or best practices. They serve as compasses, deeply rooted guides shaping what you do. If you're curious about your mindsets and take notice of them, it can change how you lead. That's because how you lead begins with how you think, and how you think begins with your mindsets.

For any leader I coach, I start with their mindsets. This book is meant to be like that: an opportunity to explore your mindsets.

Another reason I took this approach is because complexity makes past experiences less valuable. Anything I might have offered as an example doesn't consider who you are today or what is happening now in your organization. Offering you "Ten Steps to be Great at Complexity" presumes your healthcare organization is pretty much like any other and that past experiences inform the future. While that would be convenient, it is untrue. If I had made those assumptions, offering more examples for you to follow would have been a disservice.

Complexity is hard. It's hard to live with, hard to lead when you're in it, and hard to write about. You could dismiss the idea of complexity in an attempt to make things easier—many choose to do just that. In my view, making that choice doesn't go well. An inattentiveness to the nature of complexity and its consequences hurts people. Humans often suffer in complexity, including leaders. However, leaders can decrease that suffering, which is why I wrote this book: it's my effort to help you do your best to reduce the human suffering that can come with complexity.

You're not the first leader I've shared these ideas with. I've discussed complexity and the ten mindsets with hundreds of others. And I've noticed a pattern in how leaders digest complexity-fit mindsets when they first encounter them. It's not uncommon to resist unorthodox mindsets at first.

But, with some added consideration, curiosity blooms. The leader finds the ideas interesting, albeit not particularly practical. If the leader continues to consider unorthodox mindsets, what follows is a growing awareness of complexity. The leader begins to see complexity all around them. Once they start to see it, they often reconsider their orthodox mindsets.

One recent client initially dismissed complexity, but after some reflection, he saw its relevance. Then he invited complexity in for a symbolic "tea." He sat down with his mindsets, reflecting on key areas.

New insights emerged, and he began experimenting with different approaches. Within a few months, others began commenting about how he had transformed the way he led. This client started to see polarities where he previously saw only problems and began to appreciate adaptability over mere efficiency. He relaxed his need for control and began seeking multiple perspectives. He embraced the notion that his story was always incomplete.

Imagine you hear a knock at your front door. You open it to be greeted by a stranger—a stranger called complexity. Complexity looks unfamiliar and unusual. You're not sure what you should do. You could shut the door in complexity's face without saying a word. You could stand in the doorway and ask complexity something like "What are you?" or "Why are you knocking at my door?" You could invite them in for tea, too, and sit down to have a lengthy conversation.

Some will not see complexity, dismissing it as irrelevant. Some will see complexity but won't find any practical applications, so nothing changes for them. But some leaders see complexity and grasp enough about it that they invite it into their inner landscape. I've witnessed leaders interact with unorthodox mindsets in all these ways.

The leaders who sit down with complexity notice it all around them. They notice their uncertainty and wonder whether to reduce it or absorb it. They're more attentive to their power sources and more careful about which they use. And they see people interacting with change in an entirely different way.

These leaders deepen their relationship with the First Work and are driven by purpose more than vision. They hold their stories with an open hand and strive to remain perpetually curious. In summary, the pattern I've witnessed is growth—leaders growing as they go on a journey of discovery with complexity.

It's not an easy path. There are no simple answers or approaches to growing your understanding of complexity. You're not going to grasp the nature of complexity in a 40-minute presentation at a leadership conference. A brief presentation can introduce the idea that there are different and valid ways of looking at organizations that you may not be used to. But simply being introduced to that idea is unlikely to change deeply ingrained ways of thinking and behaving. This is the work of a lifetime. But it is truly transformative work, something that, as one of my clients said, "gives you a different leadership voice." He meant that you become an entirely different leader when you begin to grasp the implications of complexity.

Your mindsets will guide you as you go on your way. Stay curious and open, and let your leadership evolve with each new insight. While the discovery may not be easy, it is something to be excited about.

At MEDI Leadership (https://medileadership.org/unorthodoxy), we partner with healthcare leaders striving to transform as they journey with complexity. Reach out. I'd love to hear from you. Tell me about your journey with complexity, and please share with me what you discover. I can be reached at MEDIPublishing@medileadership.org.

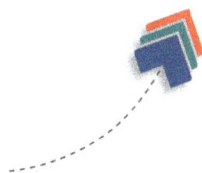

LEARN MORE

A SELECTED BIBLIOGRAPHY

As you reach the end of this book and perhaps the beginning of your journey with complexity, I want to provide you with further resources to continue your exploration. The following selected bibliography includes references that have been instrumental in shaping my understanding of complexity and leadership. They are resources I have shared with clients, and many have found them invaluable.

It is not an exhaustive list, but it serves as a robust starting point. Consider it a thoughtfully curated collection of books and articles to accompany you on your journey. I hope these resources inform you and encourage your shift toward unorthodoxy.

PART ONE: INTRODUCTION

Mindsets and Why They Matter

Achor, Shawn, Alia J. Crum, and Peter Salovey. "Rethinking Stress: The Role of Mindsets in Determining the Stress Response." *Journal of Personality and Social Psychology* 104, no. 4 (2013): 716–33. https://doi.org/10.1037/a0031201.

This article provides an example of how potent mindsets are.

Crum, Alia J., and Gregory M. Walton, eds. *Handbook of Wise Interventions: How Social Psychology Can Help People Change.* Guilford Press, 2023.

Walton and Crum describe the connection between mindsets and leaders' approaches.

Dweck, Carol S. *Mindset: The New Psychology of Success.* Random House, 2006.

Dweck's work popularized the idea of a "growth" and "fixed" mindset.

Wheatley, Margaret J. *Leadership and the New Science: Discovering Order in a Chaotic World.* 3rd ed. Berrett-Koehler, 2006.

Wheatley describes complexity, our relationship with it, and why it matters.

Systemness and Why It Matters

Boone, Mary E., and David J. Snowden. "A Leader's Framework for Decision Making." *Harvard Business Review* 85, no. 11 (2007): 68–76, 149.

An introduction to Cynefin and understanding complex systems.

Capra, Fritjof, and Pier Luigi Luisi. *The Systems View of Life: A Unifying Vision*. Cambridge University Press, 2016.

> A holistic perspective on systems, integrating insights from biology, complexity science, and systems thinking.

Laloux, Frederic. *Reinventing Organizations: A Guide to Creating Organizations Inspired by the Next Stage of Human Consciousness*. Nelson Parker, 2014.

Lawrence, Paul. *Coaching Systemically: Five Ways of Thinking About Systems*. Routledge, 2021.

> A concise explanation of different kinds of systems and why they matter.

McKelvey, Bill. *Organizational Systematics: Taxonomy, Evolution, Classification*. University of California Press, 2022.

> An exhaustive, foundational work on organizational systems.

Zuckerman, Alan. "Systemness: The Next Frontier for Integrated Health Delivery." *Veralon*. July 23, 2015. Accessed July 26, 2024. https://www.veralon.com/articles/systemness-the-next-frontier -for-integrated-health-delivery/.

> A well-constructed and typical example of orthodox systemness in healthcare.

Shifting and Why It Matters

Christensen, Clayton M. *The Innovator's Dilemma*. Harper Business, 2000.

Fisher, Dalmar, David Rooke and Bill Torbert. *Personal and Organisational Transformations: Through Action Inquiry*. Edge/Work Press, 2000.

> A methodology for shifting, anchored in behavioral psychology and adult development.

Heath, Chip, and Dan Heath. *Switch: How to Change Things When Change Is Hard*. Bantam Doubleday Dell, 2010.

An introduction to how we go about shifting our approaches.

Joiner, William B., and Stephen A. Josephs. *Leadership Agility: Five Levels of Mastery for Anticipating and Initiating Change*. Jossey-Bass, 2010.

Joiner's work profoundly impacted my leadership journey.

Kegan, Robert, and Lisa Laskow Lahey. *Immunity to Change: How to Overcome It and Unlock the Potential in Yourself and Your Organization*. Harvard Business Publishing, 2009.

Draws upon Kegan's background in adult development, informing us about how we relate to change.

Senge, Peter M. *The Fifth Discipline: The Art & Practice of the Learning Organization*. Image Books, 2006.

Using different terms, Senge describes many of the important personal and organizational shifts required to move toward unorthodoxy.

PART TWO: MINDSETS ABOUT SYSTEMS

Mindset One—Complexity: An Unorthodox Mindset about Systems

Allen, Peter M., Jean G. Boulton, and Cliff Bowman. *Embracing Complexity: Strategic Perspectives for an Age of Turbulence*. Oxford University Press, 2015.

Arena, Michael, and Mary Uhl-Bien. "Leadership for Organizational Adaptability: A Theoretical Synthesis and Integrative Framework." *The Leadership Quarterly* 29, no. 1 (2018): 89–104. https://doi.org/10.1016/j.leaqua.2017.12.009.

Uhl-Bien's work has profoundly shaped my thinking. I'd encourage you to read more of her work.

Collins, Tantum, Chris Fussell, Stanley A. McChrystal, and David Silverman. *Team of Teams: New Rules of Engagement for a Complex World*. Portfolio Penguin, 2015.

McChrystal shares his personal story of shifting toward unorthodoxy.

Garvey Berger, Jennifer, and Keith Johnston. *Simple Habits for Complex Times: Powerful Practices for Leaders*. Stanford University Press, 2015.

A sampling of Jennifer Garvey Berger's impactful contributions.

Gell-Mann, Murray. *The Quark and the Jaguar: Adventures in the Simple and the Complex*. SFI Press, 2023.

An introduction to complexity by a Nobel Laureate.

Mitchell, Melanie. *Complexity: A Guided Tour*. Oxford University Press, 2011.

Mitchell's book offers an excellent starting place for understanding complexity.

Mindset Two—Polarity: An Unorthodox Mindset about Problems

Emerson, Brian, and Kelly Lewis. *Navigating Polarities: Using Both/And Thinking to Lead Transformation*. Paradoxical Press, 2019.

A comprehensive guide to understanding and harmonizing polarity.

Garvey Berger, Jennifer. "Polarity Management." Posted July 18, 2018, by Cultivating Leadership. YouTube. Accessed July 24, 2024. https://youtu.be/yyuFr4gTzjU.

Johnson, Barry. *Polarity Management: Identifying and Managing Unsolvable Problems*. HRD Press, 2014.

The book to read for understanding and harmonizing polarity.

Leslie, Jean. "How to Manage Paradox." *Center for Creative Leadership*. November 17, 2022. Accessed July 24, 2024. https://www.ccl.org/articles/leading-effectively-articles/manage-paradox-for-better-performance/.

Mindset Three—Adaptability: An Unorthodox Mindset about Creating Value

Arena, Michael J. *Adaptive Space: How GM and Other Companies Are Positively Disrupting Themselves and Transforming into Agile Organizations.* McGraw Hill, 2018.

Arena offers an approach to creating and sustaining the adaptive space.

Grashow, Alexander, Ronald A. Heifetz, and Marty Linsky. *The Practice of Adaptive Leadership: Tools and Tactics for Changing Your Organization and the World.* Harvard Business Press, 2009.

Heifetz's insights are foundational to complexity-fit leadership.

Johnson, Steven. *Emergence: The Connected Lives of Ants, Brains, Cities and Software.* Penguin Books, 2002.

Kotter, John P. *Accelerate: Building Strategic Agility for a Faster-Moving World.* Harvard Business Review Press, 2014.

Kotter details and describes ambidextrous organizations, which are necessary for greater adaptability.

Lichtenstein, Benyamin B. *Generative Emergence: A New Discipline of Organizational, Entrepreneurial, and Social Innovation.* Oxford University Press, 2014.

The foundational textbook on emergence.

McKeown, Max. *Adaptability: The Art of Winning in an Age of Uncertainty.* Kogan Page, 2012.

Mindset Four—Power: An Unorthodox Mindset about Using Power

Boss, Alan D., David S. Boss, and R. Wayne Boss. "Power: How to Get It and How to Use It." *Organization Development Journal* 41, no. 4,

(2023). Accessed July 18, 2024. https://bconglobal.com/Resources /download/Power-How-to-Get-It-and-How-to-Use-It.
Wayne Boss has significantly influenced my thinking about power.

French, John R. P., and Bertram Raven. "The Bases of Social Power." In *Political Leadership: A Source Book.* University of Pittsburgh Press, 1986.
A foundational framework for understanding power sources.

Kotter, John P. *Power and Influence: Beyond Formal Authority.* Free Press, 1985.

Schein, Edgar H., and Peter Schein. *Organizational Culture and Leadership.* 5th ed. John Wiley & Sons, 2016.
A profoundly important body of work on organizational culture. Schein offers crucial insights into using power.

Mindset Five—Uncertainty:
An Unorthodox Mindset about Handling the Unknowable

Clark, Andy. *Surfing Uncertainty: Prediction, Action, and the Embodied Mind.* Oxford University Press, 2019.
Clark provides crucial insights for leaders dealing with prediction and uncertainty.

Furr, Nathan, and Susannah Harmon Furr. *The Upside of Uncertainty: A Guide to Finding Possibility in the Unknown.* Harvard Business Review Press, 2022.

Hansson, Sven Ove. "Decision Making Under Great Uncertainty." *Philosophy of the Social Sciences* 26, no. 3 (1996): 369–86. https:// doi.org/10.1177/004839319602600304.

Prigogine, Ilya. *The End of Certainty: Time, Chaos, and the New Laws of Nature.* The Free Press, 1996.

Nobel Laureate Prigogine introduces new laws of nature, informed by complexity science, that upend our sense of certainty about the universe and its workings.

Sutcliffe, Kathleen M., and Karl E. Weick. *Managing the Unexpected: Resilient Performance in an Age of Uncertainty.* Jossey-Bass, 2007.

Taleb, Nassim Nicholas. *The Black Swan: The Impact of the Highly Improbable.* 2nd ed. Random House, 2010.

Mindset Six—Change:
An Unorthodox Mindset about Leading Change

Akhtar, Vanessa, Gaurav Gupta, and John P. Kotter. *Change: How Organizations Achieve Hard-to-Imagine Results in Uncertain and Volatile Times.* Wiley, 2021.

Anderson, Dean, and Linda Ackerman Anderson. *Beyond Change Management: How to Achieve Breakthrough Results Through Conscious Change Leadership.* Pfeiffer, 2010.

Bridges, William. *Managing Transitions: Making the Most of Change.* 4th ed. Da Capo Lifelong Books, 2016.
Bridges describes a well-known and orthodox change model.

D'Amelio, Angelo, Jeffrey D. Ford, and Laurie W. Ford. "Resistance to Change: The Rest of the Story." *Academy of Management Review* 33, no. 2 (2008): 362–77.
Provides an insightful analysis of the mistaken belief that people always resist change.

Kegan, Robert, and Lisa Laskow Lahey. *Immunity to Change: How to Overcome It and Unlock the Potential in Yourself and Your Organization.* Harvard Business Review Press, 2009.

PART THREE: MINDSETS ABOUT LEADING COMPLEX SYSTEMS

Mindset Seven—First Work:
An Unorthodox Mindset about Leading Well

Andelman, Bob and Jack Groppel. *The Corporate Athlete: How to Achieve Maximal Performance in Business and Life*. John Wiley & Sons, 2001.
> Groppel and Andelman help us understand that we lead from our whole being.

Covey, Stephen R. *The 7 Habits of Highly Effective People: Powerful Lessons in Personal Change*. Simon & Schuster, 1989.
> Covey provides timeless truths about leading well, and many still apply in complexity.

Heifetz, Ronald A., and Marty Linsky. *Leadership on the Line: Staying Alive Through the Dangers of Change*. Rev. ed. Harvard Business Review Press, 2017.

Loehr, Jim, and Tony Schwartz. "The Making of a Corporate Athlete." Harvard Business Review 79, no. 1 (2001): 120–176.
> Loehr and Schwartz help us understand that we lead from our whole being.

Loehr, Jim, and Tony Schwartz. *The Power of Full Engagement: Managing Energy, Not Time, Is the Key to High Performance and Personal Renewal*. Free Press, 2003.
> Managing your energy is crucial for dealing well with complexity.

Nohria, Nitin, and Michael E. Porter. "How CEOs Manage Time." *Harvard Business Review* 96, no. 4 (2018): 42–51.
> Porter shows what highly effective leaders do with their day.

Rose, Charlie. "How Well Are You Investing Your Time." Posted February 9, 2017, by NEOSTARTER. YouTube. Accessed July 24, 2024. https://www.youtube.com/watch?v=nH5K0yo-o1A.

An interview with Bill Gates and Warren Buffet. Buffet's calendar inspires me and teaches Gates an important lesson.

Mindset Eight—Purpose: An Unorthodox Mindset about Why

Allworth, James, Clayton M. Christensen, and Karen Dillon. *How Will You Measure Your Life?* Harper Business, 2012.

Craig, Nick, and Scott Snook. "From Purpose to Impact: Figure Out Your Passion and Put It to Work." *Harvard Business Review* 92, no. 5 (2014): 104–11, 134.

George, Bill. *True North: Discover Your Authentic Leadership*. Jossey-Bass, 2007.

Gulati, Ranjay. *Deep Purpose: The Heart and Soul of High-Performance Companies*. Penguin Business, 2022.

Quinn, Robert E., and Anjan V. Thakor. *The Economics of Higher Purpose: Eight Counterintuitive Steps for Creating a Purpose-Driven Organization*. Berrett-Koehler, 2019.

Sinek, Simon. *Start with Why: How Great Leaders Inspire Everyone to Take Action*. Portfolio, 2009.

Mindset Nine—Stories: An Unorthodox Mindset about Reality

Garvey Berger, Jennifer. *Unlocking Leadership Mindtraps: How to Thrive in Complexity*. Stanford University Press, 2019. https://doi.org/10.1515/9781503609785.

Pay close attention to the chapter on Simple Stories.

Kahneman, Daniel. *Thinking, Fast and Slow*. Farrar, Straus and Giroux, 2011.
Nobel Laureate Kahneman explores cognitive biases and decision-making processes, demonstrating that our sense-making stories are always incomplete.

Platt, Michael. *The Leader's Brain: Enhance Your Leadership, Build Stronger Teams, Make Better Decisions, and Inspire Greater Innovation with Neuroscience*. Wharton School Press, 2020.

Roberto, Michael A. "Lessons from Everest: The Interaction of Cognitive Bias, Psychological Safety, and System Complexity." *California Management Review* 45, no. 1 (2002): 136–58.
Explores a real-life tragedy, showing the impact of our incomplete stories when we believe them to be complete.

Seth, Anil K. "The Neuroscience of Reality." *Scientific American*. September 1, 2019. Accessed July 23, 2024. https://www.scientificamerican.com/article/the-neuroscience-of-reality/.

Sharot, Tali. *The Influential Mind: What the Brain Reveals About Our Power to Change Others*. Henry Holt & Company, 2017.

Mindset Ten—Curiosity: An Unorthodox Mindset about Knowing

Duke, Bob, and Art Markman. *Brain Briefs: Answers to the Most (and Least) Pressing Questions About Your Mind*. Union Square & Co., 2016.
Markman and Duke's book is fun to read and uses stories to demonstrate the power of curiosity.

Gopnik, Alison. *The Gardener and the Carpenter: What the New Science of Child Development Tells Us About the Relationship Between Parents and Children*. Farrar, Straus and Giroux, 2016.
Gopnik provides insights into how curiosity drives learning and development for us all.

Kashdan, Todd B. *Curious? Discover the Missing Ingredient to a Fulfilling Life*. William Morrow, 2009.

Leslie, Ian. *Curious: The Desire to Know and Why Your Future Depends on It*. Basic Books, 2014.
Explores different ways to be curious.

Livio, Mario. *Why? What Makes Us Curious*. Simon & Schuster, 2017.
Livio investigates the science behind curiosity.

Loewenstein, George. "The Psychology of Curiosity: A Review and Reinterpretation." *Psychological Bulletin* 116, no. 1 (1994): 75–98.
Loewenstein offers a comprehensive overview of curiosity.

PART FOUR: PUTTING IT ALL TOGETHER

The Orthodox and Unorthodox Leader

Mintzberg, Henry. *Managing the Myths of Health Care: Bridging the Separations Between Care, Cure, Control, and Community*. Berrett-Koehler, 2017.
Mintzberg explores the interplay between leadership, organizational culture, and complexity.

Mowles, Chris, and Ralph D. Stacey. *Strategic Management and Organisational Dynamics: The Challenge of Complexity to Ways of Thinking About Organisations*. 7th ed. Pearson Education, 2015.
Stacey provides a deep dive into the dynamics of complex organizations and strategic management, emphasizing adaptive and emergent strategies. It is an essential read.

Stacey, Ralph D. *Tools and Techniques of Leadership and Management: Meeting the Challenge of Complexity*. Routledge, 2012.

ENDNOTES

1. Carol S. Dweck, *Mindset: The New Psychology of Success* (Random House, 2006).

2. Carol S. Dweck, *Mindset: The New Psychology of Success* (Random House, 2006).

3. Alexander Backlund, "The Definition of System," *Kybernetes: The International Journal of Cybernetics, Systems and Management Sciences* 29, no. 4 (2000): 444–51, https://doi.org/10.1108/03684920010322055.

4. Mary E. Boone and David J. Snowden, "A Leader's Framework for Decision Making," *Harvard Business Review* 85, no. 11 (2007): 68–76, 149.

5. Edward N. Lorenz, "Predictability: Does the Flap of a Butterfly's Wings in Brazil Set Off a Tornado in Texas?," accessed December 17, 2023, https://mathsciencehistory.com/wp-content/uploads/2020/03/132_kap6_lorenz_artikel_the_butterfly_effect.pdf.

6. "Hospital-Acquired Condition Reduction Program," U.S. Centers for Medicare & Medicaid Services, accessed February 19, 2024, https://www.cms.gov/medicare/payment/prospective-payment-systems/acute-inpatient-pps/hospital-acquired-condition-reduction-program-hacrp.

7. "About SenseMaker®," The Cynefin Company, accessed January 18, 2025, https://thecynefin.co/about-sensemaker/.

8. Dave Snowden, "Estuarine Mapping First Edition," *The Cynefin Company* (blog), October 7, 2022, https://thecynefin.co/estuarine-mapping/.

9. Michael C. Jackson and Rupert McNeil, "Mind the Gap: Overcoming the Dangerous Systems Thinking Capabilities Gap," virtual event, March

10, 2022, posted March 15, 2022, by Enlightened Enterprise Academy, YouTube, https://youtu.be/6iY-18a8FN0?si=avnHG3xg2AERT4cD; Peter G. Gulick Jr., "A Systems Thinking Approach to Health Care Reform in the United States," *DePaul Journal of Health Care Law* 21, no. 1 (2019), https://via.library.depaul.edu/cgi/viewcontent.cgi?article=1372&context=jhcl.

10. Barry S. Bader et al., *Pursuing Systemness: The Evolution of Large Health Systems* (The Governance Institute, 2005).

11. William Ross Ashby, *An Introduction to Cybernetics* (Legare Street Press, 2022).

12. Max Boisot and Bill McKelvey, "Complexity and Organization—Environment Relations: Revisiting Ashby's Law of Requisite Variety," in *The Sage Handbook of Complexity and Management* (Sage Publications, 2011), 278–98.

13. Murray Gell-Mann, *The Quark and the Jaguar: Adventures in the Simple and the Complex* (SFI Press, 2023).

14. Benyamin Lichtenstein et al., "Complexity Leadership Theory: An Interactive Perspective on Leading in Complex Adaptive Systems," *Emergence: Complexity and Organization* 8, no. 4 (2006): 2-12.

15. James P. Spillane, *Distributed Leadership* (Jossey-Bass, 2006).

16. Systems theorists sometimes refer to this pole as "Exploration" and "The Need to Innovate." See: Mary Uhl-Bien and Michael Arena, "Leadership for Organizational Adaptability: A Theoretical Synthesis and Integrative Framework," *The Leadership Quarterly* 29, no. 1 (2018): 89-104, https://doi.org/10.1016/j.leaqua.2017.12.009.

17. In Complexity Leadership Theory, these two poles are often referred to as "Exploration" and "Exploitation." See: Mary Uhl-Bien and Michael Arena, "Leadership for Organizational Adaptability: A Theoretical Synthesis and Integrative Framework," *The Leadership Quarterly* 29, no. 1 (2018): 97, https://doi.org/10.1016/j.leaqua.2017.12.009.

18. "Rounding for Outcomes," Huron Consulting Group, accessed January 18, 2025, https://www.huronconsultinggroup.com/insights/rounding-outcomes-increase-employee-retention-higher-patient-satisfaction; Ruth Harris et al., "Intentional Rounding in Hospital Wards to Improve Regular Interaction and Engagement Between Nurses and Patients: A Realist Evaluation," *Health and Social Care Delivery Research* 7, no. 35 (2019): 1–168, https://doi.org/10.3310/hsdr07350.

19. Brian Emerson and Kelly Lewis, *Navigating Polarities: Using Both/And Thinking to Lead Transformation* (Paradoxical Press, 2019); Barry Johnson,

Polarity Management: Identifying and Managing Unsolvable Problems (HRD Press, 2014); Jennifer Garvey Berger, "Polarity Management," educational video, posted July 18, 2018, by Cultivating Leadership, YouTube, accessed July 24, 2024, https://youtu.be/yyuFr4gTzjU.

20. Michael J. Arena, *Adaptive Space: How GM and Other Companies are Positively Disrupting Themselves and Transforming into Agile Organizations* (McGraw Hill, 2018).

21. Robert C. Martin, *Agile Software Development: Principles, Patterns, and Practices*, revised international ed. (Pearson Education, 2014).

22. Jens Maier, *The Ambidextrous Organization: Exploring the New While Exploiting the Now* (Palgrave Macmillan, 2015); Robert Duncan, "The Ambidextrous Organization: Designing Dual Structures for Innovation," in *The Management of Organization Design: Strategy and Implementation*, ed. Dennis P. Slevin et al. (North Holland, 1976), 167-88; Charles A. O'Reilly III and Michael L. Tushman, "The Ambidextrous Organization," *Harvard Business Review* 82, no. 4 (2004): 74–81, 140; John P. Kotter, *Accelerate: Building Strategic Agility for a Faster-Moving World* (Harvard Business Review Press, 2014).

23. "About Veterans Health Administration," U.S. Department of Veterans Affairs, accessed August 30, 2023, https://www.va.gov/health/aboutvha .asp; "Agency Profile:
    Department of Veterans Affairs; FY 2023," USAspending.gov, accessed August 30, 2023, https://www.usaspending.gov/agency/department -of-veterans-affairs?fy=2023.

24. For a thorough review, see: Gary J. Young, "Transforming Government: The Revitalization of the Veterans Health Administration," IBM Center for The Business of Government, accessed August 1, 2023, https:// www.businessofgovernment.org/sites/default/files/TransformingVHA. pdf; Adam Oliver, "The Veterans Health Administration: An American Success Story?," *The Milbank Quarterly* 85, no. 1 (2007): 5–35, https://doi .org/10.1111/j.1468-0009.2007.00475.x; Kenneth W. Kizer and R. Adams Dudley, "Extreme Makeover: Transformation of the Veterans Health Care System," *Annual Review of Public Health* 30, no. 1 (2009): 313–39, https://doi.org/10.1146/annurev.publhealth.29 .020907.090940.

25. Mariah A. Blegen et al., "Comparing Quality of Surgical Care Between the US Department of Veterans Affairs and Non-Veterans Affairs Settings: A Systematic Review," *Journal of the American College of Surgeons* 237, no. 2 (2023): 352-361, https://doi.org/10.1097/xcs.0000000000000720.

26. R. Adams Dudley and Kenneth W. Kizer, "Extreme Makeover: Transformation of the Veterans Health Care System," *Annual Review of Public Health* 30, no. 1 (2009): 313–39, https://doi.org/10.1146/annurev .publhealth.29.020907.090940. The VISNs were not consecutively numbered, hence a "VISN 23," when there were only 22 VISNs. Over the years, VISNs have been consolidated. There are now less than 22.

27. Service Lines are a business framework intended to organize and manage a subset of hospital or healthcare services around a clinical specialty grouping. For example, a cardiovascular service line or a primary care and specialty medicine service line. Each service line runs like a specialized business unit within the broader healthcare organization.

28. I served as the medical director and later, briefly, as the director of one of the service lines in VISN 23 from 2011–2014.

29. Amy C. Edmondson, *Teaming: How Organizations Learn, Innovate, and Compete in the Knowledge Economy* (Jossey-Bass, 2012); Patrick M. Lencioni, *The Five Dysfunctions of a Team: A Leadership Fable* (Jossey-Bass, 2002).

30. *Conceptualizing and Measuring Executive Presence: The Bates Executive Presence Index (Bates ExPI™) (Bates Communications, n.d.).*

31. John P. Kotter, "What Leaders Really Do," *Harvard Business Review* 68, no. 3 (1990): 103–11; John P. Kotter, "Management Is (Still) Not Leadership," *Harvard Business Review* (blog), January 9, 2013, https:// hbr.org/2013/01/management-is-still-not-leadership.

32. Hana Dib et al., *Better and Faster: Organizational Agility for the Public Sector* (McKinsey & Company, 2022), https://www.mckinsey.com/~/media /mckinsey/industries/public%20and%20social%20sector/our%20insights /better%20and%20faster%20organizational%20agility%20for%20 the%20public%20sector/better-and-faster-organizational-agility-for-the -public-sector-final.pdf.

33. John P. Kotter, "What Leaders Really Do," *Harvard Business Review* 68, no. 3 (1990): 103–11; John P. Kotter, "Management Is (Still) Not Leadership," *Harvard Business Review* (blog), January 9, 2013, https://hbr.org/2013/01 /management-is-still-not-leadership.

34. Andy Clark, *Surfing Uncertainty: Prediction, Action, and the Embodied Mind* (Oxford University Press, 2019).

35. Brandon H. Hidaka, "Depression as a Disease of Modernity: Explanations for Increasing Prevalence," *Journal of Affective Disorders* 140, no. 3 (2012): 205–14, https://doi.org/10.1016/j.jad.2011.12.036.

36. Jennifer Garvey Berger, *Unlocking Leadership Mindtraps: How to Thrive in Complexity* (Stanford University Press, 2019), https://doi .org/10.1515/9781503609785.

37. Amer Kaissi, *Humbitious: The Power of Low-Ego, High-Drive Leadership* (Page Two Press, 2022).

38. Amer Kaissi, *Humbitious: The Power of Low-Ego, High-Drive Leadership* (Page Two Press, 2022); John P. Kotter et al., *Change: How Organizations Achieve Hard-to-Imagine Results in Uncertain and Volatile Times* (Wiley, 2021).

39. Martin Heidegger, *Being and Time* (HarperCollins, 1962); Jae-Eun Shin, *Change, Continuity and Complexity: The Mahāvidyās in East Indian Śākta Traditions* (Routledge, 2023); Mark Sentesy, *Aristotle's Ontology of Change* (Northwestern University Press, 2020).

40. John P. Kotter, *Leading Change: Why Transformation Efforts Fail* (Harvard Business Review, 2007): 4, https://store.hbr.org/product/leading-change -why-transformation-efforts-fail/r0701j?sku=R0701J-PDF-ENG. Also published in a special issue of *Harvard Business Review* 85, no. 1 (2007): 59-67, https://hbr.org/2007/01/leading-change-why-transformation-efforts-fail.

41. Gary M. Grobman, "Complexity Theory: A New Way to Look at Organizational Change," *Public Administration Quarterly* 29, no. 3/4 (2005–2006): 350–82, http://www.jstor.org/stable/41288239; David Levy, "Chaos Theory and Strategy: Theory, Application, and Managerial Implications," *Strategic Management Journal* 15, no. S2 (1994): 167–78, https://doi.org/10.1002/smj.4250151011.

42. John P. Kotter et al., *Change: How Organizations Achieve Hard-to-Imagine Results in Uncertain and Volatile Times* (Wiley, 2021).

43. This quote is attributed to a range of people, including Dr. Donald Berwick, W. Edwards Deming, and Dr. Paul Batalden.

44. John P. Kotter et al., *Change: How Organizations Achieve Hard-to-Imagine Results in Uncertain and Volatile Times* (Wiley, 2021): 143-158; James Shore et al., *The Art of Agile Development*, 2nd ed. (O'Reilly Media, 2021).

45. *Dictionary.com*, "resistance," accessed November 16, 2023, https://www .dictionary.com/browse/resistance.

46. *Dictionary.com*, "adapt," accessed November 16, 2023, https://www .dictionary.com/browse/adapt.

47. John P. Kotter, *Accelerate: Building Strategic Agility for a Faster-Moving World* (Harvard Business Review Press, 2014); Stanley A. McChrystal et

al., *Team of Teams: New Rules of Engagement for a Complex World* (Portfolio Penguin, 2015).

48. Justin Carrard et al., "Diagnosing Overtraining Syndrome: A Scoping Review," *Sports Health* 14, no. 5 (2022): 665–73, https://doi .org/10.1177/19417381211044739.

49. Jim Loehr and Tony Schwartz, "The Making of a Corporate Athlete," *Harvard Business Review* 79, no. 1 (2001): 120–8, 176.

50. Matti Keloharju et al., "CEO Health," *Leadership Quarterly* 34, no. 3 (2023): 101672, https://doi.org/10.1016/j.leaqua.2022.101672.

51. "Burnout in Healthcare Executives: A Call to Action," *WittKieffer* (blog), November 30, 2022, https://wittkieffer.com/insights/burnout -in-healthcare-executives-a-call-to-action.

52. American College of Healthcare Executives (ACHE), "Hospital CEO Turnover Rate Remains Steady," news release, August 8, 2023, accessed November 1, 2023, https://www.ache.org/about-ache/news-and-awards /news-releases/hospital-ceo-turnover-rate-remains-steady.

53. Tony Schwartz, "Manage Your Energy, Not Your Time," *Harvard Business Review* 85, no. 10 (2007): 63–6, 68, 70–3, 164.

54. Stanley A. McChrystal et al., *Team of Teams: New Rules of Engagement for a Complex World* (Portfolio Penguin, 2015).

55. Stanley A. McChrystal et al., *Team of Teams: New Rules of Engagement for a Complex World* (Portfolio Penguin, 2015).

56. Viktor E. Frankl, *Man's Search for Meaning* (Pocket Books, 1984).

57. William Damon et al., "The Development of Purpose During Adolescence," *Applied Developmental Science* 7, no. 3 (2003): 119–28, https://doi .org/10.1207/s1532480xads0703_2.

58. David Sloan Wilson, *Darwin's Cathedral: Evolution, Religion, and the Nature of Society* (University of Chicago Press, 2003).

59. Satya Nadella, *Hit Refresh: The Quest to Rediscover Microsoft's Soul and Imagine a Better Future for Everyone* (HarperCollins, 2019).

60. Dare Obasanjo, "5 Things I Learned About Leadership from the Death & Rebirth of Microsoft," *Medium*, February 4, 2024, https://dareobasanjo. medium.com/5-things-i-learned-about-leadership-from-the-death-rebirth -of-microsoft-3eaf42567061.

61. Satya Nadella, *Hit Refresh: The Quest to Rediscover Microsoft's Soul and Imagine a Better Future for Everyone* (HarperCollins, 2019), 5.

62. Paul Graham, "Microsoft Is Dead," April 2007, accessed February 5, 2024, https://www.paulgraham.com/microsoft.html.

63. James K. Harter et al., "Business-Unit-Level Relationship Between Employee Satisfaction, Employee Engagement, and Business Outcomes: A Meta-Analysis," *Journal of Applied Psychology* 87, no. 2 (2002): 268–79, https://doi .org/10.1037/0021-9010.87.2.268; Marcus Buckingham and Curt Coffman, *First, Break All the Rules: What the World's Greatest Managers Do Differently* (Simon & Schuster, 2000); Amy Wrzesniewski et al., "Managing Yourself: Turn the Job You Have into the Job You Want," *Harvard Business Review* 88, no. 6 (2010): 114–7; Bryan J. Dik et al., eds., *Purpose and Meaning in the Workplace* (American Psychological Association, 2013).

64. Ashley E. Robertson and David R. Simmons, "The Sensory Experiences of Adults with Autism Spectrum Disorder: A Qualitative Analysis," *Perception* 44, no. 5 (2015): 569–86, https://doi.org/10.1068/p7833.

65. Andy Clark, "Whatever next? Predictive Brains, Situated Agents, and the Future of Cognitive Science," *Behavioral and Brain Sciences* 36, no. 3 (2013): 181–204, https://doi.org/10.1017/S0140525X12000477.

66. Andy Clark, *Surfing Uncertainty: Prediction, Action, and the Embodied Mind* (Oxford University Press, 2019).

67. Jennifer Garvey Berger, *Unlocking Leadership Mindtraps: How to Thrive in Complexity* (Stanford University Press, 2019), https://doi .org/10.1515/9781503609785.

68. Todd B. Kashdan, *Curious? Discover the Missing Ingredient to a Fulfilling Life* (William Morrow, 2009).

69. Jennifer Garvey Berger, *Unlocking Leadership Mindtraps: How to Thrive in Complexity* (Stanford University Press, 2019), https://doi .org/10.1515/9781503609785.

70. "Quotes: Leadership/Organization," Dwight D. Eisenhower Presidential Library, Museum & Boyhood Home, last revised September 8, 2023, https://www.eisenhowerlibrary.gov/eisenhowers/quotes#Leadership.

71. Walter Isaacson, *Steve Jobs* (Simon & Schuster, 2011); Ashlee Vance, *Elon Musk: Tesla, SpaceX, and the Quest for a Fantastic Future* (Ecco Press, 2015).

72. David C. Krakauer, ed., *Foundational Papers in Complexity Science: Volume One 1922–1962* (SFI Press, 2024), intro–6.

73. John P. Kotter, "Leading Change: Why Transformation Efforts Fail," *Long Range Planning* 28, no. 3 (1995): 121, https://doi.org/10.1016 /0024-6301(95)91633-4.

74. Louis Fischer, *The Life of Mahatma Gandhi* (HarperCollins, 1997).

75. Mark Juergensmeyer, *Gandhi's Way: A Handbook of Conflict Resolution* (University of California Press, 2023).

76. Carl A. Harte and Supriya Vani, *Jacinda Ardern: Leading with Empathy* (HarperCollins, 2021).

77. Mary E. Boone and David J. Snowden, *"A Leader's Framework for Decision Making,"* *Harvard Business Review* 85, no. 11 (2007): 68–76, 149.

78. Max Boisot and Bill McKelvey, "Complexity and Organization—Environment Relations: Revisiting Ashby's Law of Requisite Variety," in *The Sage Handbook of Complexity and Management* (Sage Publications, 2011), 278–98.

79. David C. Krakauer, ed., *Foundational Papers in Complexity Science: Volume One 1922–1962* (SFI Press, 2024), intro–3.

ABOUT THE AUTHOR

Michael Hein, MS, MD, MHCM, Associate Certified Coach (ACC), believes that when healthcare leaders don't fully understand complexity, it leads to burnout, turnover, and poor patient care—issues he considers preventable forms of human suffering. Healthcare is more complex than ever, and traditional top-down methods often exacerbate these challenges. Success today requires leaders who adapt, absorb uncertainty, and react quickly. For many, this means embracing new leadership mindsets.

With over 30 years of experience in healthcare, Michael is Senior Vice President and an executive coach at MEDI Leadership, the top healthcare coaching firm in the U.S. Drawing from clinical and executive roles, he helps leaders make the mindset shifts needed for success in complexity.

Previously, Michael was CEO of a nonmerger hospital network and a Chief Medical Officer in Catholic Health Initiatives. He led transformations at the Veterans Health Administration and cofounded KPI Ninja, a healthcare data company.

Michael holds degrees from the University of South Dakota, Harvard's T.H. Chan School of Public Health, and St. Cloud State University. He is a certified executive coach through the International Coaching

Federation, trained at the Hudson Institute of Coaching. His experience bridges frontline care and strategic leadership, coaching leaders to drive sustainable change in complex organizations.

His book, *Shifting Toward Unorthodoxy: Ten Unconventional Mindsets that Help Healthcare Leaders Succeed in a Complex World*, encourages a shift from outdated leadership mindsets to adaptive ones. A lifelong athlete, Michael enjoys cycling and swimming. He lives with his wife, Connie, in rural Nebraska, where the landscape's peace restores his focus and dedication to helping leaders become complexity-fit.